WHEN THE SMOKE HIT THE FAN

WHEN THE
SMOKE HIT
THE FAN

Ralph Bellamy

DOUBLEDAY & COMPANY, INC.
Garden City, New York
1979

B
Bellamy

ISBN: 0-385-14860-7
Library of Congress Catalog Card Number: 78-14693
Copyright © 1979 by Ralph Bellamy

To, for
and because of
Alice

FOREWORD

In a way this book was written twice.

Some time ago I thought I was nearing what would be the finish. On examination I realized I'd touched on areas of the theatre, electronics and pictures that are lost and gone.

So I went through what I had, enlarging on the lost areas: Chautauqua, medicine shows, tent shows, minstrel shows, tab shows, rep shows, the original stock companies, vaudeville, burlesque, early radio, early TV, original silent and sound pictures—and I wrote to friends who'd been involved in them, asking for bits that would confirm my own experiences and observations. These I've interpolated.

The response, as you shall see, was most generous and enlightening. And often amusing. The number of replies has been almost unanimous.

I'm grateful to all those who contributed and I hope the book is amusing and informative.

These are those voices, not from the past, but about the past: Robert Alda, Steve Allen, Edgar Bergen, Herbert Brodkin, George Burns, Jim Cagney, Frank Capra, Ann Corio, Michael Crichton, Irene Dunne, Lillian Gish, Freeman Gosden, Bob Hope, Walter Kerr, Sidney Kingsley, Jerry Lester, Sidney Lumet, Frank McHugh, Edward Montagne, Pat O'Brien, Senator Charles Percy, Dore Schary, George Schaefer, Phil Silvers, Milburn Stone, Lowell Thomas, King Vidor and Pat Weaver.

And a special thanks to Jerry Few, who typed and helped me to make the original form of the material.

WHEN THE SMOKE HIT THE FAN

PART I

One cold winter Saturday midnight in Chicago, after a performance of *Sunrise at Campobello,* Dore Schary's play about FDR,
at the Blackstone Theatre, I joined Irv Kupcinet at a TV studio
for his popular talk show, which was to be on the air at 12:15
A.M., to run as long as his guests talked. "Kup," as he's called, is
the night- and day-watchman of Chicago, with a daily newspaper column and the weekly TV show.

I was the first guest to arrive at the TV studio, and while he
and I stood passing the time, another guest joined us. Kup introduced us and excused himself to go into the control room. I
hadn't caught the newcomer's name. I could have said so and
asked him, but I didn't. We just stood there on the dark stage
and chatted, feeling each other out, I guess, to see if we could
find a common ground that would be useful when the red light
went on. We were to have Jack Webb, of "Dragnet," also on the
program, as well as a relative of Nehru's and a former mayor of
Salt Lake City who advocated eliminating all taxes.

My new acquaintance was younger than I. He was of medium
height, with fair, carefully parted hair, blue eyes, a resonant
voice and an easily worn sartorial impeccability. It developed
that we were both originally from Chicago.

"The South Side," I said.

"I was born there too," he replied.

"Well, I was born on Monroe Avenue and spent my early
days on Kimbark Avenue," I went on.

"My family lived on Kimbark Avenue," he added.

"We were at 5709," I said, thinking that would end it.

~ 1 ~

But he said, "*We* lived at 5709 too!" He laughed in astonishment, and I joined him. That was quite a coincidence.

Then, as one writes the finishing sentence to a chapter, I said, "When I was about five years old we moved up on the North Shore to Wilmette."

"So did we!" he almost shouted.

We could hardly get over that. Then it went like this:

"Linden Avenue," I said.

"We lived on Linden Avenue!"

"1050."

"3 (something)."

"Then we moved to Forest Avenue," I said.

"So did we."

"1214."

"*We* lived there!" he exclaimed.

His father had bought the house from my father.

It was Senator Charles Percy.

I don't think there are any odds on a coincidence like that.

I've told this story since 1959, when it took place, but on checking it with Senator Percy for authenticity and accuracy, I received the following letter from him:

"Dear Ralph:

"I remember very well indeed our appearance on Irv Kupcinet's show. The story you relate has sufficient truth to it to be credible but through the years it has become altered somewhat, very comparable to some stories I tell. The best illustration of what has happened is that old game where a person whispers a fact to the person next to them in one room, and after it has passed through sixteen people it generally comes out at the other end much different than even your tale that has survived through the years.

"I was actually born in Pensacola, Florida, on September 27, 1919, but I came to Chicago when I was six months old. It was my mother who was born on the South Side and lived there in her early childhood. We actually moved to the North Side of Chicago, Rogers Park, where I spent my childhood. We moved to Wilmette, Illinois, when I was fifteen years old and if I recall the address correctly, we did live at 1214 Forest Avenue. I am actually writing this to you from Bordeaux, France, so I will have to wait until I return home and check the address with my mother. The home we own in Wilmette now is at 308 Linden Avenue, very near the Linden Avenue el (elevated train).

"I did live on the South Side of Chicago during the years I attended the University of Chicago. My address there most of the time was 5747 University Avenue, which was the residence of the Alpha Delta Phi fraternity house.

"So you see, in principle we are quite close and I still think the story makes a good one. I would be crushed if I were omitted from your book. In any event, you are going to sell one copy to both my mother and myself, and live happily ever after on the royalties!

"Warmest personal regards,

Chuck

"P.S. I did check with my mother after I returned from France and the address on Forest Avenue is correct."

I think my oft-repeated version is better than his, even if I'm only "quite close" but slightly inaccurate. I'll make every effort to corroborate succeeding anecdotes and report them accurately.

Even though it's out of chronological order, I've chosen this tale for a beginning because it quickly places the earliest locale of the adventures and anecdotes I'm about to relate. I've met Senator Percy only that once and I admire him; and since senators are often compared to actors, I have to say I'm a better actor than he is but he'll last longer in the history books. This observation is the hardest of all for an actor to admit. So it can be seen that I'm at least starting these recollections with a degree of honesty. I hope I can maintain it.

This is not an autobiography. I can't believe the world is waiting for the story of my life. It's a collection of memories, anecdotes and impressions of, about and in various areas of the theatre, radio, TV and moving pictures over the last fifty-seven years (that sounds better than "a little over half a century") that have meaning and amusement for me. I hope they're worth passing along.

The imprints of events and observations not relating to the theatre or the profession of acting will also fall into this framework. Any actor who has pursued Thespis for a considerable time will know this, because when an incident from the past calls for identification the actor's mind refers immediately to his memory file and he says, "I remember. That was when I was playing at the National Theatre in Washington, and I was staying at the Carlton Hotel," or, "That was when I was 'at liberty' (out of a job), living in a basement on New York City's lower West Side." Those not of the theatre remember exactly where they were and what they were doing when they heard the news of FDR's death or the assassination of President Kennedy. But these unfortunate lay people don't have the actor's computerized memory and are unable to recall lesser events with the same richness and fullness that he does. So, though some of what follows may seem to be trivia, I hope it will all interrelate.

The theatre has undergone metamorphoses during my experience. We've lost many areas. I will try to report them in chronological order, with the suggestion that perhaps the order itself clarifies, to some extent, the changes. And the thread, which I hope will color the tapestry, is the recollection of pertinent anecdotes as the changing scene moves along.

And if you stay with me, in later pages you'll find colorful accounts from friends who've been active in those lost areas, in support of my own experiences and observations. In some cases they will embrace areas in which I was not active.

Reflecting on the past from time to time can be meaningful and sometimes amusing, if one keeps a good hold on the present. And seeing one's self as others saw one can keep one's ego on an even keel if one can be objective and honest. True, it can tend to fracture the image one has had of one's self. But on the other hand, if one has matured to any degree it should show up in retrospection. And that's all to the good. Anyway, everyone reflects, and everyone talks about one's self and one's observations and conclusions. That's what social communication is all about—relating experiences from the past, ranging from first-remembered impressions to those that happened this morning.

This account will start at a time some years ago in Chicago. Life was slower then. There were no airplanes, no radio, no TV, no "talkies," no rockets, no pollution (of the air, that is). There was less violence—except for a rather romantic war to make the world safe for democracy. Less population—only the Irish and the Jews had arrived here in large numbers, to encounter discrimination, and the blacks were in kitchens and shoeshine parlors. Welfare checks were not yet issued for having babies. And life was less stereotyped, if we overlook the tendency of some of today's youth, male and female, to garb and coif alike.

I was too late for Mrs. O'Leary, the Haymarket riots and the World's Columbian Exposition. I vaguely remember Samuel Insull reaching the precarious apex of his industrial pyramid and its collapsing beneath him. I remember Penny Taffyapples. The "Great Society" of Mrs. Potter Palmer was waning but I was not aware that it even existed. I was too late to be thrilled by the story of Teddy Roosevelt and San Juan Hill, which began with his Rough Riders first storming the outpost on Kettle Hill. Which, incidentally, I've seen, and it appeared to me that three boys on bicycles could have made the gentle ascent and taken the tiny sentry box with BB guns.

Sherwood Anderson, Theodore Dreiser and, earlier, Frank Norris (who was born there) and, later, Floyd Dell were drawn to Chicago by social and labor unrest that had critical national beginnings there. But I wasn't to become aware of them until later. Nor of Eugene V. Debs, the Socialist leader who perpetrated the first big strike in the country, against the Pullman Company, and who went to jail as a result. I subsequently met him when I was the leading man in a stock company in Terre Haute, Indiana. Ernest Hemingway, from Oak Park, a western suburb of Chicago, was in Paris and hadn't got started yet. I was to meet him later in Ketchum and Sun Valley, Idaho.

There was still a marked feel of the frontier about Chicago, which I feel even today. It was the railroad and industrial center of the country. Its enormous stockyards were teeming with a constant flow of bellowing, bleating, oinking animals. Clanging trolley cars rumbled along tree-shaded, bricked streets with gas lampposts at each corner, as they wove through ethnically segregated Polish, Italian, Hungarian and German neighborhoods. The canal from the Chicago River flowed through the center of the city into Lake Michigan. It was Carl Sandburg's Chicago. It loved the theatre. Some of its stars and fare then were:

David Warfield in *The Music Master*, Maude Adams in *Peter Pan*, Joseph Jefferson in *Rip Van Winkle*, William Gillette in *Sherlock Holmes*, Dustin Farnum in *The Virginian* (more of him later), Lillian Russell in *Wildfire*, William Faversham in *The Squaw Man*, Fritzi Scheff in *Mlle. Modiste*, and many other plays of romantic, melodramatic, comic and tragic nature. Dramatic fare was in the grand manner, such as *Madame X*, *The Lion and the Mouse*, *Beverly of Graustark*, many in five acts. There was lots of Shakespeare, as well as many other players, such as George M. Cohan, Tyrone Power, Sr., Harry Lauder, Montgomery and Stone, McIntyre and Heath and the Barrymores.

Another form of entertainment that was popular when I was a small child was the minstrel show, which prevailed from the middle of the last century until the early 1920s. I saw several of them. The minstrel show was probably an outgrowth of the English music hall. Richard Moody in *The American Theatre—A Sum of Its Parts,*[*] calls it the "only indigenous form of American drama."

Actually, according to Dailey Paskman in his book *Gentlemen, Be Seated,*[†] it dates back to the fourteenth century, when its members were "variously known as troubadours, jongleurs (jugglers), bards and glee men, in addition to the generic term 'minstrel.'" Paskman says the first American group existed in 1843 and was known as "the Big Four"—Dan Emmett, Frank Bower, Dick Pelham, Billy Whitlock. They called themselves "the Virginia Minstrels." They were followed, he continues, by the Christy Troupe, who conquered England, followed by another American company, "the Ethiopian Serenaders," who also won London's heart. "The Big Four," Paskman says, "increased ten-fold and became the tradition for the full-sized minstrel show."

Later minstrels, Paskman says, were Jerry Cohan, father of George M., Eddie Cantor, Al Jolson, Joseph Jefferson, Edwin Forrest, P. T. Barnum, Denman Thompson, Fred Stone, Dave

[*] Published by Samuel French.
[†] Clarkson Potter, publisher; Crown Publishing Co., distributor.

Montgomery, Nat Goodwin, Joseph Cawthorn, Raymond Hitchcock, Chauncey Olcott, Lew Dockstader, Bert Williams—and it might be noted here that David Belasco once played Uncle Tom.

In my time, the minstrel show started at the railroad station with a parade of the full troupe. The performers followed the band, in costume and black-face, to the theatre in their long-tailed Newmarket coats of startling pattern, with red lapels, large butterfly ties and plug hats.

Haverly's Mastodon Minstrels had painted on the base drum "40! Count 'em! 40!"

The show itself was in three parts. The first consisted of the raising of the curtain on the full stage, with the band on a platform at the rear and the minstrels standing in front of their chairs in a semicircle.

There were two "end men," one at each end of the semicircle. One was called "Mr. Bones" because originally his instrument was, literally, bones (later, ebony), one held between the first and second fingers and another between the second and third fingers. With a back-and-forth side-twisting movement of the wrists and hands they produced a rhythmic percussion. The other was called "Tambo" because his instrument was the tambourine. In the center, in white-face, was the "interlocutor," who conducted the proceedings in mellifluous voice, impeccable speech and grand manner. And who was the butt of most jokes.

To start the show, the interlocutor said, "Gentlemen, be seated!" And they did.

The first part was jokes, conundrums and patter—mostly at the expense of the interlocutor—songs and music to the accompaniment of the band's violins, bass viols, drums, tambourines, piccolos—and many laughs. This part was climaxed by a walk-around or cakewalk.

The second part consisted of specialties—dancing, solo singing (there was always a basso profundo, who always sang "Many Brave Hearts Are Asleep in the Deep"), monologues called "stump speeches," short sketches, female impersonations, etc.

The third part was devoted to burlesques of current plays or farcical "after-pieces."

It was an evening of fun and music. Some of the old songs were: "Arkansas Traveller," "Blue Tail Fly," "Dixie" (written on a rainy afternoon especially for the minstrel show), "Hot Time in the Old Town," "Jim Crow Polka," "Maple Leaf Rag," "Oh! Susanna," "Ring Dat Golden Bell," "When You and I Were Young, Maggie."

There's an interesting story connected with "Jim Crow Polka."

Thomas D. "Daddy" Rice, a black-face performer, was appearing in Louisville, Kentucky, in about 1828 when he saw a crippled black stablehand doing a peculiar shuffling, hopping dance. The stablehand's name was Jim Crow. And as he danced he sang a catchy song with a refrain:

"Weel about, and turn about / And do jus' so; / Eb'ry time I weel about / I jump Jim Crow."

Rice knew a good thing when he saw one. He memorized the stablehand's song, and he was off as "one of the very first stage stars. His fame was spread worldwide."‡

Overall, the minstrel show performance caricatured the Negro in a kindly but condescending way that reflected the prevailing attitude toward the Negro's imported culture, folklore, superstitions, fears, sense of humor, love of good music with good voices, rhythm and dancing. This concept of the minstrel show, born of the master-slave relationship, began to lose its popularity as white attitudes started to change—partly because of Negro riots and partly due to their newly gained access to education. Later this changing image was reflected in such plays as *The Emperor Jones* and *Porgy and Bess.*

Some of the most prominent show companies were Primrose and West, until about 1900, Al G. Field Minstrels, until the teens, and Cohan and Harris.

The greatest name in minstrelsy was the same J. H. (Col. Jack) Haverly of Haverly's Mastodon Minstrels, who introduced "40! Count 'em! 40!"

The minstrel show form undoubtedly influenced burlesque.

In 1910 Al G. Field headed the road shows. There were also McIntyre and Heath, Weber and Fields (before their Dutch act) and Harrigan and Hart (before their Irish comedy). And that brings us to a story.

That beautiful actor William Harrigan tells the anecdote

‡ From Robert C. Toll's article, "Behind the Blackface," in *American Heritage,* April/May 1978.

about his father, Edward Harrigan. It dates to the early 1900s when Harrigan was half of the vaudeville team of Harrigan and Hart. George M. Cohan wrote the song "Haitch-A-double R-I-G-A-N Spells Harrigan" about Bill's father.

Edward Harrigan was in a traveling company of *Uncle Tom's Cabin,* having gone legitimate for a season. It was an all-star company with many Negroes. Harrigan was playing Uncle Tom and Tyrone Power, the father of the fine actor we later knew in pictures, was Simon Legree. Because there were so many people in the cast it was necessary to double up in dressing rooms. Harrigan and Power dressed together.

One evening as they were making up, side by side, before individual mirrors, they were discussing things that go wrong during a performance. Harrigan, smearing on the burnt cork for Tom, said, "I don't think the audience is aware of any mishaps."

Power replied, twisting his false moustache, "I disagree, old boy. Audiences are very astute. They may not know what's gone wrong but they realize something is amiss."

Harrigan thought this over for a second as he smoothed the cork on his face and said, "I could say 'asshole' right here on the stage of the Colonial Theatre [in Boston] and get a round of applause."

Power turned from his preoccupation with his moustache and said, "Oh no you couldn't!"

Harrigan faced the evil Legree and said, "For fifty dollars I'll say 'asshole' and get a round of applause."

"You have a bet," said Power. Then, after a moment's reflection, he added, "No back to the audience."

"I'll face the audience," said Harrigan.

"Loud enough for the gallery to hear."

"Agreed," Harrigan replied.

"And," Power demanded, "a pause before 'asshole' and a pause after 'asshole.'"

"I'll do all that and get a round of applause," said Harrigan as he put the finishing smears to Uncle Tom.

They called in the stage manager to write down all the conditions of the wager and each gave him fifty dollars.

The story of the bet traveled quickly through the company and as Harrigan arrived at the stage door each night after that someone would ask, "Are you going to say 'asshole' tonight, Mr. Harrigan?"

"I'll wait for the appropriate moment," he would reply.

A night or two later Uncle Tom and Simon Legree were down at the footlights together. Just the two of them. Harrigan was facing the audience on his knees. Power was standing over him with whip, boots and moustache.

Power said, "Tom, you belong to me—body and soul!"

Harrigan whispered out of the corner of his mouth, "This is it!" Then in full voice he said, "No, Massa Legree, ma body might belong to you, but—" He rose in silence and continued— "asshole" (pause) belongs to God!"

And the audience applauded.

Bill Harrigan had another story that might produce a chuckle. It's about himself.

George M. Cohan liked Bill and wrote several juvenile parts for him. Bill was a good, reliable and handsome actor. One day in the middle of a successful run he contracted measles. He was willing to go on that night, but the New York State law said he couldn't. Cohan called a rehearsal for Bill's understudy, whom nobody had noticed because Bill had never missed a performance.

In Bill's first scene he entered a doctor's office through a door at right center (left to the audience). The doctor was downstage left (right to the audience) talking to a patient. On noticing Bill he said, "I'll be with you in a minute, son." Bill said, "That's all right, Doctor, I'll just sit down over here." And he sat, downstage right.

So Cohan, out in the dark auditorium, clapped his hands for attention and called out in a loud voice, "All right, everyone! Places for the understudy for Bill's first entrance. All right. Go!"

The unknown understudy entered. The doctor said, "I'll be with you in a minute, son."

The understudy, in a high-pitched effeminate voice with a slight lisp, said, "That's all right, Doctor, I'll just sit down over here."

As he proceeded to do so, Cohan, from the dark cavern of the auditorium, said, "That's all right, son. I'll play the part myself."

When I became aware of Chicago and its size and all its activities, even in my earliest days, I was in awe of it. Incidentally, the songs were "Oh! You Beautiful Doll" and "Everybody's Doing It Now." I guess everything seemed to me serene and ordered and sentimental, in all the treasured WASP concepts with which I was being imbued. I hasten to say that this is not meant as a criticism of my parents. It was normal middle-class attitude. One lived and died with principle, charity and pride. None of these can be faulted, but they were encased in benignity and a certain amount of snobbish hypocrisy, to the eventual lyrics of "Silver Threads Among the Gold"—the inspired work of a relative, Eben E. Rexford. This was typical middle-class, mid-American life, just pretending there was no bad. Or hiding it. Or joining it. But not acknowledging it.

This was also reflected in the theatre fare. The first play I saw was the musical version of *The Wizard of Oz* with Montgomery and Stone, to which I was taken by my parents, to view from the balcony. The next two were *Little Lord Fauntleroy* and *Buster Brown* at the stock company in Evanston, Illinois, where—many years later, at the same theatre—I had my own stock company for a season. These plays were not particularly typical, but as you can see from those mentioned earlier, the general trend was escapist—insignificant comedy, drama, melodrama and musicals. However, many musical numbers from shows of that day have withstood competition until today.

Our apartment at 5709 Kimbark Avenue, on Chicago's South Side, was near the Midway, which took its name from the main pedestrian thoroughfare of the World's Columbian Exposition in 1893. It has remained as a part of Jackson Park adjoining the University of Chicago. It was originally known as the Midway Plaisance, with White City—the Disneyland of 1893—bounded by a huge cluster of sculptured fountains at one end and the Hotel del Prado at the other.

Chicago's original airport was in the Midway before it became obsolete. There's a story about it that may be apocryphal but it's amusing. The prime advocate of a new and suitable airport was Colonel Robert McCormick, editor and publisher of the Chicago *Tribune*. He had earned his title in World War I and had clung to it. He was noted for his "right" attitudes. Liberals were anathema to him—particularly the current descendant of one Marshall Field, who bore the same name as his ancestor, who had migrated from Massachusetts to Chicago and founded the great department store that still bears his name. McCormick hated him.

The Colonel campaigned for, and probably bought most of the bonds to finance, the new airport, which has become the busiest in the world. It was built on the Skokie, a large marshland northwest of Chicago, extending almost to Highland Park, farther north. One could skate on its ice for miles in winter. It had to be drained to accommodate the new airport.

When it was completed, the Colonel, whose dream had come to fruition, claimed the right to name it.

He was a great admirer of General Marshall and wanted to name it after him. But someone called his attention to the fact that that would turn out to be "Marshall Field."

It's now called, as everyone knows, O'Hare International Airport, for the World War II pilot hero.

But to get back to first things first:

What can an adult say about his infancy with authority? Nothing, except to report secondhand pediatric assessments, and fawning parents' often repeated and increasingly enhanced accounts of exceptional infantile behavior. (Senator Percy, you make the point.)

I was told that the doctor's prediction for me was that I'd be "a six-footer and undoubtedly successful." I'm over six feet, all right, though the rest is open to question.

But any anecdotes from infancy would have to be hearsay, and that's not the purpose here. I suppose I should report that I had a nurse, even on my father's meager salary from the Barnes Crosby advertising agency. She was lovely, Hungarian Helen George. She was more than a nurse. She was my mother's household helper. Everyone had immigrant "help" in those days before heavy industry and unions. It was almost the only work immigrant women could get. Helen was part of our family. She was with us until we left Chicago when I was five. I saw her once, many years later, and she seemed happy and content. But I have a very early recollection of her almost from cradle days, and of our mutual affection.

Since I've not been psychoanalyzed, nor in any other manner

subjected to extreme retrogression—and since hearsay is ruled out—that was my infancy. There is, however, an intervening period between infancy and the "whining schoolboy" which belongs to neither age and might as well be treated here.

One deeply embedded impression from this hiatus marked me for life. I was sent to a kindergarten in the basement of the Hyde Park Baptist Church in Chicago, where we played games, sang and fidgeted with blocks and crayons. I have a mental image today, as vivid as it was when I went home and reported it, of the prettiest, neatest, cleanest young lady in the group, whose legs fascinated me. They almost hypnotized me. It might have been the beginning of things for me.

She was blond, with two long braids, big blue eyes and long lashes. Her name was Delgracia. I have determined, after habitual examination of that female area since, that her beautiful long legs were encased in silk. The rest of us, girls and boys alike, wore long, ribbed black cotton stockings. I'll never forget her legs! And though I'm still very much aware of a fine limb, I'm not too sure I'd come home and report it now. I don't have to, because I'm married to a lady with uncommonly beautiful underpinnings. But, ah! Delgracia! Wherever you are!

Psychologists say young people not only need but actually want discipline. To the very young it is supposed to be a demonstration of love and concerned attention.

Well, I had it in a most theatrical and effective manner.

As a result of any detected disobedience or misbehavior, I was taken to the bathroom by my mother. She wrapped a Turkish towel across my chest, under my chin and around both shoulders. I was then given a "talking to," which was an analysis of the crime I'd committed, the reasons it shouldn't have been committed and the prospects for my future if I didn't respect dictums and disciplines henceforth.

Then she threw a glass of water in my face.

It didn't hurt. It wasn't even too uncomfortable. But the humiliation was complete. Discipline was increasingly respected, even though an occasional Machiavellian test might have been later attempted, successfully or unsuccessfully. And eventually, recognizing its virtues and rewards, I came to respect self-discipline too.

I'm never late for rehearsal, or on the set. I know my lines. I keep my word. I affect a reasonably neat and clean appearance. I admit to a degree of squareness, but thanks to those glasses of water, I'm disciplined. Oh, what a good boy am I!

At a very early age I received what could be called my first acting lesson from my father's Aunt Ella. She was a tall, slim, venerable widow who, with her cracked-skinned, virginal/spinster sister Aunt Alma, lived on Ellis Avenue on the Southwest Side of Chicago. Their "flat" had to be reached from our "flat" by streetcar. I always got an extreme case of nausea on streetcars. It was caused by the exhaust of what they said was ozone. I had to stand on the rear platform, taking deep breaths, even when the worst almost always happened. This was not so on the el or later, going from Wilmette to Chicago on the Chicago and Northwestern Railroad. But we couldn't afford the Northwestern.

My Aunt Ella (really my great-aunt) lived in accordance with true Victorian concepts. Her husband, Charles Morgan, whose life-sized statue stood in the center of nearby Morgan Park, had left her "comfortably well off." I don't know the source of his income but I suspect he was one of the first builders of developments, which were all flats in that area.

Aunt Ella lived in a third-floor, high-ceilinged steam-heated corner flat with many ample rooms containing oriental rugs, things under glass, antimacassars, hassocks (footstools covered with carpeting), a rubber tree, a potted palm, a plate-warmer with hinged door forged into the center of the dining room radiator and gas lights.

She and Aunt Alma had a red-haired, white-capped, striped-uniformed Irish maid named Sarah.

Aunt Ella always wore black. Aunt Alma dared to splash in dark brown, the color of oak leaves in the fall after they've lost their luscious red rouge. Aunt Ella's gray (almost white) hair was pulled back severely to a bun and her clothes were nondescript except for flat heels. Aunt Alma wore steel-rimmed glasses and made a noticeable effort to dye her hair auburn and fluff it up (not as well done as my grandmother's walnut job—but all about that in a minute). She always had a coy black ribbon round her throat and a ruffled white collar beneath it. Perhaps she thought herself still in the market for a hitherto unfulfilled life.

They were colorful, charming, Victorian ladies, overflowing with Victorian love and life, and without a care, except that neither had a husband, but for different reasons.

Aunt Ella taught me a verse and commanded me onto a hassock to recite it. She also taught me gestures to punctuate the end of each sentence. These required the full use of the right arm and doubled fist in a flailing downbeat at the end of the first sentence. Then, on the word "never," a wide, palms-down, side-swiping gesture with both arms and hands starting in front, coupled with a violent shaking of the head at the end of the second sentence. And throughout was a facial expression meant to indicate complete sincerity, based on authority. Here it is:

> All that you do
> Do with all your might!
> Things done by halves
> Are never done right!

I'm aware that while this could have been the awakening of a dramatic instinct, it could also be called the origin of a style that might be identified with the term "ham acting." But I like to think the philosophical content had a continuing effect.

Incidentally, Aunt Ella opened a savings account with a deposit of one dollar for me at my birth, accompanied by the presentation of a shiny penny bank to which I contributed from time to time and made deposits amounting to three dollars or more. The Continental and Commercial National Bank of Chicago has changed its name since then. Maybe to avoid paying me the accrued interest on those deposits, which are still guarded there.

If my father's Aunt Ella started me on an acting career, my mother's mother introduced me to make-up and hairdressing.

My widowed maternal grandmother lived with us—my mother and father, my brother and sister and me. She was born in Canada and her maiden name was Urquhart, like the plaid. My grandmother and I were great friends. She was big, tall, heavy, jowly and jolly. She made all my mother's and her dresses. And she was a good cook. Some years before, she had had red hair, which was eventually passed along to my sister, skipping my mother. Her hair was always red as long as I knew her, and that's the point of this fond, conspiratorial recollection—the first secret I was ever asked to keep.

At sporadic intervals, when I must say I noticed her hair was turning dull and somewhat puce-colored, she'd wink at me and motion toward her room. She'd lock us in and uncover, on her dresser beneath a towel, in front of a tall mirror, a large soup dish of black walnuts in some kind of vinegar solution, a glass of water, a toothbrush, a comb and some more towels. It was mystic. We whispered. It was a ritual.

She'd dip and flourish the toothbrush as deftly as Mary Cassatt ever approached a canvas. Then, after toweling and brushing, she'd place the combs that held the tresses high in a pompadour and she was a radiant redhead again. And with a dash of powder and rouge to her face, she swore me to secrecy, and I honored the oath as long as she lived. My first lesson in make-up.

But I still can't figure out how black walnuts produce bright red hair.

Probably my first real acting experience occurred about this time. I was often left alone in our flat, and to amuse myself I had two imaginary characters who would visit me: "Mrs. Sophardie" and her daughter "Gretchel," who was about my age.

Our conversation wouldn't have made sense if it had been taped because I, of course, was the only one who spoke. But we talked about many things and there was lots of simulated action, such as cooking and dining and driving through Jackson Park with a horse and buggy.

A kind of Jonathan Winters streak. But I never got anywhere with it.

It's wondrous and difficult to be young. Each new discovery is exciting, and its revelation is a personal and permanent addition to what one will become later: one's first realization of the four seasons and all that goes with them; the realization of friends, of learning, of growing. Also of disappointments to be avoided in the future. Then heroes and heroines, which mean the beginnings of ambitions and goals. And certainly one's first experience with death is unforgettable—in my case, a younger brother twenty-four days old, but more profoundly, later, my "red-haired" grandmother.

When you open your eyes in the morning, you can tell what kind of day you're going to have. If it bodes ill, there's nothing you can do to change it—you learn to accept it without challenge. If it foretells good spirit and accomplishment, you enjoy the day even more. There's an infallibility about it. Maybe it has something to do with the moon. Maybe we'll soon find out.

Also, in these days of political corruption and bombs and skyjacking and kidnapping and guerrillas and marijuana and heroin and inflation and depletion of morals and ethics, maybe the moon has nothing to do with it—or maybe we shouldn't have left our traces there.

Or maybe the very young should ignore us and sing "Over the Rainbow."

Certainly today the resistance to the establishment by even the very young has affected the entertainment world. We have a subjective, introspective theatre that is defying—even flouting—concepts and ethics, manners and morals, testing society and fracturing it.

I believe the theatre is a process of reaching out to the audience. Shaw said, "The theatre reflects the times." There never was a more distracted time. It's true that as one grows older, tolerance magnifies. This would seem to be a recognition of our own misconcepts, based on bigotry, tradition and self-interest. If only we could pass on this tolerance and preserve the respectable concepts.

If this sounds lofty, I don't apologize, nor do I hold myself blameless, nor apart from the very young. After experiencing four major wars, a serious depression and the threat of another possible one on the way, I'd have to say something's wrong. It may just be that we're human beings. But I'd like to be more optimistic. I believe we'll overcome. I look for one world, with all it implies.

PART II

Wilmette is a suburb of Chicago. One way to get to and from Chicago was by electric elevated trains (the el), which had three terminals—one in Wilmette at Linden Avenue, up where Senator Percy lives; one at Jackson Park on the South Side of Chicago, Steve Allen's territory; and the third at Hemingway's Oak Park out west. They formed "the Loop" in downtown Chicago.

The other means of transportation was the Chicago and Northwestern Railroad, which ran on left-hand tracks because of the English engineer who laid it out. He was accustomed to left-hand right of way in England and neglected to take our right-hand system into account.

We moved up to Wilmette when I was about five, and the Northwestern was a half block from each of our two houses. The one on Linden Avenue my father remodeled from a small rococo Victorian shelter with an outhouse into a bungalow, done with the expert carpentry of a Mr. Solomundson who lived with us while he did the work—which was obviously non-union. The other house was on Forest Avenue. There was a definite "right" and "wrong" side of the tracks. We just made it in both cases. Incidentally, I think there was a time when Allen, Hemingway and I were all in residence at the three el terminals.

Wilmette had many small-town characteristics. I used to walk under the elms and oaks, catalpas and thorn apples, past the parochial school on my way to the public school each day. A group of us WASPs always clashed with the Catholic kids (I was raised a Baptist). We called them "catlickers" and they called us "doglickers," and we threw things at each other. I didn't know why, and I'm sure they didn't either. It was just the thing to do. But when I got into the third or fourth grade, I was told that the Catholics were stashing guns back of their altars and I would have to be prepared to take up arms against them in defense of the country someday. I was not told this by the Baptist Church, I hasten to say. It was my mother—God bless and forgive her.

But there was definitely one reason for animosity. We always got dressed up on Sunday, really dressed up, and went to Sunday school and church. Everyone, catlickers and doglickers. The rest of the day we WASPs were allowed to do nothing. Even running and talking loudly was forbidden. But the Catholics went to Mass and afterward they had fun.

In Grosse Pointe, right near Wilmette, there was a big Catholic cathedral, whose priest was Father Vatman, I remember. After the Masses, many of his parishioners would beat a path to the saloon across the street. Catholics enjoyed life more than we WASPs. I can remember envying them that—the fun on Sunday, not the saloon. I didn't drink then. I was only about six or seven years old.

I can't remember a single "colored" pupil in grammar school. That's what we called them then. Not "black."

But there were lots of kids my age and we played together and had fun on weekends. In the summer we went swimming in Lake Michigan at the east end of town, and I used to walk to Mahoney's farm with milk pails to get our milk. Mahoney's farm was on Sheridan Road on a county strip between Wilmette and Kenilworth. It's now a fashionable high-rise and shopping complex.

In the winter there were sleigh rides, and all milk and grocery deliveries were made by sleigh. We kids had sleds and ice skates. We used to skate out on the Skokie, northwest of town. It was marsh then.

Art Stoepen, the lamplighter, rode by on his bike (a girl's bike) each evening and stopped at the corner street lamp. He'd put a kitchen match in a socket on one side of the two-pronged tip of his long-handled lighter and scrape the match up the lamppost. Then he'd turn on the gas with the key on the prong on the other side of the lighter tip and light the street lamp on each corner.

Wilmette was a typical upper-middle-class Midwest Republican village. I had a good time there. I delivered papers, and groceries for Brinkman's Grocery Store, ushered at the movie theatre, worked in the Wilmette State Bank, jerked sodas at Snyder and Kazel's Drug Store, and at home I cut the lawn, raked and burned the leaves (a pungent autumn aroma one never forgets) and beat rugs, developing a house-dust allergy that still persists.

I must confess to a comfortable feeling of snobbish superiority because we were just on the right side of the tracks with the Northwestern a half block away from both houses.

In the middle of the night in the autumn of 1910, I was awakened by my mother and father and bundled into a blanket. Half asleep, I was carried out into the night and stood on the carriage step that was in front of every house in those days before there were many automobiles.

I was told that at any moment Halley's comet would appear in the heavens and wouldn't be seen again for seventy-five years.

I had seen shooting stars and had heard about comets and I wasn't too impressed.

But suddenly there appeared a large ball of fire with a tail moving through the black night at enormous speed. I became fully aware, and I was impressed.

As the years have passed I've been more and more impressed because I'll see it again. It has appeared every seventy-five years —1759, 1835, 1910. And no one knows how many years before that. But after 1985 there won't be many who'll be able to say they saw it twice.

When I started in first grade in Wilmette, my regular "habit" was "Buster Brown." This was bobbed hair, Eton collar, Windsor tie, long coat-like jacket buttoned down the front and extending to between hips and knees, wide loose belt over this, short pants like modified bloomers, long stockings coming up under them and shoes that buttoned outside to above the ankles.

I was dressed like this until I was well into first grade. As I came home from school one day, another boy rode by on a bicycle and shouted at me, "Oh, look at the girl-boy!" My embarrassment forced me to rebel at home and it was met with understanding. For some reason I thought I would progress to long trousers, to which no one my age had yet arrived. But I only got as far as another comic strip character, Little Lord Fauntleroy. This was: tight pants to the knees with three buttons set perpendicularly close together on the outside of the leg just above the knee. From the waist up there was a loose sailor blouse with a wide sailor collar that began at my stomach and extended up over my shoulders and halfway down my back. Today no such embarrassment would occur. All young people seem to dress like comic strip characters, or as if they were going to or coming from a Halloween party.

I was taken one day, in this Fauntleroy getup, to the office of a friend of my parents in the Quaker Oats building on Michigan Avenue in Chicago which overlooked Grant Park—now Soldier Field. From a top floor we watched the Wright brothers and Lincoln Beachey fly their airplanes. In retrospect, it was rather like stunt flying in moving pictures today. I've since worked in pictures in which airplane stunt men Paul Mance and Jimmy James (both gone now) have flown as crazily, but deliberately, for large fees.

A small circus came to our town when I was a good-sized nine or ten years old. I was being punished for some misdeed and was denied the price of admission to the circus.

But when I visited the grounds where the tent was being pitched, I found that I could see the show that afternoon if I'd drive a parade cage-wagon to Lake Michigan, along with several others, and help wash the wagon and the horses and then later, in a yellow jacket and peaked cap, lead a cockaded stallion in the parade.

This all worked out fine until the parade passed the village hall, which was across the street from a row of shops, the grocery store, hardware store, drugstore and the millinery store.

There was a horse and buggy standing in front of the village hall. The horse was a mare. My stallion took a fancy to the mare and reared, whinnying, and he wasn't going to let the carriage stand in his way. The mare understood what was happening. She was obviously aroused, but she was hitched to the carriage and prevented from moving by a piece of leather harness clipped to her bridle with a huge chunk of lead at the other end in the street. I lost my head and my cap trying to control the situation, and a circus man came to the rescue.

My mother happened to be shopping and witnessed this confusion. She made me surrender my cap and jacket there and then in the middle of the street, with half the town looking on, and took me home.

I missed the circus after all. I never pursued that area of show business further.

I had a degree of shyness when I was eight or nine years old which I've outgrown completely, I like to think. But my first public appearance was at that unfortunate age.

I was invited to a dance at the Wilmette Women's Club by the parents of a schoolmate. I couldn't believe it. I didn't know how to dance (and still don't). I remember thinking maybe they were having me on.

My mother bought me a new blue serge suit (short pants) and high-button patent leather shoes and off I went for the evening at the Wilmette Women's Club.

When I got there I could see that others had already arrived. I walked around the block twice before mustering the courage to go in. I went in. I didn't dance—I more or less clung to the walls. And I went home.

My mother took my sister and brother and me to see the 1915 World's Fairs in San Diego and San Francisco. We went by Santa Fe Railroad, tourist class—four days and three nights from Chicago. There was no air conditioning (the windows remained open) and there were no dining cars, so we carried a large basket of sandwiches and cookies, etc., to avoid having to go to the Fred Harvey restaurants that were located at points where the Santa Fe could stop for thirty minutes at breakfast, lunch and dinner hours. We couldn't afford this but we went once or twice for the experience, with the admonition not to order too much. The waitresses wore knee-length bouffant, dairymaid skirts that hiked up when they leaned over the tables. And I was alert to the thrills provided by Delgracia. Incidentally, Bob Cobb adopted the same costume later for his Brown Derby Restaurant waitresses in Hollywood.

This trip included my first visit to a moving picture studio. Silent pictures then. There was no studio tour as there is today, but one could get to Universal City from Los Angeles via Pacific Electric trolley cars: big red cars that went to all the beaches and suburbs and points of interest in Southern California. Would that they were running today! The trolley fare for the trip through the sparsely inhabited neighborhoods and the densely cultivated citrus and walnut groves to Universal City was a nickel. Admission through the front gate of Universal Studio was two bits. "Uncle" Carl Laemmle ran the studio then.

There were actors in make-up wandering the lot and animals of all kinds in cages. Around one corner was a man with his cap on backward, looking through a lens and cranking a camera. Another man in puttees and riding britches and his cap on straight, sitting in a director's chair with a megaphone to his lips, was telling the actors in front of the camera what to do. It was thrilling.

As we were leaving the lot near the front gate, I saw a man coming toward me whom I recognized as Dustin Farnum. I asked him if I could take his picture with my Brownie 2A.

"You don't want my picture," he said.

"Yes, I do," I said, snapping the shutter.

As we passed through the gate I asked the gate man if I wasn't right, if that wasn't Dustin Farnum.

"No," he said. "He's the animal keeper."

That was my first experience at Universal, but not my last, by any means.

At that time, California was having its second "discovery."

The gold strike was washed out but the blue skies, temperate climate and golden sunshine were just being recognized as pleasant surroundings in which to live.

Everyone was selling real estate. Inducements to buy were free bus trips through hills and groves to a pitched circus tent near a gravel road where a high-powered salesman pleaded for purchases at fifty dollars a lot to a hundred dollars an acre. After this the suckers were given a substantial box lunch, descended upon by an army of lieutenant salesmen and returned to Los Angeles. All for free.

My mother, sister, brother and I saw most of Southern California this way. We never had any intention of buying real estate. And didn't.

I wish we had.

It's now selling by the front foot, on paved roads and highways.

In 1919 my mother took us to California again.

A friend of mine, Bill Ostrander, and I became bored with life and got ourselves jobs as bellboys at the Palisades Tavern, which I believe still stands near the channel entrance to the Pacific Ocean from Balboa Bay.

A movie company moved into the Tavern and headquartered there for location work at sea. The stars were William Farnum and Louise Lovely, and the picture was *Wings of Morn*, directed by J. Gordon Edwards.

I was cleaning Miss Lovely's white shoes a day or two after their arrival and we chatted. She was charming and friendly, and I told her I was going to be an actor. Where this urge came from, I didn't know. The only other theatrical decoration on the family tree was a George Anne Bellamy (a mixed-up mistake of some kind for Georgiana), who played Juliet to David Garrick's Romeo in the mid-1700s and who had six illegitimate offspring. But though her surname was the same as ours, *she* was the illegitimate daughter of a British diplomat named Lord Tyrawley and probably didn't deserve to hang on the Bellamy tree at all. Anyway, that was around two hundred years ago, and the records seem to indicate that she was an extraordinary actress.

Miss Lovely asked me if I'd like to be in *Wings of Morn*. Naturally I said I would, and she arranged it. I had to get permission to leave my bellhop job for the required one day, and I was told to report at the dock the next morning.

A rather large group of us were taken in boats to our location, which was one side of a completely equipped deck of an ocean liner built on a barge that was anchored about five miles offshore.

I had a brief acting experience with Mr. Farnum in which, as a cabin boy, I delivered a telegram to him on a silver salver, on deck. Then our group (extras) were told to assemble at one end of the deck, back of a rope that we'd find there. I hurried to the rope, wanting to be in the foreground, but the rest of the group seemed to take their time, and when they did appear they were in different clothes.

Mr. Edwards explained to us through his megaphone that this was to be the beginning of a shipwreck and we were to be panicked. He directed us to move forward on "Action" and circle around the set and come back again to make our number look twice as large.

Then he said, "Action!"

Two airplane propellers and three fire hoses were directed straight at us. The rope was pulled away and Mr. Edwards said, "Camera!" and the cameraman, with cap on backward and eye in the lens, started cranking. I, at the head of the group, was thoroughly drenched and out of breath immediately but I was forced forward, around the set and back again.

The rest of the group changed clothes again. Someone had neglected, or forgotten, to notify me of the costume change and I dried off the best I could on a pile of rope.

Late in the afternoon we were taken back and I got five dollars. My first job in pictures.

Those early silent pictures had captivated everyone in the country. Everyone went to the movies. The admission had jumped to ten and fifteen cents and the big productions, such as *Ben Hur, Intolerance* and *Orphans of the Storm,* had additional publicity build-ups with limited runs, called road shows, and they cost a quarter after you stood in line for an unreserved seat.

Serials, such as *The Perils of Pauline, The Million-Dollar Mystery* and *Elmo the Mighty,* usually preceded the feature. Also *Fox Movietone News* with Lowell Thomas and an occasional Keystone Kops were included.

Lillian Gish says of early silent pictures: "The difference between Mr. Griffith and today: he rehearsed and rehearsed and rehearsed which we don't do today. Film is the only performing art form that doesn't rehearse. I still firmly believe that if we did, we'd have better films."

In *The Movies, Mr. Griffith and Me,* Lillian writes a moving account of her early struggles in the theatre as a child actress with her sister Dorothy, accompanied by their mother, who made all their clothes. They played in separate companies frequently, mostly on the road. Their father had deserted them.

The two sisters were introduced to D. W. Griffith by their friend Mary Pickford at the old Biograph Studio at 11 East Fourteenth Street in New York City. Their first picture with Griffith was *The Unseen Enemy.*

In her book, Lillian traces the development of pictures from their birth to the early heyday of silent pictures:

"In the tail end of the nineteenth century, a new phenomenon had captured the imagination of the American public. In places called 'penny arcades,' which were usually rented stores, people could see 'moving pictures'—strips of film on assorted subjects— by dropping a penny into a slot and peering into a machine called the Kinetoscope. A few years after the Kinetoscope made its appearance, it was superseded by the Mutoscope, a peep-show machine owned by the American Mutoscope and Biograph Company, one of the leading motion picture companies. By 1896 film images were projected on screens, usually in vaudeville houses. These early movies, which were mostly photographed vaudeville acts, were greeted enthusiastically, but the novelty was short-lived. By 1900 movies were the last act on the programs in the vaudeville theatres in which they were shown.

"Movies seemed to have no future until, in the first year of the century, vaudeville actors struck for higher wages. Theatre owners had no choice but to show movies exclusively. Film equipment was purchased in large quantities—until the end of the strike. Projection manufacturers, who had responded to the demand while it lasted, suddenly found themselves overstocked; theatre owners were willing to sell their machines cheaply. The penny arcade owners, who had long wanted to show films on screens but had been unable to compete with the theatre owners, now had an opportunity to buy the equipment at a bargain price.

"Not only arcade owners but small-time entrepreneurs everywhere found a new and quick source of income. They rented unused stores, fitted them with projection machines, a screen, and some chairs, and charged a nickel admission. Called 'nickelodeons,' these new movie houses, cheap and accessible to everyone, enjoyed phenomenal success, and were established in small towns and large cities throughout the country.

"The average program lasted thirty minutes and consisted of several short subjects, each running from 100 to 200 feet of film. The nickelodeon stayed open twelve hours a day. As the average film rental was about $15 a week and a well-situated nickelodeon could make $60 a day, the venture could be very profitable. Often the projectionist ran color slides with words of popular songs between shows. There were also suggestions on the audience's decorum and always the admonition 'Ladies Please Remove Hats.' Advertisements for local emporiums soon began to appear on the screen, adding to the owners' sources of income.

"By 1908, there were already between 8,000 and 10,000 nickelodeons in the country. Originally dark and ill-smelling places, patronized in the cities by the poor and uneducated, the nickelodeons became cleaner and more well-appointed as they gained in popularity. But 'respectable' people continued to look down on them and the movies that were shown in them. Stage actors called them 'galloping tintypes,' and considered working in them only slightly better than starving."

Times and budgets have changed. Lillian says *The Birth of a Nation* cost $61,000 and another $30,000 was spent on exploitation, advertisements and making duplicate prints. Up to 1969, Lillian says, "*The Birth of a Nation* has been the all-time money maker in film history, there have been so many black market prints in circulation that no one will ever know its true gross. A man closely associated with the business side of the film once told me that the total box office take was much more than $100,000,000." (*Star Wars* is expected to gross between $250,000,000 and $300,000,000.)

Incidentally, King Vidor, who has one of the longest and most distinguished careers in pictures and who directed *The Wedding Night*, in which I appeared with Gary Cooper and Anna Sten, says that in the nickelodeon days he "took up tickets and then ran the projection machine."

The Midwest was booming. Everything seemed to be in place. Labor was being held fairly well under control, despite a few malcontented obstructionist leaders, and no one paid too much attention to politicians, who were getting fat on food, money, liquor and smugness, in about that order. Maybe, in our complacency, we were planting the bare roots of hypocrisy and self-deceit that have led to today's disenchantment among the young and the minorities. Anyway, an atmosphere of progress and happy days and affluence gently veiled those who didn't have to scrape for a living. Until a German submarine sank the British ship *Lusitania* off the coast of Ireland with a hundred twenty-eight Americans aboard.

If all this seems irrelevant to what's been suggested in the title and Foreword, it was really the beginning of the awareness from which those of my generation and social stratum began our struggle with things to come.

Our first colorful contact with society was the introduction of military training in high school, so we would be ready in case the Germans got out of hand.

The fact that our fathers were members of the Home Guard, meeting to drill with wooden guns in uniform once a week, didn't have the significance of our own uniforms and wooden guns. Not even when our fathers were dispatched to the South Side of Chicago to quell a smoldering racial unrest, with their wooden guns.

We were preparing to defend our country if necessary, and the propaganda machine was at work.

Woodrow Wilson was President. Kaiser Wilhelm was on the rampage. Paul Whiteman had just reached his pinnacle. Eugene V. Debs, the perennial Socialist candidate for President—whom I was to meet later in Terre Haute—was arrested and imprisoned under the Espionage Act for incitement against enlistment and the draft (fifty years later he might have got away with it). Forts and naval stations that had previously been simply symbols of patriotic gallantry were now alive with friends and relatives. And then we were at war. World War I. It was called "The Great War"—until World War II.

In the teens every young person on the North Shore went to high school. Many of them, especially young men, went to college and prepared for a business, scientific or professional career if they were lucky enough to have felt a calling, or had a father who would leave them his business.

Those young men who were not called found a fine living selling bonds when their education stopped, because the stock market was booming.

The young ladies "came out" if they were socially eligible and Father could afford it. But no matter what, they "got married."

New Trier High School was in a small section called Indian Hill between Kenilworth, which is just north of Wilmette, and Winnetka. There were some eight hundred students then. The last I heard, there are now over four thousand. Among its graduates are Charlton Heston, Rock Hudson, Ann-Margret, Bruce Dern and Hugh O'Brian.

I have reported that I have no remembrance of the dawning of my urge to become an actor, which at this time had become colossal. And I'm sure I had become a colossal nuisance, posing before mirrors and assuming mannerisms and stances of past tragedians of whom I'd read. But I really began life, in its vital aspects, in high school. And my urge eventually led to a presidency—of the Dramatic Club.

Waldo Wynekoop was a health nut. He lived on our block, on Linden Avenue in Wilmette, and we considered him an oddity. He was one of eight or ten of us in the neighborhood of about the same age. His father was a judge in Chicago. Waldo was more than medium height, muscular, with dark hair and the beginnings of a premature moustache. He was a disciple of Coué ("Every day, in every way, I am getting better and better") and he chewed each mouthful of food one hundred times. It was disgusting to sit with him in the mess hall at high school and watch him chew everything a hundred times. The trouble was, he couldn't keep the food in his mouth as he masticated it, so that it dribbled and drooled from the corners of his mouth before he reached the count of a hundred.

Waldo didn't walk; he strode, much as the Beefeaters do as they guard the Tower of London. Except that he didn't carry a halberd, so his arms swung counter to his step as he strode. And while he strode he was so full of life and energy that he had to let it out.

All of us from the neighborhood walked from Wilmette through Kenilworth to New Trier High School. I had a newspaper route before leaving, and breakfast was the last function. The signal to leave for school came from Waldo. As he strode up the street he made a sound like a distant train whistle by protruding his lower teeth in front of his uppers, spreading his lips, pressing his tongue forward against his teeth and blowing. Most of us can do this, but Waldo included his voice, which had changed, combining the whistle with a guttural bass moan—thrv —thrv—thrv—thrrvvv—

When this peculiar sound was heard, someone would invariably say, "There's Waldo—time to go." And I had to move right along from Wilmette through Kenilworth in time for the eight-thirty bell at New Trier, because Waldo was a fast walker.

While I was at New Trier we had the worst flu epidemic the country has ever seen. It was centered in Chicago and its suburbs. Initially it didn't get out of those bounds because of drastic precautions. (It later became a national epidemic.) Many shops were closed, including department stores, and we were advised to stay at home. The schools were closed, and for us students that was the good from the ill wind. But people died by the thousands—so fast that undertakers and cemeteries were unable to manage.

I was in good health and I got a job in Chicago, sorting sheep pelts during the recess period of about two weeks. I rode the el from Wilmette to Chicago and back each day. There were few passengers and the streets were nearly deserted. But at the ends of many blocks were stacks of thirty or forty boxlike coffins piled on top of each other, awaiting disposition. It was like a scene from a horror movie. It cast a gloomy pall over our normal Midwest complacency.

My job with the sheep pelts was to select them according to size from mound-shaped piles, and toss them up into large burlap sacks, whose mouths were stretched open at the tops of racks standing about eight feet high. The pelts were just as they had been shorn on the range or the plains, wired crudely to hold one sheep's offering in one piece, as it were. And when I say "offering," I mean everything that could be divested from the outside as well as generous gratuitous contributions from the inside. Those pelts were the foulest things I've ever encountered—with the exception, perhaps, of a couple of directors who come to mind.

Frequently it was necessary to climb the rack and jump down onto the sorted pelts, while bracing myself by flattening palms on the sides of the open mouths of the sacks, in order to pack the filth solid.

At the end of the day, after scrubbing with some kind of detergent jelly and industrial soap and changing clothes for the ride home on the el, I always felt people were keeping their distance. Probably the flu germs did too, because I survived the epidemic in fine, foul fashion.

In 1917 we were at war, with its gas and trenches and biplanes and heroes and songs: "It's a Long, Long Way to Tipperary," "Over There," "Keep the Home Fires Burning," "K-K-K-Katy," "Ja Da," "How Ya Gonna Keep 'Em Down on the Farm?", "My Buddy" and "Roses of Picardy."

Mary Pickford and Douglas Fairbanks sold Liberty bonds. Meat, butter and sugar were rationed.

I was too young to go to war, but I felt it would be the thing to do if I could, and I'm sure my fellow students did too. How envious we all were when an upperclassman who had joined up as an ambulance driver in the Red Cross appeared at school in uniform to say goodbye to us. It made us swell with pride, and hatred of Hohenzollern and his "Huns." But I was really consumed by my actor's urge, to the exclusion of all other interests.

Military training continued. There was a false armistice, just as in World War II, and we were sent to Chicago to march in celebration. The parade was in thrilling progress when word came of the error, and we all went home. There was no parade and less demonstration when the real armistice was announced two days later. There can be only one climax. But we were safe for democracy. Until Pearl Harbor.

Wrist watches came in during World War I, and they were considered effeminate for men. "A slap on the wrist" dates to that time. They were introduced for the Navy. Previously it was pocket watches, many times given to young men at age twenty-one for not smoking until then, or as college graduation gifts.

I spent a memorable summer during the war as an usher at

Ravinia Park, up near Highland Park. The Chicago Symphony Orchestra and Metropolitan Opera singers performed opera in an open-air pavilion, financed in large part by Louis Eckstein of Cracker Jack and Julius Rosenwald of Sears, Roebuck. This was close to the theatre, although I found the acting somewhat bombastic. But, coupled with the afternoon orchestral concerts, it bred a lasting love of music—and the beginning of a fondness for classical music. My favorite symphony is Dvořák's "New World". I also love Tchaikovsky's "Pathétique" Symphony and "Romeo and Juliet," and I'm fond of Sibelius and Respighi. My favorite instrument is the harpsichord. But this is beside the point.

Sophie Braslau was singing Carmen for her first time one night. Richard Hageman, who was about six feet five, was conducting and Bruno Steindel, who had played a virtuoso concert that afternoon, was in the pit with the orchestra for the fun of it. He was positioned just in front of Hageman.

I was instructed to take some flowers down the center aisle to Miss Braslau after the second act. I didn't know the opera well, but I figured that if I started down as the curtain was closing it would time about right for me to arrive after the finishing bars.

So down I went with a basket of American Beauty roses in water, about four feet tall, under each arm. I arrived too soon. Hageman made a sweeping flourish with the baton that caused me to turn quickly to avoid being struck. As I turned I swished water all over a gentleman in the front row who was in tails. He rose, wiping the water from himself, and said, "You son of a bitch." I said I was sorry, which didn't help.

As Hageman turned to acknowledge the audience's applause I was standing squarely in front of him, preventing him from bowing. I managed to draw to one side as the curtains parted and Miss Braslau appeared for a bow. She said, "Give me the flowers." I stepped down into the orchestra pit, but I couldn't reach up high enough to present the roses.

Steindel saw my predicament and, drawing his Stradivarius cello to one side, offered me his chair to stand on. One leg was shorter than the others and I fell, pouring the rest of the water and the roses all over his Stradivarius.

Steindel was famous for his profanity as well as his virtuosity.

Many people wouldn't attend his concerts because if he hit an off note or chord his swearing could be heard in the gallery. He was that loud. And now Miss Braslau was taking another bow as the curtain parted for the second time, and she repeated, "Give me the flowers." I was picking up roses from the floor of the orchestra pit, the gentleman in the front row was cursing me and so was Steindel. Hageman had left in a rage. I finally got the flowers delivered on the third curtain call and somehow got back up the aisle.

Many years later, at a cocktail party in New York, I met Miss Braslau. She remembered, and we both laughed.

Back at school that fall, trips to Chicago were not uncommon now—I skipped classes for a matinee occasionally. The theatre was flourishing and seats were inexpensive compared to today. A dollar and a half to two dollars provided a fine orchestra seat, seventy-five cents and fifty cents bought good balcony seats, and the gallery, scaled for my budget, was available at a quarter.

The actors appearing then belong to our national history: Sarah Bernhardt, George Arliss, the Barrymores, John Drew, Frank Bacon, William Collier, Raymond Hitchcock, Al Jolson, Otis Skinner, Sothern and Marlowe, Robert B. Mantell and Genevieve Hamper, Mrs. Thomas Whiffen, Katharine Cornell, Jane Cowl, and many others. They were all great in their day and many of them could still be considered great today. The theatre was ascending into its greatest period of activity and popularity, which would last for the next twelve years or so.

Interest in scholastic pursuits was not only waning: it had waned. My only interest was the theatre. I kept a notebook for entries of quotes from biographies I was devouring. One that impressed me was a bit of advice of Madame Duse's to aspiring young actors. I can't remember it verbatim, but its essence was an admonition to work, to watch others work and to keep working. I was willing to work, but the New Trier Dramatic Club offered only sporadic opportunities, and they were interrupted by classes in such irrelevant subjects as Latin and mathematics.

Even presidents can be capable of personal revenge. And at least one president has been humiliated by being passed over for honor and recognition.

I was president of the New Trier High School Dramatic Club. But because I had been caught smoking on the school grounds I wasn't allowed to participate in the forthcoming production of *The Admirable Crichton,* in which I had anticipated the lead. My best friend, Harlan Ware, got the part. I was happy for Harlan, who was a good actor, and I gave him the benefit of my assistance in preparing for the part.

But adding further insult in the meantime, the French Club chose to do some poetry and songs at the assembly in the auditorium and had neglected to consult me about arranging for the piano and some furniture on the stage. Whether this was deliberate or an oversight didn't matter. The president of the Dramatic Club reigned over the stage, front and back, and something had to be done which would demonstrate that when any group planned to use the stage they had to consult him first and thus have not only orderly procedure but supervision.

Parenthetically, it could be said, in those days of Valentine's Day celebrations and funeral processions following $50,000 coffins, that there was precedent for this rationale. In Chicago, just fifteen miles or so to the south, people were machine-gunned for as much or less.

But in this case there was only one thing to do. Surreptitiously I slipped pie tins onto the strings of the grand piano just before the French Club program started. It didn't stop the performance but it did create some raucous amusement for the audience, from which the French Club never recovered. I hoped it would serve as an example for the future. I was never found out. Incidentally, I've since been informed by Hugh O'Brian that I was considered not too good an actor in those days.

The performance of *The Admirable Crichton* was imminent. You will recall that it's the story of an English family with servants, shipwrecked on a deserted island. After struggling to land, like clumsy seals, they dry off and revert to class and position. Soon Crichton, the butler, has a fire going by striking stones together, and a meal cooking. He serves the meal in semblance of baronial style and retires to have his own repast and to relax, sitting against a tree at a discreet distance. A social comment!

My *pièce de résistance* for Harlan's portrayal was, since Crichton was an Englishman, to light his pipe after this. You will remember that smoking on the school grounds was forbidden, so this was a risk that had to be taken in the interest of artistic perfection. It couldn't be done at rehearsal for fear of having it censored, so it was saved for the one performance.

The moment came when the action previously described had taken place—the fascinating striking of the stones to start the fire, the meal prepared and served and then retirement to the tree to enjoy his own relaxation. Then Crichton rose, produced his pipe, filled it from a pouch, struck a kitchen match on his trousers and lit it.

I think the audience is still laughing.

As president of the Dramatic Club, I had the keys to everything backstage at the auditorium. One lunch hour in the midwinter of 1922 I wanted a cigarette, but it was raining. Smoking, of course, was prohibited on the school grounds but I was not to be denied.

I unlocked a door below the stage and found myself in a corridor that I'd never seen before. There was a gentle warm draft coming toward me as I followed the corridor to its end, where there was a window up at ground level and a room off the corridor from which the draft seemed to emanate. There was another window in that room, also up at ground level. This room was almost completely occupied by a huge spinning wheel about three feet wide and about eight feet in diameter, encased in an open frame and spinning furiously as it hummed.

I lit my cigarette and stood hypnotized by the wheel. I blew a puff of smoke into it and the speed of it pared off the smoke gradually until it vanished. I was fascinated and I blew in another puff, and another. As I stood there enjoying my cigarette, I was suddenly aware of Mr. Windoes, the chemistry and physics teacher, standing in the corridor doorway. He always seemed to be the one to catch me at anything I shouldn't have been doing.

"What are you doing, Ralph?" he asked.

"Just having a smoke," I replied.

"You know the rules," he said. "Do you want to go over and tell Mr. Tubbs (the principal) or shall I?"

"I'll go," I answered as I put out my cigarette and ambled back through the corridor and up into the auditorium, which reeked of cigarette smoke. I'd been blowing the puffs into the ventilator fan.

This was the latest of many violations and Mr. Tubbs said, "I think you'd better take your books and go home."

My education was interrupted, but I wasn't too upset. I had somehow got the name of a man in Chicago who produced plays for one-night-stand performances under tent on the summer Chautauqua circuit, and on my way out of New Trier I stopped at the pay phone in the hallway and called him.

To my surprise the man, Warner Wales, answered the phone himself. But I was ready for him. I had read biographies and autobiographies of actors and I knew the procedure. "Mr. Wales?" I asked.

"Yes," he said.

"This is Ralph Bellamy," I asserted with total confidence.

"Oh, yes," he replied, which stopped me briefly, because there was no way he could have known me. But rising to the moment like a pro, remembering the biographies, I put the traditional actor's question: "I wonder if you have anything for me this season?"

After a slight pause he asked, "Let's see, what do you do?"

I wasn't prepared for this one but I heard myself saying, in a deep resonant tone: "Ingénues." I wasn't even sure what an ingénue was.

There was a somewhat longer pause, and he said, "You mean juveniles, don't you?"

"Yes," I replied hurriedly, and I wasn't too sure what they were, either. I don't know why, except that he turned out to be a very nice man, but he said, "Come in and see me."

I did, and I got the part of Old Matt, the leading man's father, and doubled the part of Wash Gibbs, the "heavy," in Harold Bell Wright's *The Shepherd of the Hills*. The leading man was ten years older than I, and the leading lady was seven or eight years older. I would turn eighteen right after we started the tour in June.

PART III

While I was waiting for the tour to start, I organized a little theatre group called the North Shore Players. The "little theatre movement" began in the late teens. It embraced local, adult, amateur performances of inoffensive plays, the rights to which were usually contracted through the Samuel French Company, which is still publishing plays. The stages were the Women's Club, the high school auditoriums, the church Sunday school rooms, etc. The players took themselves and the theatre quite seriously. George Kelly, Princess Grace's uncle, wrote a very funny and successful comedy about the little theatre called *The Torch Bearers*.

The North Shore Players consisted of those I considered to be the most talented of the New Trier Dramatic Club; a few Northwestern University students who had theatrical ambitions, among them Bernard (Dummy) Szold, their football fullback hero who was also a ballet dancer and scene designer; and a group of special friends of mine whom we called "the Five Fools." The other four of this special group besides myself were Harlan Ware, the star of the New Trier performance of *The Admirable Crichton*, an aspiring actor and writer; Montgomery Major, another aspiring writer who later wrote a seven-volume biography of Benvenuto Cellini, so voluminous that no publisher could afford to publish it, and who wrote an original one-act play for the North Shore Players; Earl Fox, a gifted musician who put together a thirty-piece orchestra that he conducted before and between our plays, which consisted of three one-acts on each program; and Fenn Germer, who seemed to be a genius at everything. He and I wrote a one-act play together called *Nothing*. We gave the playwright the nom de plume of "Robert W. Rooms." It was a travesty on Robert W. Chambers, whom we considered to be a cheap commercial writer. The last I heard of Fenn, he was the editor of *The Theosophist*, the official organ of the followers of Krishnamurti, brought to this country by Annie Besant, who claimed he was the personification of the second coming of Christ.

We were one of the first little theatres and we certainly took ourselves seriously. Jessie Royce Landis, who was married to Mr. Landis of Sosman and Landis, Chicago scenery builders, took over the North Shore Players when I left to conquer Chautauqua in *The Shepherd of the Hills*.

There were many Chautauqua circuits, consisting of from three- to seven- or eight-day programs of lectures, music, plays, poetry, singers, religious speakers (William Jennings Bryan was a perennial), entertainers (rated G), etc. The tent crew pitched the huge tent the first day and the various programs arrived daily for as long as the local sponsors had contracted. Then the crew moved the tent to the next town.

Chautauqua was an outgrowth of a practice of local "lyceums," so called after the place where Aristotle lectured to the young people of Greece. Its first meeting, under Methodist-Episcopal auspices, was held at Chautauqua Lake, New York, in 1874, to study the Bible and Sunday school methods. Gradually it expanded its program to include the whole field of education, with popular entertainment added. It still conducts an annual ten-week assembly.

This assembly was copied by communities across the country. Each contracted its programing independently through lyceum bureaus, which later organized local Chautauqua committees in circuits of towns, then supplied them by contract with programs of lectures, music, readers, entertainment of various sorts, sketches and drama.

There are many memories of *The Shepherd of the Hills*, but one in particular shines. The play was in four acts, laid in the Ozark Mountains. Our scenery consisted of three diamond dyed drop curtains of the Ozarks, Aunt Molly's kitchen and the mill, pinned over a frame of borrowed one-inch gas pipe that was fas-

My mother in her wedding dress

Me at age three

Wilmette Public School—I'm on the extreme right, front row

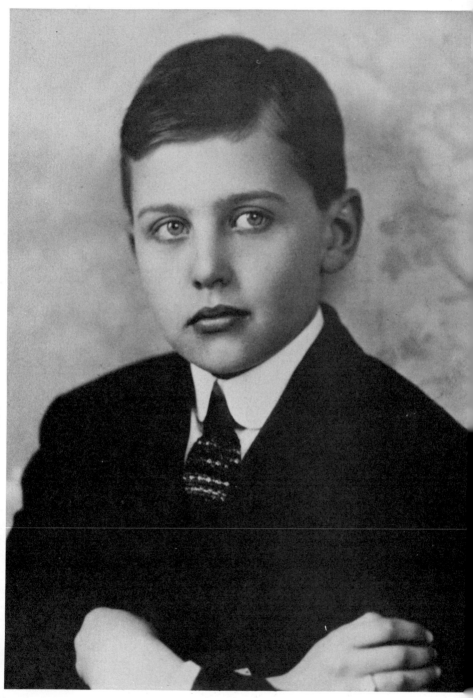

Graduating from Wilmette Grammar School

RALPH BELLAMY PLAYERS

PRINCESS THEATRE

Week of September 19, 1926

RALPH BELLAMY
Leading Man

My father in 1927

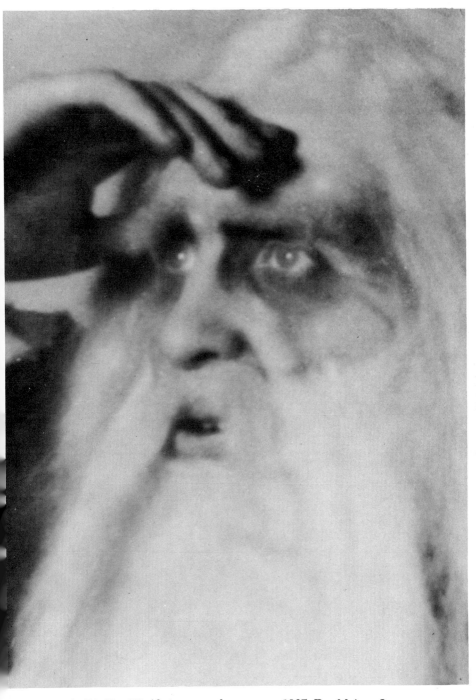

As Rip Van Winkle in my stock company, 1927, Des Moines, Iowa

Way Down East, Ralph Bellamy Players, Des Moines, 1928, with Charles A. Browne

In a scene from *Roadside,* 1929, Plymouth Theatre, New York

tened to borrowed two-by-twelve planks laid across borrowed bales of hay. The footlights were inverted green-shaded drop desk lights, tilted upstage. They were ours.

The play called for twelve principals, as I remember, and some supers. We were doing it with eight actors. I was doubling two parts. Mr. and Mrs. Wales were playing Ollie Stewart and Aunt Molly. The Waleses had just been married and they were making a honeymoon of our tour in a secondhand coupé.

One night, the Waleses hadn't shown up at curtain time. The tent was sold out to twelve hundred people who'd come by horse and buggy and Model T Fords, and the cast decided to start the show without Aunt Molly and Ollie Stewart. Now six actors were doing a play that originally called for twelve principals and a mob scene during a fight at the mill. But we had played it so many times we felt we could handle it until the Waleses arrived.

Then in the middle of the third act the leading lady, playing the part of Sammy Lane, had a severe attack of appendicitis and had to be stretched on the grass in the back of the tent while one of the tent crew went for a doctor. The Waleses still hadn't arrived yet, so that left us with five actors doing this twelve-principal play. But we were ad-libbing and getting along fairly well when someone backstage said in a horrified voice, "Listen! There's no one onstage!"

All five of us started for the planks, but the leading man said, "Wait! I'll go on and do a soliloquy. I'll take it up to" (a certain point; I don't recall his exact words) "and then someone else come on." Whereupon he stepped out and, picking up an apple box that was against the Ozarks, went downstage to the "footlights" and sat on the box with an elbow on one knee and the heel of his hand under his chin and stared at the audience. And he sat, and he sat, and he sat. Then he got up, carefully replaced the box against the Ozark Mountains and came offstage saying, "I couldn't think of a goddamned thing to say."

We all rushed on after that—all except the leading lady, who was still on the grass, but with a doctor now (in attendance, that is). Soon the Waleses appeared—their coupé had broken down—and they joined us, much to the confusion of the audience, I'm sure. But when it was over we got a fine hand and took several curtain calls. All except the leading lady.

Knowing that Edgar Bergen had had Chautauqua experience, I asked if he'd contribute a few words. Here they are:

"So you want to talk about Chautauqua. Well, I was there, three years with Redpath (the name of a circuit). My first year right out of high school I spent with the Travers and Newton people (producers like Warner Wales—R.B.). I opened in South Dakota to an audience of farmers and Indians (in blankets yet).

"I boast of playing to the smallest audience in Chautauqua. It was one woman and her dog and during my act the dog walked out.

"It is sad how few performers today have voice projection. Everything is through a microphone. They are at a loss if they have to speak to a hundred people. I was looking at my Redpath program. The price of a season ticket was $2.75 for seven days—afternoon and night shows—with different entertainment every day."

Lowell Thomas, from whose autobiography I will quote later on, contributes this unexpected bit about Chautauqua:

"As for the Chautauqua period, well, I was on what I laughingly call 'a speaking tour of the world.' When I got home Chautauqua was fading and I only recall getting their white handkerchief greeting on one occasion, at the Chautauqua national headquarters at Jamestown, New York: similar except for the opposite reason to what Princeton rooters do in the closing seconds of a game if they have trounced either Yale or Harvard.

"As you know, William Jennings Bryan was the number-one Chautauqua star. I heard him on one occasion. Not his 'Cross of Gold' speech. It was his next most famous one, 'The Prince of Peace.' This was 1919, when I was a college freshman. When he finished his oration he allowed me to ride with him in his buggy. I remember only one thing he said to me: 'My boy, I always make my best speech on the way to the railway station!'

"As you undoubtedly know, he had a talented and stunning daughter. Ruth Bryan Owen was our first woman diplomat—ambassador to Denmark. We often met on the platform and to me she was even more eloquent than her silver-tongued father. When he spoke I sometimes felt as though some of it was malarkey. But his fabulous daughter made you think everything she said was so.

"Mark Twain of course was one of the early stars under the big tent."

On my Chautauqua tour—my first professional engagement—I had to join Actors Equity Association, which, three years before, in 1919, had been recognized by management after all but a handful of the actors on Broadway had walked out of their plays on strike. Membership in Equity was now mandatory. I resented this. It was, in effect, comparing actors with bricklayers, plumbers and carpenters as members of labor unions, I reasoned. With all due respect to these craftsmen, actors were artists, above unionism and the attendant ugliness between management and labor at the time. But the union movement was now quite validly under way, and thirty years later I became president of Actors Equity Association, to serve for four three-year terms.

The formation of Actors Equity came about as the result of many years of inhumane abuse of actors by management.

The Actors' Society of America was formed in 1896 to combat the Theatrical Syndicate, an organization of managers which dictated casts and theatres to be played both on Broadway and on the road.

The Society was ineffective, and in 1913 it dissolved itself, leaving a few adamant actors at the same meeting, on December 22, to organize Actors Equity Association. But it took continuous ugly battling to gain final recognition in 1919. It's now one of the most highly regarded of all labor unions affiliated with the American Federation of Labor.

Colorful and moving details of this struggle, led by the leading stars, can be found in Alfred Harding's accurate and exciting book *The Revolt of the Actors.** It will even captivate the layman.

The contract with Mr. Wales at forty dollars a week to play two of the five male characters in *The Shepherd of the Hills*, as

* William Morrow & Co., 1929.

~ 41 ~

well as a one-act sketch each afternoon, for sixty-seven "one-night stands" provided me with the security, self-confidence and what was, I'm sure, boorish conceit that led me to decide to forgo the balance of my schooling and prepare to tread the boards. If only we could cling to a respectable degree of that self-assurance till the last of Shakespeare's seven ages! But alas! The intervening ages tend to shatter it, don't they? And somewhere during this inevitable evolution, whether we admit it or not, the fact of our individual insignificance becomes painfully and at the same time—if we're lucky—amusingly evident.

My father was an advertising man. He headed his own agency in Chicago. He was disturbed at my decision to leave school. He wanted me to go to college. But he was even more concerned at my determination to give myself to the theatre. In a serious parental confrontation in his office, he warned me that if I pursued this calling and later changed my mind, I probably wouldn't be able to get a job of dignity and honor in any "reputable" field. It voiced the universal image of actors at that time. But it couldn't even scratch my steely ambition. We compromised on an agreement for me to go to work temporarily in his office.

I'm sure my father hoped I'd see the wisdom of his persuasion and come to the realization that acting was an infantile pursuit and really just a passing fascination. It was considerate and generous of him, too, I've realized later. It provided an income which made it possible for me to pay for a room on the Near North Side of Chicago, which was flourishing with writers and artists and where I made the acquaintance of a retired actor who was surrounded, literally and figuratively, by a Bohemian group of colorful iconoclasts.

My job as an advertising man was master of the files of clippings of the company's ads in all the periodicals. There were many clients and therefore many periodicals. They were all boring to me. So was the advertising business. I had a shelf-lined room in which to conduct the majestic task of keeper of the files, but I wasn't too precise about the filing of the newspapers and magazines that were entrusted to me. I was more interested in reading everything I could get my hands on that had to do with the theatre.

So, with the door to my filing sanctuary closed, I sat each day, with my feet on the long table, devouring biographies and autobiographies, current as well as past, of those of the theatre. Many of the past biographees, incidentally, were drunkards and/or lunatics. But I attributed this to their glorious eccentricities, in which I felt I could also indulge to some extent, but always keep under control, so that I wouldn't end as tragically as they did.

One day my father burst unceremoniously into my sanctum with a prospective new client, to whom I was proudly presented. He asked for certain of the files that would pertain to what he proposed for the P.N.C. I couldn't find them. My father, and then the P.N.C., joined the search. We never did locate them. The P.N.C. left and my father didn't get the new account.

He called me into his office and with admirable control spelled out the import of my felony. I truthfully said I was sorry but that I had an abhorrence for the whole dishonest business of advertising. It was, really, forcing people to buy something they didn't want or need. If it were done honorably, a splash of red paint at the top of the page and under it the message "We sell——," whatever, would be sufficient.

After a moment to exercise a little more admirable control, my father said, "Son, I guess you're not for the advertising business."

That ended my career as an advertising man—and my income from it. It's the only job from which I've ever been fired, and I must say it wasn't a traumatic experience. It rather served to solidify my ego. This is an example of the value of reflecting on the past, of "seeing one's self as others saw one" and being "objective and honest" and realizing how obnoxious one was.

Of course my father wasn't aware then that some years later he'd join me in my stock company.

I wish I could remember how I met William Owen. He was a "retired" actor—a Shakespearean actor, really—in his early sixties. He lived in a glorified rooming house at 18 West Delaware Street on Chicago's Near North Side. In the same building lived Julian MacDonald, an artist who did the scenery for the Chicago Grand Opera as well as stunning portraits and landscapes. He also did a mile of outdoor landscape with a crew every year in

Toronto, to be adorned with fireworks for some annual celebration or fair.

William Owen, who was called Billy by all his friends despite his age and commanding theatrical presence, had been an actor all his life, as far as I know. He said he was afraid of the big cities but he played almost every town in the country comfortably away from the big cities. I never saw him act, but I'm sure the big cities were the losers, as were the small towns that were beginning to ignore Shakespeare and demand modern fare.

Julian MacDonald became a lifelong friend until his death from cancer years later. He was removed on a stretcher through a window of a railroad car in Chicago on his way from New York to spend his remaining days with me in Beverly Hills.

Billy Owen moved from 18 West Delaware to 17 East Ohio Street and I moved there too—another rooming house. This is where I dwelt while in the advertising world and after my severance from it.

I met Melvyn Douglas at 17 East Ohio Street. He'd been a student of Billy's before my time. He'd just come in from an unsuccessful Shakespearean tour with John E. Kellard in the fall. They'd been stranded, given peremptory notice without salary or return railroad fare (which can't happen any more because managers are required to post bond even before rehearsals start, thanks to Actors Equity Association) somewhere in the hinterlands, and each of the company had to get back to civilization the best way he could. Melvyn and I became fast friends. And he got me a job the following summer as stage manager and "general business man" (more about this later) in Madison, Wisconsin, where he was the leading man at the Orpheum Theatre in the Dorothy Lavern stock company.

Through Julian MacDonald I developed a friendship with another artist, Rudolph Weisenborn, who was later to head the Chicago Art Institute.

There were many gatherings and gab fests among artists and literati in which I was privileged to be included. I met Ted Miller, one of the founders of the Taos, New Mexico, artist colony. And Stanley Zukalski, who designed the Polish Embassy in Paris, for which he received an international architect's prize.

When Melvyn had his own stock company in Madison, Julian

MacDonald did the scenery. And when I had my own company in Des Moines, Julian did my scenery and program covers.

Billy Owen had a group of young aspirants like me, and we rehearsed plays together under his direction, intermittently playing them (for nothing) in women's clubs, schools, churches, etc. The plays were classics for the most part—Shakespeare, Anatole France, Oscar Wilde and others. My special part was in *The Servant in the House,* by Charles Rann Kennedy.

With the encouragement to continue in the theatre, Billy Owen instilled in me a deep sense of respect and obligation to the responsibility of being an actor, and I've never lost it. In fact, it's increased as my luck has led me on. I'm eternally grateful to Billy Owen.

During this time I met a man who was about to produce a vaudeville skit. He wasn't a producer, he was a lawyer. But he had influence somewhere, because he got a tryout booking at an outlying theatre and Harry Weber, the biggest Chicago vaudeville booker, agreed to look over the act.

At one point in the sketch, after a violent scene with his wife, a man in an "English walking coat" puts out the lamp on the table beside him, leaving the stage in darkness, and goes to sleep on the couch downstage left (that's near the footlights, on the right of the stage as one sees it from the audience). Presently "the Phantom Death" enters in a spotlight and stands in the door in the back wall, above and a little toward center stage of the couch.

"The Phantom Death" has a recitative that includes almost everything from Omar Khayyám ("The Moving Finger writes; and, having writ,/Moves on . . .") to the Bible ("O death, where is thy sting?") to the Book of Common Prayer ("Ashes to ashes, dust to dust") and much more. This represents the sleeping man's dream. After this, "the Phantom Death" crosses the stage between a table and two chairs in the center and a piano lamp above them against the back wall, wraps the girl in the folds of his sleeve and exits stage right (left, from the audience's point of view). This is Death taking the girl away.

I was "the Phantom Death."

When the day came to present this masterpiece to the public and Harry Weber at a hideaway theatre on the outskirts of Chicago, it meant taking three streetcars, transferring twice—a trip of well over an hour. We were finally made up and ready for the matinee performance, the first of three that day. The curtain rose and the sketch started, and our hearts were pumping hard. At least mine was. The actor in the English walking coat eventually lay down on the couch, reached over and put out the light and went to sleep, leaving the stage dark. Presently I appeared in a spotlight in the upstage door. My face was made up like a skull, I had a black hood and a loosely folded floor-length cape. In my right hand I had a small spotlight concealed in the folds of my sleeve with which I focused a green light on my face.

I finished the recitative in the doorway and started my trek to the girl, whom I would fold in my free sleeve, and exit: Death taking her away stage right, followed by the spotlight from the lantern house out front. But when I got to stage center I tripped on a cable running between the table and the piano lamp, and fell, taking the lamp with me.

In the melee that followed I got entangled with the cable. I was on the floor, in the spotlight from out front, which had been instructed to follow me. I was a writhing figure of death, with the face of a skull, waving a green spotlight in one hand and kicking trousered legs from under the black shroud. I couldn't get loose but I found a plug connection in the electric cable and pulled it apart. I then rose, wrapped in cable, and taking the piano lamp with me, left the stage in the spotlight and the girl to her own fate. The girl, quite sensibly, made her exit too, and they pulled down the curtain.

There was silence in the dressing room, which I shared with the gentleman in the English walking coat. What was there to say? Soon the producer came in and just stood looking at me. Finally I said, "Do I have time to take off this make-up and go out for something to eat?"

"Yes, you'll have time to go out and get something to eat," the producer replied. "But don't bother to come back."

I never heard what Harry Weber thought of the act.

And I didn't pursue a vaudeville career.

Vaudeville was a group of specialty acts: jugglers, acrobats, tumblers, dancers, singers, magicians, comedians, monologists and play sketches.

Early variety shows in the United States were performed in dives and on waterfronts and in frontier honky-tonks. They were coarse, vulgar sucker-traps, including rigged gambling games and floozies along with suggestive songs and dances.

These shows were denounced from pulpits and the actors were outcasts. Boardinghouses exhibited signs saying, "No Dogs or Actors Allowed."

In 1842 P. T. Barnum tried to clean up the stigma by calling his "freaks, fakes, monstrosities and exotic animals" a museum, "an educational exhibit."

But in 1881 Tony Pastor really cleaned things up by publicizing "No drinking, no smoking, no vulgarity or rough talk permitted on stage"—thus making his variety shows entertainment for the whole family.

As in minstrel shows—and no doubt borrowed from them—the variety shows frequently finished with an "afterpiece" that involved personnel from the entire program in a sketch or "bit."†

Vaudeville was eventually designed after the English variety show or music hall by Benjamin Franklin Keith, a former circus performer, in 1883.

His first "museum" and show were housed in a vacant candy store, which he called the Gaiety Museum.

His principal attractions were Baby Alice, a midget who weighed one and a half pounds, and an "ancient mermaid" (stuffed). Later he added "the Circassian beauties," a chicken with a human face and a pair of rising comedians, Weber and Fields.

Keith was joined in his venture by Edward F. Albee in 1885. Together they acquired theatres in Providence and Philadelphia. These became the nucleus of a chain of approximately a thousand theatres, located eventually in every city of a hundred thousand or more, entertaining a daily aggregate of two million people in the United States and Canada.

Among early vaudeville acts were the Four Cohans, one of whom was George M. Cohan. Others were Montgomery and

† A good part of this material was obtained from *Once Upon a Stage* by Charles and Louise Samuels, Dodd Mead, 1974, and the Columbia Encyclopedia.

Stone, David Warfield, the Barrymores, Sarah Bernhardt, Lenore Ulric, the Foy family and Harrigan and Hart.

Other circuits followed. Kohl and Middleton in Chicago. In San Francisco Gustave Walters opened the Orpheum Theatre, which was taken over by Martin Beck, who established the Orpheum circuit and merged with Keith-Albee. F. F. Proctor, John J. Murdoch and Oscar Hammerstein (the father of Richard Rodgers' partner) operated vaudeville theatres in New York City. Gus Sun operated in Ohio, and Alexander Pantages and John Considine in the Northwest.

Martin Beck's greatest achievement was signing Sarah Bernhardt for $7,000 a week.

In 1905 the Keith and Proctor interests formed the United Booking Office, which became the official clearinghouse and engagement bureau for all artists and acts.

In 1916 the National Vaudeville Artists Association Inc. was organized to deal with the United Booking Office. By 1928 this association listed about fifteen thousand members, and it's still active.

As moving pictures and radio developed, Keith-Albee in the East and Orpheum in the West absorbed movie interests to become Radio-Keith-Orpheum (RKO).‡

Although vaudeville is virtually gone now, many of our comedians and dramatic actors and actresses learned their business there—among them Elsie Janis, Nora Bayes, Sophie Tucker, Frank Fay and Mae West.

The nearest things to it today are the variety and talk shows on TV, such as the old "Ed Sullivan Show" and the Johnny Carson, Merv Griffin and Mike Douglas shows. Actually, it was these very shows that finally finished vaudeville as we used to know it, because the familiar acts couldn't continue to go out over the circuits year after year. They reached millions of people who saw them in one performance over TV. But it was great in its day.

A close friend of mine, William McCaffrey, became a noted vaudeville agent through the United Booking Office. He's still an agent in all areas and was my agent in New York during early radio and TV. His most prominent client today is Art Carney. Bill contributed the following:

‡ Credit Encyclopaedia Britannica for a lot of this—R.B.

"Anent vaudeville: I was E. F. Albee's office boy and in the latter days of the vaudeville business he was a czar. The vaudeville business was started in Boston by B. F. Keith and when he became deceased it came under the jurisdiction of Albee, and became the Keith-Albee circuit. It was designed essentially as family entertainment and it flourished until the Depression and the advent of radio and talking pictures caused its expiration. The management was very strict about performers not doing risqué material. For instance, Sophie Tucker sang a song at the Palace called 'Who Paid the Rent for Mrs. Rip Van Winkle When Rip Van Winkle Was Away?' She was immediately canceled and paid off, inasmuch as her contract had a clause that prohibited censorship of her material.

"Some great performers evolved from vaudeville, such as Jack Benny, Burns and Allen, Olsen and Johnson, Joe Cook, etc.

"Incidentally, Keith-Albee was sued at least three times for anti-Sherman violations, and they beat it every time."

And here's a word or two from one of the greatest.

He not only starred with Gracie in vaudeville for years, but they practically took over TV too.

I made the picture *Oh, God!* with George Burns. He had just celebrated his eighty-first birthday and a couple of days later he had a long scene to do in the picture. They were ready for him with TelePrompTers and cue cards.

He did the scene in one "take" without TelePrompTers or cue cards and he went home at noon.

George tells this story:

"Years ago in small-time vaudeville your contracts had a cancellation clause, and if the manager didn't like you, he could cancel you after your first performance. So every Monday and Thursday afternoon they'd play eight acts, and then after the first show the manager would only keep four.

"I was doing an act then called Brown and Williams, Singers, Dancers and Roller Skaters, and we were booked into the Dewey Theatre on 14th Street in New York. So after the opening show on Monday all the performers would stand in front of their dressing rooms, and the manager would come down and cancel four of the acts. He'd walk past and say, 'You're closed . . . you're closed . . . you're closed . . . and you're closed.' These acts would go into their dressing rooms, take off their make-up, pick up their pictures and go home.

"The Monday after we opened at the Dewey Theatre the manager passed right by us and canceled the acrobatic act next to us. This big husky acrobat grabbed this little manager by the seat of his pants and lifted him up in the air and said, 'Who's closed?' And the manager pointed to my partner and me and said, 'They are.'

"But I've been canceled many times. However, the manager had nothing to do with it, it was the audience.

"I hope you can use that story, Ralph. If you can't, let me know and I'll use it. And you know it's a true story—'God' never lies."

Burlesque saw its heyday during the first thirty years of this century. I saw a good deal of it, and maybe I learned something from it. But I always had a good time. And oh! those strippers!

Under the delusion that my old friend Jerry Lester had been a part of burlesque, I found out the following:

"*I've* not only *been* but headlined and starred in all the areas you've mentioned, i.e., vaudeville, clubs, Broadway, TV, radio— well, *not movies*. I'll kaleidoscope my entire 'movie' career in one sentence. Ready? I played the love interest to Judy Canova in *Sleepy Time Girl* at Republic—any questions? I love Judy but none of the leading men in town are worried.

"You asked about 'burlesque' bits. Funny, but I was never in that one medium until just a few years ago when Ann Corio asked me to co-star with her in *This Was Burlesque,* which I thought would be fun—and really was—*and* enormously successful. You're aware, I'm certain, that *all* the sketches in burlesque are handed down, given the particular comic's 'version'—i.e., 'We'll do the schoolroom scene' and the straight man (whoever) will immediately say, 'Which version?' So the answer could be 'the Jack Albertson,' 'the Benny Rubin.' Now! Corio allowed me complete latitude for ad-libbing, which is unusual for her; she's a great editor and disciplinarian. And I had a picnic because she *trusted* me, knowing my background, plus having been great friends. Though 'friendship' exits when the show starts. If you really want a rundown on the fun Ann Corio and I have had, I suggest you contact her.

"Incidentally, she wrote a book called *This Was Burlesque.*"

I wrote Miss Corio as Jerry suggested, and here's her reply:

"Dear Mr. Bellamy:

"I note that you said you were getting a copy of my book, *This Was Burlesque,* and I feel that it will supply you with most of the information you are seeking. It is a history of burlesque, both before and after our time.

"But if there is anything specific that you would want that is not covered in the book please feel free to contact me. I will be happy to help you in any way that I can.

"Fondly, from one of your many admirers,

Ann Corio"

In *This Was Burlesque* Miss Corio says, "Burlesque is as old as Aristophanes, who was the first to satirize people, human tragedies and contemporary ideas and events. He laughed at the world in his plays and he made people laugh too. And that's what burlesque means. It comes from the Italian word *burlare,* which means to laugh at, to make fun of."

The Columbia Encyclopedia confirms this and says further that burlesque took the form of low comedy, coarse slapstick, in a series of short turns. A sort of vaudeville characterized by low comedy, backed by a display of nudity.

In tracing burlesque from early to latter days, Miss Corio says that in the early 1900s an American playwright named John Brougham burlesqued Shakespeare, the classics and current drama. And that many actors, including Edwin Booth and Sydney Greenstreet, participated, often burlesquing their own legitimate performances.

In 1868 Lydia Thompson brought her "London Blondes" to America and made burlesque an American institution.

Weber and Fields deserted the minstrel shows for burlesque,

and they were the greatest comedy team of the day and for many years afterward in vaudeville and musical comedy.

Others who immortalized the old Columbia circuit, known as the "Columbia Wheel" (later challenged by the Mutual and Empire wheels and the Hirst circuit) were James Barton, W. C. Fields, Will Rogers, Bert Lahr, Jackie Gleason, Red Skelton, Ed Wynn, Joe E. Brown, Leon Errol, Buster Keaton, Fanny Brice, Joe Penner, B. S. Pully, Hal Skelly, Eddie Cantor, Bobby Clark, Paul McCullough, Al Jolson, Danny Thomas, Jimmy Durante, Red Buttons, Joey Faye, Rags Ragland and Abbott and Costello.

Ann Corio indicates that there may be a difference of opinion about who was the first "stripper." There is documentation of its having been Hinda Winssau in Chicago in 1928, she says.

Hinda did a shimmy in a chorus girl contest. She was underdressed in a short beaded and fringed costume for the shimmy. She left the chorus line to remove her chorus costume in the wings, but it got stuck on the beaded costume beneath. Her music was playing and the manager was urging her onstage. In desperation she went on, with the outer garment still half on and half off, and started her shimmy. As she shimmied, the chorus costume started to come loose. She removed as much as she could and the audience howled. She shimmied more, and more came loose, and she removed that. At the climax of her shimmy the chorus costume came completely loose and she tossed it aside. After that she became a featured attraction.

But Miss Corio thinks the "mother of strip tease" was Carrie Finnell.

In an effort to prolong her engagement in Cleveland, on the first week Carrie removed one garment and promised there'd be more the next week. She continued removing a garment a week for a year—and originated the "tease."

The G string, Miss Corio says, is "a tiny jewel-like bauble on a string around the waist, which covers up its specific subject, along with the pasties on the bosom. They were the last garment still attached to the stripper when she finished her act."

In addition to Hinda Winssau and Carrie Finnell, latter-day strippers who became household names (?) were Gypsy Rose Lee, Margie Hart, Georgia Southern, Lois de Fee, Lily St. Cyr and, of course, Ann Corio.

Ann was approached by Broadway, but declined. She says she's never regretted it.

Billy Minsky of the Minsky family was the most prominent burlesque producer.

Burlesque has had its impact on TV, movies and Broadway, but it's almost gone now because of those media.

Ann Corio and Jerry Lester keep the nostalgia alive by going on the road each summer with *This Was Burlesque*.

An old burlesque "top banana" friend of mine, Phil Silvers, contributes these words:

"When I was working in burlesque during the Minsky era the strip women were the attraction and the comics were, in a sense, walking towels, cooling the audience off between strips. But it was great training for comedians if they had the guts to hang in there and make their presence felt. Now—

"There was a most beautiful lady named Christeen Ayres who was a Ziegfeld show girl whose top salary was in the area of $250 per week. She must have said 'The hell with this' and changed her name to 'Charmayne' and became a strip woman for Minsky. She was a beauty, especially stripped, and in burlesque her salary rose to $2500 per week.

"The loudspeaker would announce, 'Harold Minsky proudly presents the beauty of Miss Charmayne,' the orchestra would play a few strains of 'Charmaine' and she would glide through the center curtain and proceed to do her bit, finishing with the nakedness of her strip routine.

"Well, there was always a heckler or two in the audience, and I use the term audience loosely, but the particular instance I refer to is one of complete hilarity. This one never-to-be-forgotten heckler yelled, clearly and with great authority as the curtain parted to reveal her after the announcement, 'Miss Charmayne, if that's chow mein I'll eat it!' Bedlam of laughter from the audience and indignation from Christeen. Even at this late date I ask you, how indignant can you be in a spotlight, naked?"

And here's a surprise. Who would have thought that Robert Alda, star of the musical hit *Guys and Dolls*, is a product of burlesque? He's not only made a name for himself in pictures, but his son Alan is mashing out a name for himself too. Here's a note from Bob:

"Dear Ralph:

"In your search for anecdotes and stories about burlesque, I have come up with the following. There was a young kid, hardly twenty-one, who went into burlesque as a singer. Unless you were a comic, that's the way you started in the early days. Then if you had ambition and talent, you graduated to a straight man. This kid became a 'talker' in his first month, when a blind comic by the name of Mike Sacks asked him if he could 'talk.' Of course he said yes and he went on to become one of the youngest straight men in burlesque. That kid was me, Robert Alda.

"I spent five years in burlesque, for which I'm not the least bit sorry. Where else could you get a show-biz education like that without paying for it? Who could afford to go to an acting school in the middle of the Depression?

"Now, in retrospect, I find I really had some great opportunities. While other aspiring actors were scrounging around looking for their next part, I was doing everything from derelicts to song-and-dance men. I had the chance to work with a lot of people who later were destined to make their mark.

"I worked with Abbott and Costello before they were a team. I worked with Rags Ragland, who went on to Broadway and films. With Red Marshall, who went to Broadway musicals; Phil Silvers, the ever lovable Sergeant Bilko; Red Buttons, whom 'they never gave a dinner for'; and eventually teamed up with Hank Henry, who became legendary in Las Vegas. We became one of the highest-paid comedy teams in burlesque until he was drafted and went into the Army in 1940. Six months later I quit burlesque and went on to other things which eventually brought me to Hollywood.

"Some of the gals I 'sang' for did pretty well too. Ann Corio, Margie Hart, Gypsy Rose Lee, just to name a few. There were dozens more. 'Singing' for these gals meant singing a torrid ballad in the wings, over a mike of course, while they did their strip-teasing.

"It was more teasing than strip in my early days of the mid-thirties. At one time greater New York, which included Newark and Union City, New Jersey, had seventeen burlesque theatres operating at one time. You could stay in the Big Apple for years, without ever hitting the road, if you so desired.

"But then the bomb exploded. Mayor La Guardia put a ban on burlesque and the theatres countered by changing the spelling of the word. They called it burlesk. From that time on, in my humble opinion, it slowly went downhill, until today a good burlesque show is hard to find.

"Believe it or not, when I went into burlesque, it was at the tail end of the old Columbia Wheel days. That was a circuit that covered most of the country, and if you signed for a season, that meant about forty weeks' work. Other circuits cropped up after that, but they were still doing burlesque where a lot of families used to attend, mainly for the funny comedy sketches and routines.

"Then family attendance began shrinking as the comedians began losing favor to the strippers, who began the fine art of 'teasing.'

"Unfortunately, burlesque has just about disappeared. It's a lost art. 'Lost' because it's just one place less where young talent can learn the ropes, work in front of an audience and build themselves a solid foundation for the future.

"My fondest regards,

"Sincerely,
Bob Alda"

A strange kind of entertainment had been delivered to the "sticks" for some time—

The medicine show.

Even though it's part of our early Americana, the medicine show undoubtedly derived from the European strolling mountebank. He operated all over Europe from the seventeenth century on. His *raison d'être* was to sell cure-alls—magic ointments, soaps, smelling salts and "medicines." He attracted crowds at fairs, street corners, market squares or wherever people were likely to gather. Even in the Piazza San Marco.

I never saw a medicine show, but I remember the casting of them in agents' offices in Chicago.

American newspapers, mostly in the Middle West and South, carried ads for such medicine shows as "Dr. Duponco's Golden Periodical Pills," "Dr. Sappington's Vegetable Febrifuge Pills," "Dr. Hemmold's genuine preparation of highly concentrated compound fluid extract of Buchu," "Dr. Williams' pink pills for pale people," "Hoofland's German Tonic," "Schiffman's German Asthma Cure," "Mexican Mustang Liniment," "Kickapoo Indian Sagwa," "Turkish Pile Ointment," "Merchant's Gargling Oil," "Kickapoo Indian Oil," "Buchu-Paiba, the great kidney cure," "Ka-Ton-Ka, the great Indian medicine," "Wa-Hoo Bitters," "Snake Oil," "Wizard Oil" (containing camphor, ammonia, chloroform, sassafras, cloves and turpentine and, at various times, 55 to 70 per cent alcohol) and of course "Lydia E. Pinkham's Vegetable Compound." They were guaranteed to cure anything from corns to constipation. The last of the line was probably "Hadacol."

The average medicine show of my time traveled in wagons pulled by horses or mules. If they were among the few of greater size, playing in larger cities and fairs, they traveled by rail with their "equipment" in the baggage cars. They carried as few as two or three performers and as many as forty.

Later the smaller shows converted to housecar-trucks, with accommodations for eating and sleeping. A tail gate dropped, forming a small stage.

The audience stood. And for night performances, illumination was by gasoline or kerosene pan torches or calcium floodlights on a pole.

About one third of most shows consisted of lectures, demonstrations and sales, and the rest was devoted to some kind of variety show.

Many small shows played country towns, where there was no other entertainment, and often the country people bought whatever was being sold out of gratitude.

Many preparations were concocted in washtubs carried under the wagon or platform, or were ordered from patent medicine manufacturers, who either would bottle the showman's own formula or paste his personal label on their own stock liniment, soap or herb remedy.

Some of the medicine show entrepreneurs had colorful names, such as "Calculator Williams," "Doc Ruckner," "Silk Hat Harry," "Electric Bill from Over the Hill," "Big Foot Wallace," "Chief Sheet Lightning," "Dr. Yellowstone," "Texas Charlie," "Nevada Ned," "Red Fin."*

My friend Milburn Stone, who played Doc in "Gunsmoke" for twenty years, came from "med show" country.

The following is a transcript of a tape Milly sent me.

"The 'med shows' didn't change very much. They were all about the same so when I describe one or two of them, I think I've described them all insofar as my knowledge of them is concerned.

"Naturally, the early ones were horsedrawn, which is the case of the first one I ever saw back in 1910 or 1911 when I was six or seven years old in western Kansas.

"First, let me describe the wagon itself. It was a kind of enclosed panel wagon with a high seat up front very much like a stagecoach. The unique thing about it was that the entire rear end—not just the tail gate but the whole back end of it—hinged and dropped down and was held up and supported by two permanent stanchions and provided the stage room for the two performers to work. The old doctor and the entertainer, which in this case in my early recollection was a young fellow who was very clever. He worked in black-face and played the banjo, and he was damn good.

"Quite naturally, both ends of the wagon and the rear end, and every place there was room for lettering, there was a sign proclaiming all the virtues of this magic potion that the old boy was selling. I can't recall the name of it, let's just say it was 'Dr. Southerland's Kickapoo Indian Magic Herb Remedy.' And, believe me, it claimed to cure everything—everything from pneumonia right on down to chilblains, and everything in between.

"Now as I've said, that is my earliest recollection of a medi-

* Most of this from *Step Right Up* by Brooks McNamara, Doubleday, 1976.

cine show and the thing I remember most about it is that it thrilled the hell out of me to see this old boy sell his medicine. He was just great. Did the damnedest fast-talking pitch you ever saw—marvelous slapping on the bottle—and he would give you all kinds of bargains and everything. But the thing that impressed me the most was this young guy who worked in black-face and played the banjo. My God, he was clever! At least I thought so then. He danced and sang and told jokes and I think maybe it might have been right then that the bug bit me, I don't know.

"Now I'm sure the way they worked was they went from town to town in this rig and they lived in it, slept in it, ate in it and carried all of their personal gear and their medicine in great supplies. They had possum bellies under the wagon. And they carried a great deal of paraphernalia in there.

"I recall another thing. They had carbide lamps on the side of the rear end, and I'm sure you might recall what carbide smells like when it's lighted. If you've ever smelled it, you'll never forget it. Boy, it stinks, and puts out one ungodly glare, too!

"Now, my recollection is that they were well treated in the town. Nobody seemed to be angry about anything they did. And I don't recall any aftereffects. That is, I don't recall any irate citizens wanting to find them and get their money back. They might have been crooks. I don't think so. I don't think they got arrested anyplace. They just sold their medicine and, obviously, they did bilk the public because it was nothing but colored water, I'm sure, and a little sugar in it, maybe.

"But I'm going to tell you about some others that I saw when we moved over to the little town where I was born, Burton, Kansas. Now Burton, being a small town of about four hundred or five hundred population, attracted this type of entertainment. I saw two or three 'Med Shows' and I recall them pretty well, I think. They were much more sophisticated versions of the ones I saw out in western Kansas but only in the fact that they were motorized. They all had trucks. Their vans were on truck chassis, but they worked the same way exactly. There was the high-pitch man, the doctor and the entertainer or entertainers.

"I remember one outfit that came through had two entertainers and they worked in black-face and, as I recall, they were much like Amos and Andy. They told jokes, they sang and they danced and they played banjos, and they were damned good. They might have been more accurately like the 'Two Black Crows.' You remember them—Moran and Mack.

"The entertainment was corny jokes. It was all corn but they were damn good at what they did. The pitch men were absolutely fantastic. These birds were just a different breed of cats. They were personable. They inspired confidence and by the time they talked to you a few minutes, they could charm the gold teeth right out of your mouth. They all had the same cure-all, the same great elixir, that was bound to cure everything in the world that was wrong with you. And they all, I think, had the philosophy that the public was invented to be bilked and they were the privileged few sent on earth to do it.

"It was at this stage of my life that I was fortunate enough to meet the Proctor brothers. I got to know them quite well and I watched them work. They were just absolutely fantastic. I watched them sell medicine, and I remember I said to one of them one time, 'Now I want to ask you something. You admitted that this medicine is no damn good. You make it yourself out of water and color it and sweeten it and whatever.' And he said, 'That's right.'

"I said, 'Well, it won't do anybody any good, will it?' He says, 'Well, it won't do 'em any harm.' I said, 'All right, you play the same towns year after year. You go into a town and you sell them a whole case of this stuff—and you come back the next year and it hasn't done them a damn bit of good and they're mad as hell and they want their money back and they tell you, "It's no good." What do you do then?' He says, 'We just tell 'em they haven't had enough and sell 'em another case.'"

PART IV

In the late teens and early twenties, Chicago was experiencing what may have been its most exciting period. Certainly they were exciting days for a small-town kid like me.

Irene and Vernon Castle were the rage of the ballrooms, and flagpole sitting was the fad.

Ben Hecht did a daily two-column true story on the back page of the Chicago *Daily News*. Some of it was unquestionably his best writing. They were searching and touching stories of people, people he met as he wandered through the various ethnic and class-divided neighborhoods, and they carried underlying social and human statements and problems.

George Bellows was teaching at the Chicago Art Institute.

District Judge Kenesaw Mountain Landis became the first commissioner of baseball in 1920.

Clarence Darrow was one of Chicago's prominent lawyers, later to defend Loeb and Leopold and then Scopes at the famous "monkey trial."

Samuel Insull was pyramiding his mammoth industrial empire, which later collapsed in ignominious failure.

Republican Mayor William Hale Thompson was reigning on the spoils system, to be defeated by Democrat Anton Cermak, who built the Tammany-style machine that has been entrenched since then and who was later killed accidentally by a bullet meant for FDR in Miami, Florida.

Jane Addams was drawing national and international attention to her progressive and innovative social concepts, so successfully being exercised at Hull House.

Percy Hammond of the Chicago *Tribune*, later to go to New York, was one of the country's most erudite drama critics.

John T. McCutcheon, also of the *Tribune*, was one of the most outspoken and respected social cartoonists.

Al Capone, in his twenties, reigned supreme. He owned the town.

Chicago has always had a restlessness, a rebellion against the status quo, a look beyond the frontier. Someone has said the difference between Chicago and New York is that if you telephone an executive in New York, a secretary says he's in a meeting and tries to get the message from you. But if you call the president of a company in Chicago, he answers the phone himself.

Chicago was seething creatively in those days, but it also took note of the lighter side. All newspapers carried thick comic sections on Sunday—"Old Doc Yak," "The Katzenjammer Kids," "Mutt and Jeff," "Buster Brown," "Barney Google," "Bringing Up Father" and "The Gumps."

Crowds jammed the Aragon and Trianon ballrooms every night to dance to the music of Paul Biesie, Ben Bernie and Paul Whiteman.

The large colony of self-styled intellectuals lived on the Near North Side, the area bounded by the Chicago River to Division Street, and Clark Street to Lake Michigan. They were writers, painters, revolutionaries of all kinds, almost all of them in pursuit of some form of expression against prevailing concepts.

The Industrial Workers of the World was the radical organization of its day, corresponding in its iconoclastic ideas to communism today. It was a labor-oriented movement that wanted to improve conditions of workers of all kinds everywhere. The IWW was depicted in conservative newspaper cartoons as a man with wild hair, stringy full beard and a smoking bomb in his hand.

There was a dead-end alley running east off Newberry Square, in front of the Newberry Library on the Near North Side. It was dubbed "Bug House Square," for the odd people who lived around it. For some reason the alley bore the name, on a city street sign, of "Tucker Place." It served the houses on Delaware and Chestnut streets and contained, on both sides, buildings that had once been carriage stables, with living quarters for livery-men above the stalls and carriages.

A fellow named Jack Jones came to Bohemian prominence on the Near North Side in the early twenties. He bore the aura of a story that he'd had both arms broken as an IWW strike agitator in a mine strike in Idaho. He talked two sisters who lived in adjoining houses on Delaware Street into letting him use their carriage stables, knocking out the wall that separated them and making one building for a meeting hall.

As I remember Jones, he was short, stocky, blond and blue-eyed, quiet but fierce-looking.

The downstairs of his new edifice was a kind of gathering place for the intelligentsia, with provision for art exhibitions and refreshments.

Upstairs, there was a small auditorium with a raised platform at one end with seating room for seventy-five to a hundred people. Each Sunday there was a speaker in the auditorium. I remember Clarence Darrow and Judge Landis—before he became the first baseball czar—being among them. Frederick Starr, the University of Chicago anthropologist, was another.

Admission was ten cents for these lectures, with the stipulation that anyone who interrupted the speaker would be ejected. But after the speaker had finished he would be available for a question-and-answer session at which anyone could say anything he liked. And they always did.

This procedure had an attraction for these brilliant men. It was a form of intellectual exercise, I guess, because they seemed to relish the Q&A session, which was more of a debate with a mob, and which included a fair amount of profanity and frequent fist fights. Of course, only the audience indulged in the fist fights and there were times when the police had to be asked to intervene. But I heard, was awed by and shook hands with many of the speakers.

Jack Jones called his establishment "The Dill Pickle Club" and everyone referred to Tucker Place as "Tooker Alley." If my memory is good on this, I believe the city was persuaded to acknowledge this preference on its street sign.

There may have been more opportunity to effectively defy the status quo at that time because "the system" more securely prevailed. With the exception of unions and women's suffrage, not much effort had been made to resist it. True, it took more courage to protest, because the trend was to comply. This condition, therefore, bred innovations in all creative fields. It was an exciting period, not only here but abroad. It would seem that World War I had, in large part, been responsible for probing and questioning past mores and customs by dispersing soldiers to new social, ethnic and economic areas in strange countries. Also, the objections were more solidly and understandably based than the kind of non-specific protests for the sake of protest we see in a good deal of today's non-conformists because those were so blatantly obvious and needed immediate correction. Today's protests are leveled at abuses of the trust and power embedded in our original concepts.

The energy and excitement and frontier-like individualism of Chicago and its people were not only an education but an inspiration for this very receptive, eager, restless neophyte.

All of this, the training, the introduction to the colorful Chicago life of this incubating time—but most of all the profound and consecrated devotion to the theatre—was welded into me by Billy Owen.

World War I, while it was being waged, had slight effect on the theatre insofar as subject matter was concerned. That was to come later with *Buddies*, *What Price Glory?*, *Journey's End* and others. But many actors enlisted, and theatre attendance dropped, due in part to increase of ticket prices to two-fifty to three dollars, plus a war tax.

I was not too aware of modern plays and actors before the war, but the substance of most of the popular fare on Broadway, and from there to the road, seems to have been, in comparison to later seasons, escapist, romantic and somewhat unsophisticated. There was a considerable number of Shakespearean plays running almost all the time. Acting was beginning to become natural, as opposed to the theretofore flamboyant and elocutionary style.

There was an impressive list of stars, such as the Barrymores, John Drew, Montgomery and Stone, Jane Cowl, Margaret Anglin, Lowell Sherman, Sarah Bernhardt, Wilton Lackaye, Nance O'Neil, Maude Adams, Holbrook Blinn and George M. Cohan, just to name a very few. And they worked literally all the time.

If a play was unsuccessful on Broadway, the actors either took it on the road or went into another play on Broadway. It was not uncommon for an actor to appear in two plays on Broadway in the same season.

The actors' strike in 1919, with the backing of the AFL-affiliated unions, closed every theatre in the country until Actors Equity Association was recognized. After that, the theatre flourished as it never had before in the United States, and we saw the beginning of a literary, sophisticated American theatre, as typified by such playwrights as Sidney Howard, George Kelly, Eugene O'Neill, Sidney Kingsley, Laurence Stallings, George S. Kaufman, Elmer Rice, Marc Connelly and S. N. Behrman.

Prohibition was enacted in 1920 and that was reflected in a few plays such as *The Old Soak*, *The Great Gatsby* and *12 Miles Out*.

There was a sudden release. Life everywhere, in big cities and small, included "going out." Speakeasies were plentiful and stocked with bootleg liquor and good food. There were big dance bands in palatial dance halls. All this nocturnal activity overflowed into the theatre. Once again it was thriving, on Broadway and on the road and in stock.

PART V

In the twenties, before radio and talking pictures and television, almost every city of fifty thousand or over had at least one resident stock company (not to be confused with what we know today as "summer stock"). The larger cities sometimes had two or three. Everyone in these cities and towns went to see the stock company every week, usually in the same seats, at fifty cents to a dollar a ticket. At Wednesday matinees, flowers were frequently sent to the leading lady and pies or cakes to the leading man. An usher delivered the gifts over the footlights.

A stock company consisted of a basic complement of ten actors, a director, a stage manager and a scenic artist. The actors were all good. They had to be. They did ten performances a week—seven nights and Wednesday, Saturday and Sunday matinees. At the same time they rehearsed every day, usually with the exception of Thursday (but had an all-day dress rehearsal Friday), preparing for the following week's play.

The plays were recent Broadway successes.

The scenery was built for each play by the stagehands and painted on the "paint frame" on the back wall of the stage. The scenic artist worked on a catwalk some twenty feet above the stage, extending horizontally and hanging about two feet from the back wall, allowing the frame that bore the newly built flats of scenery to be raised between the catwalk and the back wall.

The basic acting company consisted of leading man, leading woman, second business man and second business woman (they usually played the heavies), juvenile, ingénue, character man, character woman, comedian and general business man (who played the small parts that were left over). Sometimes the director and/or stage manager would play a part, and if a large cast was called for, additional people were brought in from the nearest pool of actors. They were called "jobbers."

It was customary for actors to go to the production centers— New York, Chicago and Los Angeles—in August to see the agents for jobs. Those who didn't get a Broadway play or a road show would go into stock.

A stock company run could be from fifteen to forty weeks a season in the same city. Many actors did only stock, and some Broadway stars and featured players reached a point where they could afford not to play stock any more. But everyone starring on Broadway started in stock, including the Lunts, the Barrymores, Helen Hayes, Katharine Cornell—everyone. It was earning one's spurs. It was the great training ground for young actors, as well as professional security for older actors who didn't want to risk Broadway or the road any more.

When Melvyn Douglas got the job as leading man in the stock company in Madison, Wisconsin, and got me on as general business man and stage manager at forty dollars a week, he was getting sixty dollars and later seventy-five. That was my first stock job.

The last conscious impression of my first night in Madison was the sound of the huge town clock striking in the distance. Twelve slow, resonant bongs. It produced a feeling of security, a feeling of satisfaction with the day and anticipation of tomorrow. It was akin to that disappearing sensation of comfortable isolation that used to come with the far-off midnight train whistle.

Arriving in Madison was associated with a sense of responsibility and obligation. It meant a different part each week. It meant organization of props and furniture and cues for lights and offstage effects such as bells, doorslams, rain or snow, etc. It meant rapping on each dressing room door, calling, "Half hour, please," "Fifteen minutes, please," "Five minutes, please," before each performance—all the duties of the stage manager. It was wonderful.

Madison is a beautiful city, between Lake Monona and Lake Mendota. It's cold with lots of snow in the winter. Buddy and leafy and fresh in the spring. Green and lush and hot, with frequent lake breezes, in the summer. Blazing with color and sunsets in the fall.

The university inspired an intellectual excitement.

Cop's Cafeteria on the Capitol Square was a gathering place for students at night, and they were friendly.

The poet William Ellery Leonard was a kind of local intellectual mystery man, with the odd phobia that prevented him from venturing beyond the square block containing his house. He was writing one of his most famous works, *Red Bird*.

Madison was a spirited, progressive city.

Glenn Frank, who had been editor of *Century Magazine*, was coming to head the University of Wisconsin. His arrival brought faculty, students and citizens to the Northwestern Railroad station along with the band. Mr. Frank descended from the train wearing spats and carrying a stick. The band didn't play and the welcoming horde retreated in silence.

This was certainly not a reflection of the attitudes of the university or the Madisonians, who were disturbed at this boorish reaction. It had to be by order of one, or a very few, unenlightened and unrepresentative university potentates. Subsequently, of course, Frank introduced innovations at the university which added further distinction to his already glowing literary and academic aura.

"The Great War" was over and life was back to normal. The war had not yet had a marked social effect. Life was perhaps a little more sophisticated, but the unrest of the awakening youth, and labor, and enlightened thinkers hadn't moved society yet from its self-deluding lethargy. But there was an air of expectancy, a distant rumble. Prominent lecturers were popular and drew respectable audiences.

Alexander Woollcott came to Madison on a lecture tour and Melvyn Douglas and I met him. We drove together to Spring Green to see Frank Lloyd Wright's house, Taliesin. We met Wright, who was just leaving on an errand with his beautiful black-haired paramour. He ordered a tour for us that included the workrooms where his staff, many of whom were Japanese, was busy. We were told that everything structural in the house had come from within a radius of seven miles. An hour after we left it burned to the ground.

Melvyn and I had other adventures. We jointly owned a Model T Ford, which cost about $800 brand-new, and which we were paying for out of our weekly salaries. In the rolling hills outside of town one afternoon we stopped at a cheese farm and asked if we could buy some cheese. We were told that their total production was contracted for in Europe, where it was packaged and labeled and sent back here as "imported cheese." They gave us a generous piece.

We were young and curious and daring. It was during Prohibition. We had a bootlegger. He wouldn't deliver. We had to go to his house on the outskirts of town. He was a friendly, smiling Italian with a friendly, smiling Italian wife, who offered home-made red wine at fifty cents a pint. It was potent, and it always made the tippler pretty sick. In extremis.

I lived in a rooming house at 222 Monona Avenue. I still have a laundry mark from Madison that has persisted on some things that have always gone to the laundry. Not the same things, of course, but in the same sartorial classification. Anyway, the laundry mark is 222.

I have many memories of that engagement, but three stand out.

The first was one Sunday matinee when we were getting ready for the first performance of *Seven Keys to Baldpate*. I was playing "the chief of police of Askewan Falls." While we were in our dressing rooms making up, Melvyn fell off his chair with an attack of appendicitis. He was rushed to the hospital and there we were.

He and I were the same size and I volunteered to play his part, in his clothes, reading the part from his script, in which he'd written all the stage directions, which were rather involved. I quickly took off my boots and broad-brimmed hat, my gray wig and moustache, in which I was going to play the amusing part of the chief of police of Askewan Falls. The company manager, who had played the part in the past, put on my clothes. They were too large, but it didn't matter.

He went before the curtain and announced what had happened to Melvyn and what we were about to do, offering money back to anyone who wanted to leave. No one left and we got through the play, and the curtain came down.

The University of Wisconsin is in Madison, as everyone knows, and many students came to our Sunday matinees. When the curtain touched the floor, the company lined up for a curtain call. When it rose again, through the applause came a loud, prolonged "Hiss-ss-ss," and the curtain dropped. I was pretty upset because I took the hiss to be for me. The curtain rose again to continued applause, and through it came "Boom! Bah! Bellamy—Bellamy—Rah! Rah! Rah!" I felt pretty good.

The second memory of Madison was an incident in the first act of our performance of *Lightnin'* at the Sunday matinee. Incidentally, the Frank Bacon star part was played by our director, Roy Hilliard, the father of Harriet of "Ozzie and Harriet."

Our scenic artist had his sixteen- or seventeen-year-old son with him. He was tall and thin, with a large nose and a larger Adam's apple. He had a consuming ambition to be an actor, and the scenic artist was constantly at the manager and Roy Hilliard to give the boy a part. The only difficulty was that he stuttered violently.

But at last there came a chance to give his career a start. There was the non-speaking part in *Lightnin'* of the boy who has driven the prospective divorcee from the train to the hotel on the Nevada-California border to get her divorce. He enters the empty lobby with her, carrying her two bags. She tips him, he leaves and the prospective divorcee is alone.

At our opening performance they made their entrance and after a few seconds those of us offstage heard the biggest laugh we'd had all season. We rushed to the wings and saw the poor fellow with a quarter in his half-raised, palm-up hand, saying, "Th-th-th-th-th-hank you." He was padding his part, but he was told to leave it in. It was a sure-fire laugh for the rest of the week.

The third outstanding memory is the assembling on the outskirts of town of Ku Klux Klan members from several northern states. In their hoods and robes they silently marched to and around the Capitol Square and back to their starting place from about five in the afternoon till about nine at night. They were protesting some proposed legislation before Wisconsin's governing body. Access to the theatre, just off the square, was blocked, and we had to hold our curtain until nine-thirty to allow the audience to arrive. It was a dramatic and sinister spectacle.

The constant preoccupation with creating parts and all the demands of the theatre were, of course, the greatest training a young actor could have. Unfortunately, this kind of opportunity doesn't exist any more. The stock companies, the tent shows and the traveling repertory companies are all gone.

After many weeks of stock one could become so engrossed in the daily pattern that the demands of the clock could get confused. Several times I awakened with a stroke of panic in my hotel room, grabbed my clothes and started for the elevator, dressing as I ran, thinking I was late for the curtain, only to realize that it was four o'clock in the morning. Every actor who has played in the old stock companies has had a similar experience.

I was in Madison at two different times. After my first experience, I later went back to join a company that Melvyn Douglas had put together. Typical plays of both companies were such popular fare as *Nice People, Six-Cylinder Love, Madame X, The Best People, Scandal, Kempy, Lightnin', Miss Lulu Bett, Experience, Smiling Through, Cappy Ricks, Clarence, Three Wise Fools, Wedding Bells, The First Year, Welcome Stranger* and *The Bat.*

At the close of that season Melvyn and I went to different companies and didn't see each other for a while.

Ishpeming is in the upper peninsula of Michigan. The deepest iron ore mine in the world was there—one mile deep.

I arrived in Ishpeming around two or three o'clock one morning to join the Beach and Jones Repertoire Company—"Rep Show," as they were called.

I checked into the Railroad Hotel, which fronted on the platform to which I'd just descended from the train, and I was walking to my room, bag in hand, when I heard a woman scream on the second, and only other, floor. I went to the foot of the wide stairway in the lobby and started up, when I saw a screaming redheaded woman in a blue kimono run across the hall above. She was followed by a half-clothed, running man with a bottle raised over his head.

As the man was passing the top of the stairs he looked down

and saw me with my bag. He lowered the bottle and held out a welcoming hand. "Hello, Bellamy," he greeted me.

It was Guy Beach, of Beach and Jones, and the red-haired lady was his wife, the leading lady and star, whose stage name was Eloda Sitzer. She was billed on the posters around town as "Eloda Sitzer, the Little Red-Head."

I was to be the carpenter, stage manager and general business man with the Beach and Jones company. I got the job through the O. H. Johnstone Agency, one of two in Chicago. The other was the Milo Bennett Agency. Rep shows did eight plays a week, beginning on Monday—six nights and two matinees—then on Sunday moved to the next town.

I thought Eloda Sitzer was beautiful and a great actress.

I told her she was born to play Nora in *A Doll's House*. I followed her around. I was infatuated, even though she was a good ten or twelve years older than I, and married to one of the managers.

One cold, slushy, winter night after the show in Ironwood, Michigan, I was having supper with Eloda and the character woman, Adelaide Melnott, in the Chinese restaurant next to the theatre. We had ordered, and I remembered I'd left my copy of *Billboard* in my dressing room. I excused myself and went through the lobby of the theatre next door into the dark auditorium.

The janitor was cleaning the balcony, lighted by a one-bulb work light, and he couldn't hear me. The rest of the theatre was dark. I started down the steeply sloping aisle to go backstage. I was fine till I hit the iron post in the center of the aisle about halfway down. When I came to, in the aisle, the theatre was completely dark and all the doors were locked.

I had a painful lump through my eyebrow over my left eye, but I was determined to get my *Billboard*, return to the Chinese restaurant some way and say nothing about it. I got *Billboard* and left through a fire door that opened out to the alley. I trod through the slush to the restaurant and sat down to my chop suey, which was waiting. The ladies had finished and they were reading *their Billboards*.

Suddenly Addie Melnott screamed. She had looked up and seen blood all over my forehead and face and an open gash in the lump over my left eye. We found a doctor and I had four stitches taken. I still have the scar—a memento of Eloda Sitzer, "The Little Red-Head."

Every Saturday night the juvenile man, who was also the prop man, and I would load the freight car with the help of the local house crew of stagehands. We had to get the scenery and props for eight shows into one freight car. We wore leather jackets and had a gallon jug of the local liquor (it was during Prohibition) against the cold. And we used to take turns each week sliding backward on our stomachs out of the end of the car from on top of our load, which reached the ceiling. We worked so hard in the cold that the liquor which we shared with the local crew didn't affect us.

One winter night on that tour, we arrived in a small, cold northern city only a few hours before the first performance Monday night. After getting the scenery and props to the theatre from the freight car, I heard the juvenile/prop man giving instructions to the local house prop man.

He said, "For the last act, an after-dinner coffee service on a tea cart."

"I know what a tea cart is," said the local man, "but what the hell's an after-dinner coffee service?"

"Cups and saucers and spoons and cream and sugar and a coffee urn with a spigot," our juvenile explained.

"Oh! Okay," replied the local man.

Later, during the last act, there was a commotion offstage and a rattling of china and silver. Then the butler entered, pushing a large tea cart on which were thick restaurant coffee cups, a large thick cream pitcher, a large thick sugar bowl, teaspoons and a huge coffee-shop coffee urn with a big-handled spigot—all of which had been borrowed from the local diner. All except the tea cart.

It was difficult for the actors to contain themselves. But we managed.

I'm sure the audience thought the people in the play had strange customs. But they didn't let on.

Recalling the fact that one of my duties with the Beach and Jones company was carpenter brings to mind a somewhat embarrassing incident which occurred many years later.

Carpenter with a rep show was, at least in this case, a misnomer. The scenery had been built and it was actually in use when I joined the company. My responsibility in that capacity was, as I've already described, getting the scenery from the baggage car to the theatre and back and properly set up with the assistance of the local stage crew and the juvenile man, who was also the property man.

One Sunday in the above-mentioned later year when I was playing on Broadway, my wife and I visited friends in their new apartment in Ridgefield, New Jersey, Susan and Norman Varney, who had just been married. Norm was in the publicity department of the J. Walter Thompson advertising agency. He's now a vice-president of the company.

We arrived about 6 P.M. for dinner. They had been completing the furnishing of their new apartment and there was a group of four or five small paintings or pictures to be hung. I volunteered.

With yardstick and pencil I worked out the geometry of the arrangement and put nails into the plaster wall. The plaster cracked in some places and left white holes around the nails in others. But this didn't worry me too much because the pictures would cover the blemishes.

But when I hung the pictures on the nails they were in complete disarray with nothing resembling order or design. And I'd held up the dinner.

Now everyone had gathered with suggestions for a new start. My wife and Susan Varney, without yardstick or pencil, but with just a decorator's eye, spotted the pictures and I hung them.

But now all the cracks and white holes were exposed. I'd scarred the wall so drastically that they eventually had to have it replastered and painted.

And we had dinner at eleven o'clock.

The next morning at his office, Norm found a biography of me. Among my accomplishments, it was noted that I'd been the carpenter with the Beach and Jones company. He roared with laughter, phoned Susan and shared the story of the picture hanging with cohorts.

They're still close friends and Norm frequently alludes to my carpentry skills.

Three major entertainment business publications today are the daily *Hollywood Reporter* and the daily *Variety*, which cover principally Hollywood and pictures, and the weekly *Variety*, which covers all of the entertainment world.

In the late teens and twenties, *Billboard* was the major weekly publication for all live entertainment. Actors used to refer to it as "the Bible." It carried news and ads for everything from carnivals to Shakespeare. It also carried the views of the most erudite and caustic drama critic that we've ever had, Patterson James.

I have three recollections of *Billboard* from the early twenties. Two were ads in the "personal" columns.

One read: "(man's name). Juveniles and pathos. Have dress suit."

The other was a full single column which bore, at the top, a lady's name in bold type. Under it, also in bold type, was the single word, "Leads," and under that, "Rep." Beneath that, in smaller type, was a list of the names of repertory companies with which she'd appeared. A lengthy list it was, too. And below the list, in the same bold type as her name at the top, was: "Can I act?" And directly under that, also bold: "Seven trunks of wardrobe!"

Then there was Patterson James's cruel account of the appearance of a Shakespearean actor and his company in repertoire at the Century Theatre in New York. It read, to the best of my memory:

"Mr. Fritz Leiber and his company have just completed a six-week engagement in the plays of William Shakespeare at the Century Theatre. In the lobby of the theatre were fifty-six pictures of Mr. Leiber as various Shakespearean characters. Mr. Leiber and his fifty-six pictures of Mr. Leiber as the various Shakespearean characters have departed, with his company, for the hinterlands. God speed!"

Of course we must remember that a critic's reaction is one man's opinion. Unless they all agree.

The John Winninger Players was a repertory company that traveled through Michigan, Wisconsin and Minnesota. It was a company like Beach and Jones.

John Winninger had three brothers, Frank, Adolph and

Charles. They started their careers in their back yard in Neenah, Wisconsin, a German beer garden run by their father. After a time they organized a repertory company which, I was told, included not only all the Winningers but some of the Marx brothers and Houdini. Charlie married Blanche Ring, the vaudeville headliner, and finally went to Hollywood. His departure broke up the company and each of the other brothers formed companies of his own. I was John's leading man one season.

John was short and stocky. He had a magnificent untrained baritone voice and a glass eye. He also had a bride, Minette, who was a member of the company doing small parts.

There were many repertory companies at that time. They played theatres in the fall and winter.

Other repertory companies played under tents in the summer. They were called tent shows.

It was the custom in rep shows and tent shows to do "specialties" between the acts—singing, dancing, playing musical instruments and telling jokes by members of the cast, who would step out of the character they were playing and entertain in front of the curtain while the scenery was being changed. John sang spirituals as his specialty. He sang loud and clear, down on one knee in "Mammy" fashion, as Al Jolson used to do. I can still hear him singing "A Pharisee Came into the Temple to Pray."

Salaries were small in rep and tent shows. I was getting fifty-five dollars a week, out of which I had to provide and maintain all my wardrobe for eight plays, pay my hotel bills and buy three meals a day. Everyone had to draw an advance before the week was out.

Our opening week, which was in Sheboygan, was going pretty well when we were faced with a play that we had rehearsed only once. The second act was in the district attorney's office and the whole cast was onstage, including the stage manager and the director, who was playing the district attorney. It was one of those interrogation scenes: "Where were you that night?"—"You! How did you happen to be there?"—"Did anyone else come into the room?"

No one knew his lines very well and the director said, "Everyone forget stage directions for this scene. Just find a comfortable position and stay there. I'll sit at the desk in the center of the stage with the script. If anyone feels uncertain or 'up' in their lines, walk to the desk. I'll have my finger on the place in the script."

We started out all right, then one at a time we sauntered to the desk and finished the scene with the entire cast reading the script over the director's shoulder.

I went to John and Minette's room in the hotel one time to draw five dollars. I rapped on the door and John's muffled voice inside said, "Hold!" Then loudly, "Come!"

I entered, to find John and Minette both in long winter underwear, standing on the double bed with their hands on each other's shoulders. I started to back out with an apology, but John said, "That's all right. We're just wrestling."

"Well," I said, "could I draw five dollars?"

"In my trousers on the chair," John said.

I peeled a five-dollar bill from his roll, said, "Thanks, John," and left. In the hall outside the door I heard John say, "Go!" I must confess I listened. And I think they were really wrestling.

In one of his letters, Frank McHugh included the following: "Did you ever hear of *The Opera House Reporter?* A news publication for theatre managers and show owners in Iowa and adjoining states. It was much like *Variety* with a very rural atmosphere. It had 'at liberty [out-of-work actors—R.B.] actors wanted', ads asking for show bookings, reports and criticisms, knocks and boosts, personal notes on hifalutin conduct of certain actors with the rep shows, gross receipts, and general news concerning house managers. It was a reliable publication in the years I was there, 1916–17. I thought it might be good for a paragraph."

It is, and I never heard of *The Opera House Reporter.*

Frank also included this: "Did you ever hear of the heavy man who would never take the job with the tent or rep show unless he was given the concession of selling 'frozen sweets candy' between the acts? 'Frozen' were ordered from a wholesale house. A good big box with six or eight candy kisses wrapped in wax paper, selling at twenty-five cents. A high price in those days. In about every twentieth box, marked of course, there was a pair of good silk stockings. These marked boxes were sold in the most visible part of the audience. It was a bonanza for the heavy man."

Robert Sherman was a Chicago producer who started in business with a rep show, playing one-week stands in small towns under a tent. Later he formed companies, playing one-night stands, also under tent, of current Broadway plays in the smallest towns, which no road company would ever reach. He was successful with his one-night-stand companies, but he kept the week-stand repertory company active for reasons of sentiment and profit.

Roy Hilliard—Harriet Hilliard's father, remember—told the following story about Robert Sherman's tent repertory company:

The company had opened and been successful one season, when word came to them that Mr. Sherman, who considered himself a playwright, had written a play called *The Girl Without a Chance*. And further, since he also considered himself an actor, that he was going to join the company long enough to rehearse and open in the "blue-shirt lead" of his new play. The "blue-shirt lead" was theatre parlance for the "engineer" or some such hard-working, open-shirted, high-booted, high-principled young man who, by having all these virtues and surmounting many frightening obstacles, always got the girl.

Robert Sherman was universally known as the worst and loudest actor out of Chicago. His only rival was Corse Payton, out of New York.

The evening arrived for the debut of *The Girl Without a Chance*.

The tent was packed. The play was bad. Mr. Sherman was bad. And Mr. Sherman was loud.

Soon there was a contest, under the tent, between Mr. Sherman and the audience. The louder he talked, the louder they talked to themselves about what a wasted evening it was.

Finally Mr. Sherman couldn't stand it any longer and he stepped to the footlights. Putting a foot up on the lip of the footlight trough, leaning out and pointing a finger at the audience, he said, "Now listen! If you goddamned people will only keep quiet long enough, in a minute you're going to see some of the goddamnedest acting you've ever seen in your life!"

That was the last performance of *The Girl Without a Chance*, and I don't think Mr. Sherman ever appeared on the stage again.

American plays were just as modern then as now. They were not *all* escapist, as is sometimes said. They depicted life much as it was, and certainly as we thought it was.

Foreign playwrights like Ibsen and Shaw were more concerned with social problems—though we did have an occasional *Within the Law* and *The Lion and the Mouse*. But it was a fulfilling experience to go to the theatre. It had popular appeal, as pictures came to have later. This was before the pressures we know today.

It's true that there were a few serious strikes, but they were romantic, in a way, as World War I had been. We hadn't become aware of the mounting population. Transportation was still slow, without airplanes. The influences of two-way foreign travel were experienced mostly by wealthy Americans who could afford the transatlantic steamers and foreign immigrants who came here, in steerage, hoping to find a better life. Material demands were simple compared to today. Industry hadn't yet produced the conveniences we now accept as necessities. Values were easier to analyze and categorize.

This simplistic life was reflected in our plays—*Beggar on Horseback, The Front Page, Anna Christie, The Green Pastures, Men in White, The Children's Hour, Victoria Regina, The Petrified Forest*. War plays were beginning to appear. There were serious American playwrights developing and about to come into their full capacities, such as those mentioned earlier. They were involving themselves and their works with social problems. These were the avant-garde, along with foreign playwrights with the same concerns, such as Drinkwater, Galsworthy and Molnár.

But there still remained the old lulling, dulling and romantic subject matter, as in *Nice People, White Cargo, The Best People, The Student Prince, The Ghost Train, The Desert Song, My Maryland, This Thing Called Love*, all good plays, to be sure, and we played all the straight dramatic ones in stock. But there was a new excitement brewing.

There was considerable theatrical and gourmandizing activity in the Catskills during the twenties. Some of it, as typified by the most famous resort of all, Grossinger's, continues today, but without the old-time theatrical excitement.

Much of our well-known talent was incubated there.

The following account of a talented gentleman who was part and parcel of that era tells all in detail:

"The Borscht Circuit, like the old days in Hollywood, has become a fond memory to the people who once worked there and perhaps to those old enough to have stayed in some of the hotels that flourished in the Catskills.

"I came to work in the Borscht Circuit in 1928 as as assistant to Moss Hart. Each one of the big hotels which catered mainly to the Jewish population of New York and its environs had a large staff including musicians, dancers, actors, and so-called 'tummelers' whose main duty was to keep the guests in good humor.

"The cuisine was essentially food that was enjoyed by people who lived in Jewish homes but today much of that food is popular with the entire American population: I speak of lox, bagels, cream cheese, marinated herring, scrambled eggs and fried onions, blintzes, hot pastrami, and other delicacies. An unidentified comic once said that if you entered the dining room at Grossinger's as the milk lunch was being served you could get snow blind from the sight of the plates of sour cream which were poured over dishes of chopped vegetables.

"The schedule of work for the staff was demanding. Moss was an excellent director and a martinet when it came to running the staff. Monday night was usually rather quiet because it followed a hectic weekend. So Monday nights were usually occupied with storytelling at a bonfire or the playing of games.

"Tuesday night was dance night where we socialized with the wives who had been abandoned by their husbands until the next weekend. It was a night that usually ended up with many of the staff enjoying the favors of merry 'grass' widows.

"Wednesday night in some places was amateur night. This gave the guests an opportunity to perform and in most cases to make fools of themselves.

"Thursday night was hit or miss entertainment. Friday night was used to present a straight play. Moss was ambitious. We did plays such as *Redemption, The Trial of Mary Dugan, The Emperor Jones,* Ibsen's *Ghosts,* and programs of one-act plays such as the hardy *The Valiant.* Rehearsals for these Friday night shows would take place during the days, at the beginning of the week, or at night after some of the activities closed down.

"Saturday night we would do an original musical which Moss and I would outline during one day and then, having sketched it out, Moss worked out some rough casting from his staff. We would then put the company into rehearsal, tell them the story scene by scene and would ad-lib the dialogue. Believe it or not, we did some pretty good musical shows. We also stole dialogue from successful plays and musicals.

"Then on Sunday night we would stage a vaudeville show and specialty acts. The dancers would do numbers, the singers would sing, the comedians would do familiar and funny sketches, and the orchestra would stage musical numbers with orchestral specialties. Most of the guests would leave Monday morning and the staff would usually take a break for a few hours.

"Every other week there was a baseball game with a team from one of the neighboring hotels, and in my spare time I had to write a one-page daily gossip sheet. That season I also designed the scenery and did most of the make-up which I had learned during my experience with Paul Muni in *Four Walls.* Moss, as I remember, got $1,200 for the season; I got $400. Of course, our food was free. We had a room in the back of the theatre, and the management did the laundry as an added 'perk.'

"At the end of the summer I returned home having lost twelve pounds and having learned fascinating things from a number of attractive women, but most important I learned more about the theatre than I could have learned in a couple of years on Broadway.

"You most likely know that veterans of the Borscht Circuit included Moss, Don Hartman, Garson Kanin, Sid Caesar, Red Buttons, and Danny Kaye.

"A few years later the large staffs were disbanded and hotels began to import famous entertainers for a weekend and everything changed.

"I think those of us who worked the Borscht Circuit had more fun and worked harder and absorbed more than any of the young people breaking into the theatre today.

"'Affectionately,'
Dore (Schary)"

I had never seen a "tab show" and had only a vague idea of what they were. "Tab" is the diminutive of "tabloid." I was the leading man in the stock company in St. Jo, Missouri, and there was a tab show playing at one of the picture houses. Through some unusual happenstance, I had a couple of hours free one afternoon and I determined to find out what a tab show really was.

The musical tab show played for about an hour before the silent picture came on. Usually there were two completely new shows each week, both tab and picture. The scripts, such as they were, were cut versions of musicals or plagiarized and altered scripts written just for tab use. A company consisted of leading man, leading woman, second business man and woman, ingénue, juvenile, comedian, a couple of small-part people and a chorus of six or eight girls. They stayed in town for a season, much the same as stock companies.

Every theatre had an orchestra in the pit in those days, even stock companies, and most of the tab show consisted of singing and dancing. What little "book," or script, there was was raced over rapidly by the actors, almost unintelligibly, to get to the next music cue. It was really pretty bad. But it seemed to bring people into the theatre to see mediocre pictures. The tab companies never appeared at the larger theatres that showed big and important pictures. And it was work for the actors.

I don't know what the story was about at the one I saw in St. Jo. They spoke so fast I couldn't even guess at the plot.

There were six or eight young men sitting in the fourth or fifth row of the center section of the theatre who seemed quite engrossed in the proceedings onstage. They whispered to each other and giggled a lot.

The leading man was about six feet tall, had slick black hair, heavily made-up eyes, a dark suit and patent leather shoes. He had a prissy, flouncy demeanor and, though he had volumes of lines to speak, one couldn't understand a word he said.

Toward the end of this cantata, in the midst of a long rapid-fire speech, this apparition lit for a few seconds in his prancing tour of the stage, addressing the leading lady. And as he rattled on, one of the boys in the fourth or fifth row shouted loudly through cupped hands, "Are you?"

The leading man, not hesitating, turned to the heckler and said without interruption, as if it were part of his never-ending speech, "Ye-e-e-s-s!" And then he continued his speech.

He and the leading lady then went into a song, and soon the girls came out and danced around the romantic couple. As they embraced, the curtain fell.

That was my introduction to the tab show. I've only seen a couple since but, I hasten to say, the St. Jo leading man was not typical of all tab show performers.

One famous veteran tab show actor, Bob Hope, says:

"I started with the Tab shows for Fred Hurley's Jolly Follies in 1924 when I opened in East Palestine, Ohio. Then I went to Ottawa, Ohio . . . then I played the smaller towns. In Ottawa, we all sat on the trunks on the stage waiting to rehearse the three-piece orchestra. After about twenty minutes, I went down to the piano player and said, 'What are we waiting for?' And he said, 'We're waiting for the violinist. He works at the butcher shop.' I think that was a very colorful period of my career.

"I remember trying to do black-face in McKeesport, Pennsylvania. My partner and I were a singing and dancing team, Hope and Byrne. We wanted to do some comedy, so they let us do some black-face bits. We put on black grease, and we were in the basement until three in the morning trying to get it off! The more cold cream we put on, the more the grease worked into the pores in our faces. We looked like a polka-dot dance team from there on out for about three days.

"Another thing that stands out is the theatre in Orangeburg, South Carolina, where we played with Hurley's Smiling Eyes, which was the next season. It was a Tab show, booked out of Gus Sun Time in Springfield, Ohio. The theatre was very small and the street drop, which was a roll curtain, was so small that our heads were above the buildings! But the dressing rooms were fine—I dressed in an old coal bin, downstairs in the theatre.

It's hard to believe, but these are the true facts . . . May I never get another laugh. And it was great experience. When I got to Broadway and walked out on the stage at the New Amsterdam Theatre, Jerome Kern walked up to me and said, 'How can you do these things in such an easy manner?' And I said, 'Well, I've had a little experience.' I didn't tell him I was from Tab shows. We had a lot of fun.

"I also have a story about Kern and Otto Harbach. After Tamara sang 'Smoke Gets in Your Eyes,' I sat there smoking a cigarette listening to her, and she had said before the song she was in love with a football player—my buddy, who was Ray Middleton. She said, 'You know, in Russia we have a proverb, "When your heart's on fire, smoke gets in your eyes."' And then, with that Hassard Short lighting and that great orchestra with the Russell Bennett orchestrations, she sang 'Smoke Gets in Your Eyes,' which was a great high spot.

"When she finished, the music continued and I said, 'You know, we have a proverb in our country, too, "Love is like hash. You have to have confidence in it to enjoy it."' It was the biggest laugh. I had a lot of trouble getting it in the show, because Otto Harbach did the book and he was very jealous of the book—and I don't blame him. I kept going to him with jokes and I must say, he was very fair. But he didn't dig this particular joke!

"When he went back to New York, and we were at the Forest Theatre in Philadelphia, I went to Jerome Kern and I told him the joke and I said, 'What do you think about it?' And he said, 'Try it this afternoon.' It was such a big laugh it almost lifted the seats out of the theatre. Otto Harbach came back that afternoon, and at the night show he heard the joke and he walked back to me and he said, 'That's a good joke.' He's a beautiful guy, and that was one of my great experiences—working with those two guys. Great talents.

"Regards,
Bob (Hope)"

Most young people revolt against the establishment.

I was the very young leading man in the Sherman Stock Company at the Hippodrome Theatre in Terre Haute, Indiana, in 1924. I had found a fine friend in a local baker, who was the constant unsuccessful Socialist candidate for mayor. I spent many nights, after the performance, in the back of his bakery with him and a young newspaperman friend, talking political philosophy and utopia—neither of which I was qualified for, nor even informed. I would hate to have known me then. We'd talk until we had coffee with the next day's bread and rolls and cake that came from the oven. Then I'd go to my hotel and shave and shower and study and go to rehearsal. I couldn't do it now. For many reasons.

One night the baker said, "Gene'll be in town tomorrow. Just for one day. He's coming in from a lecture tour and he's going out again the next day. Would you like to meet him?"

"Gene" was Eugene V. Debs, regular but unsuccessful Socialist candidate for President, who was then seventy or over. I said I certainly would like to meet him, and the date was made for ten o'clock the next morning.

It meant I'd have to be late for rehearsal, which was held at ten o'clock every morning, and punctuality was a part of the actor's discipline and credo. Tardiness at rehearsal was the cardinal sin in the theatre. It was tough on the whole cast because of the peculiar theatre schedule, getting to bed after midnight and having to be at the theatre at 10 A.M., with lines studied and learned. So one got to rehearsal on time, no matter what, out of consideration for everyone else.

This was a hard decision. But meeting Gene Debs was, to me, like a private audience with the Pope to a Catholic. To me, Debs was the fearless spokesman for honesty and truth and reason. He was awesome.

At ten o'clock I rapped on the tall, solid door, which had a glass panel marked "Debs Real Estate Company." It was on the second floor of a typical Midwest, late Victorian red brick office building with a flat façade whose only relief was keystone arches over tall windows and doors. Inside, the halls were generous and the stairs were wide.

When I entered the office in response to a "Come in," I surmised that the real estate business Debs and his brother ran was a modest one. Everything was yellow with age—the large roll-top desk, the wall adornments, even some of the papers on the desk.

Debs rose from the desk to meet me. He was tall, lean, gaunt, with sparse gray hair and pronounced but undistinguished features—except for his wise, compassionate, but foreboding blue eyes, which twinkled as he stood in shirt sleeves with arm bands, collarless, with a brass collar button securing the collarband, and wide galluses over a shirt with tiny figures forming perpendicular stripes. In toto, not unlike the man in Grant Wood's "American Gothic."

It's not enough to mention meeting a man who was part of history. The depth of your impression is the thing. To me, Debs was a monument to the First Amendment and the true meaning of patriotism and humanity. He was the Patrick Henry, the Milton, the Voltaire of his day. In prison he'd lost his citizenship in the country he loved for speaking up and saying what he thought.

I don't remember anything of our conversation, except that he asked me if I was related to Edward Bellamy of *Looking Backward* and I replied that I was. He put both hands on my upper arms, as though to make a kind of lineal contact with a dead hero, and he said, "A very great man. I was the only one at his bedside when he died."

It was a memorable day for me. It still is.

When I appeared an hour late for rehearsal, I told the truth to the manager of the company and my fellow players. They accepted it without visible or audible reaction.

I guess they were aghast.

I played in stock companies in Terre Haute, Fort Wayne and Evansville, Indiana. And before that, in small Indiana towns with Chautauqua. I also played in Evanston, Illinois, with my own stock company. And the Chautauqua tour included Vandalia, Carbondale and small towns along the Mississippi River down in "Little Egypt."

Both these states still have a feel of the early settlers, particularly in the smaller towns. Some of the architecture of the nineteenth and early twentieth centuries still stands. Central Illinois has retained the atmosphere of the Lincoln legends in the back country. My father was born in Mattoon.

Indiana is still reminiscent of Booth Tarkington, James Whitcomb Riley, George Ade and the Midwest atmosphere that

Hoagy Carmichael captured, just as western Missouri, in the country surrounding St. Joseph and Kansas City, Kansas, still recalls the jumping-off place of the Old West. The legends of the Mississippi, the Missouri, the Wabash and the Ohio rivers during their busy pre-Civil War days are still intact.

The Midwest is a sturdy part of the country and the people are individualistic.

This is an account of perhaps more trouble in one performance than in any other single performance in the annals of the theatre.

Three Weeks, an adaptation of Elinor Glyn's somewhat overly romantic novel, was a favorite stock company bill. We were playing it in Terre Haute or Fort Wayne or St. Joseph—it's so long ago I've forgotten.

I was the leading man and my part was that of Paul, the lover. My concept of Paul's image was a dark jacket, white flannel trousers, patent leather shoes, a Windsor tie and as much profile as possible. Through the play, the character of Paul's uncle appeared briefly from time to time. There was always a warm hearty greeting, and Paul would relate everything that had happened since they last met. This helped the audience keep up to date with the very complicated plot. Then the uncle would be off to Timbuktu or the Ural Mountains until the playwright needed him again.

The trouble started in the second act. Paul and his uncle are dining on the terrace in front of the chalet in the Swiss Alps. Paul is in the process of bringing his uncle and the audience up to date when the Queen of Sardalia, the leading lady, arrives through the wood-wings with a retinue of handmaidens. She sits at a table on the other side of the stage, for some reason. Her eyes meet Paul's and something happens. She dismisses her retinue, Paul embraces his uncle and sends him off to the Orinoco or somewhere, and the Queen retires to the chalet, upstage center, and presently reappears on the balcony over the entrance. Paul climbs the rose trellis to the balcony and a tender Romeo and Juliet scene follows in the spotlight, and the curtain comes down.

That's what should have happened. But as my uncle and I sat dining on the "prop" food—consisting of a large lettuce leaf, a lengthwise slice of banana, some crackers and a bottle of hock

Hildy Johnson in *The Front Page*, Rochester, New York, Stock Company

The Secret Six, l. to r.: Lewis Stone, Paul Hurst, me and Wallace Beery, 1931 (*From the M-G-M release* Secret Six © *1931 Metro-Goldwyn-Mayer Distributing Corporation. Copyright renewed in 1958 by Loew's Incorporated*)

With Fredric March and Ann Sothern in *Trade Winds* (*Photo by Jerry Weisfeldt*)

With Barbara Stanwyck and Adolphe Menjou in *Forbidden* (*Courtesy of Columbia Pictures*)

Marian Nixon and me in *Rebecca of Sunnybrook Farm*, 1932 (*Rebecca of Sunnybrook Farm Copyright © 1932, Fox Film Corp., All rights reserved. Courtesy of Twentieth Century-Fox*)

Pat O'Brien and me in *Air Mail*, 1932 (*From the motion picture* Air Mail. *Courtesy of Universal Pictures*)

With James Cagney and Patricia Ellis in *Picture Snatcher*, 1933 (©
copyright 1933 Warner Bros. Pictures, Inc. Copyright renewed 1960)

Spitfire with Katharine Hepburn, 1934 (*Courtesy of RKO General
Pictures*)

Another scene from *Spitfire* (*Courtesy of RKO General Pictures*)

The Racquet Club, Palm Springs, l. to r.: Me, Charlie Farrell, Rudy Vallee and Lester Stoefen

How to foot fault, New York City (*Photo by Leo Friedman*)

The Awful Truth with Cary Grant and Irene Dunne, 1937 (*Courtesy of Columbia Pictures*)

Boy Meets Girl with l. to r.: Dick Foran, Pat O'Brien, James Cagney and Marie Wilson, 1938 (© *Copyright 1938 Warner Bros. Pictures, Inc. Copyright renewed 1966*)

Spencer Tracy and me in *Young America* (Young America, *Copyright © 1942, Twentieth Century-Fox Film Corp., All rights reserved. Courtesy of Twentieth Century-Fox*)

With Carole Lombard in *Hands Across the Table* (*From the motion picture* Hands Across the Table. *Courtesy of Universal Pictures*)

wine (burnt sugar and water)—I swallowed a cracker the wrong way and had a coughing spell that sounded like a baritone saxophone solo. I drank the whole bottle of hock to no avail. In fact, it made things worse. My uncle was slapping my back and I was gasping as the Queen of Sardalia entered and passed us on the way to her table. I did my best to hold in my wheezes and chokes long enough to flirt with her through my tears and leave the stage to get a real back treatment from one of the stagehands.

When I returned, somewhat disheveled, the Queen had got rid of her retinue. In a high-pitched, uncertain voice, with teary and swollen eyes, I sent my uncle on his way and the Queen went into the chalet, giving me a moment to compose myself. Then, there she was on the balcony. I strode to the trellis, started my ascent and got halfway up through the paper roses. The trellis fell, all right. But slowly. So slowly that I had time to look over my shoulder and plan my landing. But I looked up through the roses to see the whole balcony, bearing the Queen of Sardalia, collapsing like an orange crate and slowly moving down on top of me. I just had time to roll out of the way of the balcony to let the leading lady land beside me, and the curtain came down.

The audience liked it better than if things had gone right. But we had to go on.

The next act is laid in the Queen's sanctum sanctorum in the castle on the canal. It's an ancient stone castle with a large open portal in the center of the back wall, which gives onto the canal. As the curtain rises, the Queen is lighting incense pots and arranging the leopard skin on the stone seat, all in excited anticipation of her impending tryst with Paul. Then it happens. Paul arrives, in a gondola. They meet, and after a violent love scene, she tells him about the King of Sardalia, who is very unpleasant and who, she believes, has discovered their radiantly blooming friendship. I don't remember the rest of the act, and in the light of what happened, one can perhaps understand why.

The Queen proceeded, as indicated above, until my entrance. The gondola was a cut-out piece nailed, on the audience side, to a low platform on wheels. The gondolier was standing in the bow (the wrong end) with a large paddle, with which he swept the air in a rowing gesture, and I was standing behind him in the center of the boat with my Windsor tie and profile. A stagehand was pulling us by rope from offstage.

As we got nicely in the center of the arch, the wheels of our gondola contraption struck a stage brace, which someone had forgotten to pick up, and stopped dead. The gondolier, with his oar, was thrown forward, slapping his feet offstage in the canal. I was thrown forward too, but to avoid colliding with the gondolier, I veered toward the stage and came charging full force through the portal, running into the leading lady and knocking her down. I picked her up and dusted her off and we tried to play the scene as it would have been if I had made a more dignified entrance. But because of what had happened, everything each of us had to say to the other had an indecent, bawdy, lecherous connotation, to the audience as well as to us. And it got worse as we continued. So, because we each knew what the other was about to say, we couldn't look at each other and we played the scene (which was supposed to start in each other's arms) with our backs to each other, trying to keep from laughing. The audience was rolling in the aisles.

Later, again in the Queen's stone boudoir on the canal, she's alone and brooding when a large secret panel in the wall opens and there in splendorous regalia stands her husband, the King of Sardalia. He's in white uniform, with medallions and gold buttons and epaulets and shiny patent leather boots. The secret panel closes and he confronts her. He has some serious problems: he has no heir to the throne because he's impotent; he desperately craves an heir; he knows about the carrying-on with Paul; he's jealous; he's embarrassed; and he's angry about all of it. He backs her accusingly around the stage, exploding his wrath. Part of his confused denouncement, I remember, was: "Get me an heir, woman. Get me an heir!" Finally, in the spotlight, center stage, he draws a dagger from his belt and in a wild rage says, "And now, Madame, greet your lover!" as he stabs her in the stomach.

The King was played by our director, whose right side was paralyzed so that he walked with a decided limp. He was a fine actor, and extremely profane at times. He entered and played the scene beautifully, backing the Queen around the stage, demanding, "Get me an heir, woman. Get me an heir!" and finally maneuvering them both into the spotlight and drawing his dagger, he growled, "And now, Madame, greet your lover!" and he plunged the dagger.

But before entering he'd picked the wrong dagger from the prop table. Instead of the one with the blade that slid up into the handle when it made contact, he picked the balsa wood dagger. So when he stabbed her, it hurt and she winced, and the dagger broke in two, the blade bouncing on the floor.

So the climax went: "And now, Madame, greet your lover!" She winced, the blade fell and he finished with: "Goddamn son of a bitch!" and he limped off into the canal.

I really don't remember what happened after that.

In one stock company, there was a leading lady who never quite knew all her lines. She knew her own big moments verbatim, but she didn't bother too much about anyone else's scene. She had a habit in such a case of looking you in the eye, having received a cue that didn't stir her to remember her reply in your big scene, and say, "Well, what are you going to do about it?"

She did this to the second-business man one time in his big scene. And he replied, "I'll tell you what I'm going to do. I'm going offstage into the prop room and get a prop cigar and I'm going to sit down and smoke it until you think of your next line." And he left the stage.

The stage manager, who was following the script offstage, shouted her line to her, but too late. The second-business man wasn't there, and she couldn't just say the line to the empty stage.

They finally persuaded the second-business man to return, and with the help of the stage manager they finished the scene.

New York and Broadway being the goal of all actors (today I suppose it would be Hollywood), I left Terre Haute, where I'd been the leading man in the stock company, in the early summer of 1924 to put my name in lights on the Great White Way. I must have had a couple of hundred dollars to my name. Whatever it was, I was sure it was sufficient to carry me until I got the job that was going to raise me to national stardom.

Julian MacDonald was living at the Pennsylvania Hotel in

New York City, where I joined him in a double room. After two nights I awoke the next morning to find Julian gone. He told me later that he could see what was ahead in the way of work for both of us. He went back to Chicago and I moved into a hall bedroom at Seventy-ninth Street and Amsterdam Avenue.

Like all actors, I made the rounds of the agencies every day: Chamberlain and Lyman Brown, Paul Scott, Richard Pittman, Wales Winter, Pauline Boyle, the Packard Agency, Jane Broder, and Liebling-Wood. Among them, they did almost all the casting for Broadway. "Anything for me today?"

My money was disappearing. I found a restaurant on Eighth Avenue just above Forty-second Street where I could get a bowl of vegetable soup with bits of beef in it and a quarter loaf of rye bread all for ten cents. That was my one meal a day. Then, as the bankroll got smaller, only jingling money, I found raw peanuts for fifteen cents a pound. If you're ever in my predicament, try eating fifteen or twenty raw peanuts, shells and all, and drinking a couple of glasses of water, and then go for a walk. It's a filling, nutritious delicacy, and a pound lasts a little less than a week.

Finally the inevitable happened. I was flat broke. Early one morning I was in the act of appropriating a bottle of milk from a doorstep on Seventy-ninth Street and to my horror a cop came by. I straightened up as we looked each other in the eye. Then he went one way and I went the other without a word. I've always thought he must have been a good guy.

At the moment of complete desperation, I got a call from the Milo Bennett Agency in Chicago to go to Waterloo, Iowa, for leads in the stock company at a hundred dollars a week. At that moment that job seemed as good as Broadway with my name in lights. But there was a catch: I had to pay my own way out there. I borrowed the railroad fare from Irene Homer, Melvyn Douglas' leading lady in his stock company in Madison, whom I'd seen in town.

We played a long season, 1925–26, in Waterloo, a pretty little city divided in its center by the Shellrock River. The company all lived at the Russell Lamson Hotel on one side of the Shellrock and the theatre was on the other side. In the middle of winter, to get to the theatre, the company would meet in the lobby, proceed to the bridge and, single file, leaning forward with hands on the hips of the person ahead, we'd slug against the wind and snow that was tearing down the Shellrock River. We did good plays and it was a good company (all broke like me, I guess) and we did a sell-out business.

In the spring of 1926 I got a telephone call from Morgan Wallace, who had the stock company at the Princess Theatre in Des Moines, Iowa, a hundred miles or so south, asking me if I wanted to come down and finish his season as leading man when we closed in Waterloo. It worked out fine, and I got a hundred and fifty dollars a week. But it didn't last long. Wallace was reducing his players one at a time after a so-so season, thereby reducing the salary list and playing short-cast plays to end the season.

He began by replacing his leading man, who was getting much more than he paid me. The cast of our last play, *The Handy Man,* consisted of Wallace and his wife, the leading lady and her husband, the stage manager and me.

When that season ended I got a lease on the theatre for the upcoming season. It was owned by a tailor, Oscar Lofquist, who built it some years before for two Des Moines stock company producers, Elbert and Getchell. They had conducted probably the finest stock company in the United States. Conrad Nagel was the leading man and Fay Bainter was the leading lady. Frank McHugh and Robert Armstrong were in the company, and Priestly Morrison was the director. All went on to Broadway.

PART VI

Before going back to Des Moines to open my company, the Ralph Bellamy Players, I went to Jamestown, New York, for a ten-week season as leading man in the Fiber and Shea Stock Company. It was uneventful.

We played two thirty-six-week seasons in Des Moines, 1926–27 and 1927–28, to phenomenal success, doing such plays as *Seventh Heaven*, *The Show-Off*, *Silence*, *The Goose Hangs High*, *White Cargo*, *Liliom*, *Smiling Through*, *Rip Van Winkle*, *Sherlock Holmes*, *Irene*, *What Price Glory?*, *Cradle Snatchers*, *Rain*, *Craig's Wife* and *The Barker*.

My father put up the starting money and profits carried the venture afterward. He and my brother ran the "front of the house." Julian MacDonald, as I've said, designed and painted my scenery and program covers.

My brother, Dick, never had theatre aspirations in any department. He's been associated with business ventures and served as a first lieutenant in World War II, distinguishing himself dispatching air traffic "over the hump."

My sister Carolynn did have a feeling for the theatre and later, in Hollywood, did some acting at the Pasadena Playhouse under Gilmore Brown. But her interest didn't last. She married and has a daughter and three grandchildren.

Some people feel most comfortable without clothes. I don't mean nudists or nudism in its common connotation. The people I mean start to disrobe immediately on entering their private quarters. They enjoy the freedom, the absence of shackles, that undressing produces. There's a name for these people, I think. Anyway, I'm one of them.

While I had my stock company at the Princess Theatre in Des Moines I lived at the Savery Hotel, which was diagonally across from the theatre at Fourth Street on Locust. I was single and I lived in a single room. Those were more friendly and less perilous days and many people didn't lock doors. I was one of those, too.

Usually after the performance at night I had work to do: paper work, play reading, learning lines, studying a part, etc., and I was in the habit of doing these things in my hotel room, *au naturel.*

One night I was sitting at my desk stark naked when the hallway doorknob on my room rattled and the door was pushed slightly open, enough to allow the house detective to put his head in and say, "Lock your door, please!" Then he withdrew and closed the door.

I was somewhat annoyed with the house dick for bursting in like that, but I locked my door and went about my work.

A night or two later the same intrusion was repeated under similar conditions. Except that before he withdrew I said, "Don't burst into my room like this! Rap on my door and I'll open it and you can tell me anything you like. But don't open my door again without announcing yourself!"

He was a mousy little fellow, probably around forty years old, with a moustache that looked like a nail brush and a shiny dark blue suit. He carried a flashlight and a gun stuck out under his jacket which gave the impression, because of his slight, short physique, that it might be a Thompson submachine gun. He mumbled something about "For your own protection" and departed.

It happened a third time and I was furious. I stood stark naked and said, "If you come into my room again without knocking I'm going to hit you!" I'd never hit *anyone* up to that time, which of course he didn't know. But my threat didn't seem to bother him. He just looked at me. I said, "This room is my home, don't forget! I could shoot you for breaking in." He muttered something and was gone.

Incredible as it seems, the very next night he rattled the knob and put in his head. I leaped at him and he ran down the hall. I pursued him as if I'd been propelled from a slingshot, until I came to a corner in the hallway and realized I was naked.

I stopped short. The dick, some fifteen to twenty feet ahead of me, stopped too and turned to me, laughing. I must say I laughed pretty hard myself as I hurried back to my room and locked the door. The house dick and I became good friends after that.

Early one morning, about three or four o'clock, my phone rang, and it was my protecting friend. He said that from the lobby of the hotel he could see someone in the theatre office, which was just above the marquee. I hurried downstairs in trousers, jacket and slippers. Sure enough, we could see activity in the theatre office across the street. I asked him to come over with me, but he said he couldn't leave the hotel. So I asked him to let me take his gun and flashlight and, scared to death, I went over to my theatre.

I knew every inch of it, and my plan was to open the outer lobby door quietly with one of my huge bunch of keys, quietly cross the lobby to the inner doors that led to the auditorium, open one of those with another key and slowly and quietly ascend the stairway that led to the office door.

At the top step my heart was pounding so hard that it could have alerted the burglar. But I hurriedly reviewed all the stage directions I'd ever exercised in this circumstance and proceeded in professional style. With the gun in my right hand and the flashlight in my left, I quietly turned the knob and then kicked the door open, banging it against the wall in case the interloper was lying in wait there for me. I entered and, from the doorway, scanned the room. There was no one there. Not under the desk, nor in the closet, which I investigated.

There was, however, a drop-cord lamp with a green shade hanging from the ceiling over the desk. It was swinging gently in the breeze from a window that had been left open. Every now and then it flickered, the result, I guess, of a mild short circuit caused by worn wires that had been exposed to each other by friction from several hours of buffeting in the breeze.

I turned out the light, locked up the theatre and returned to the hotel, where I told the story to my protector friend. I gave him back the tools of his trade and went up to my room, shaking from the delayed reaction.

I used to select plays that would give each member of my company a chance to play a star part. Our character woman was a fine actress, Laurett Browne—"Brownie." It was her turn for the star part. The play was *Dancing Mothers,* originated the preceding season on Broadway, to great acclaim, by Mary Young.

Brownie was tall and thin and she made her own clothes, which always had panels hanging from her shoulders and sleeves. She had studied Delsarte, a system of calisthenics designed for co-ordination and grace. Applying Delsarte gestures when she crossed the stage, with the panels flying from her shoulders and sleeves, she gave the impression of something floating in midair on a wire. And when she read a line standing still, she resembled Don Quixote fighting the windmills. I say this in amused kindness, as both the audience and I loved her and had great admiration for her acting talent.

At the opening performance, Sunday afternoon, Brownie came to her big scene, in which she had a long speech. I was the only one on stage with her. Our director, Walter Gilbert—John Gilbert's stepfather, who had given him his name—had me sitting downstage on a settee, looking at Brownie upstage, while she wallowed in her great moment. But alas! She "went up" in her lines in the middle of the speech and began ad-libbing with hesitance. I knew what she had forgotten and tried to interrupt to say something that would bring her back, but she would have none of it. It was her crowning moment and she would fight any intruder to protect it.

Finally, in her ad-libbing, she said directly to me, Delsarte, panels and all and apropos of nothing in the script—in fact, relating to nothing at all—"Who was your father?—Did he marry your mother?—Why?—Tell me!"

I could only drop my head between my knees and erupt with laughter. So did Brownie. And so did the audience.

Drake University is in Des Moines and I made several good friends among the students and professors and learned to ride horseback at the cavalry post. I still have good friends in town there.

Toward the end of the second season, after fabulous business for over a season and a half, there was a slight drop-off. Not alarming, just a few empty seats in the last couple of rows. We weren't used to this, so I investigated. With my hat pulled down and my overcoat collar up, I followed groups from the vaudeville theatre to our theatre, to the burlesque theatre and to the big new Paramount picture theatre, before curtain time.

They would look at the billboards in the lobbies and the ticket prices and talk it over. There was no question about it—they were being lured to the Paramount Theatre, where they thought they'd get more for their money: a big two-hour movie and an hour stage show. The stage show was provided by the Publix Circuit, a subsidiary of Paramount Pictures Corporation.

The motion picture companies owned most of the movie houses in the big cities and now they were moving into the hinterlands, where they were competing with other forms of entertainment.

The Paramount Publix Circuit provided the stage show companies that traveled to the Paramount theatres, staying for the duration of the run of the picture that was booked at the time of their arrival. Each company consisted of a master of ceremonies who was young, good-looking, with a lot of personality and a singing voice; a comedian, as a rule; maybe a magician or a vaudeville act; and a dozen or so chorus girls. Of course there was a fifteen- or twenty-piece orchestra in the pit, too. This was the beginning of the end for vaudeville, stock and burlesque.

We moved our company to Nashville, Tennessee—from practically the heart of the North to the heart of the South. And I didn't know a soul there. The new movie palaces hadn't yet come to Nashville and there was no vaudeville or burlesque, so we had a good two years there, doing many of the plays we'd put on in Des Moines.

Dinah Shore has since told me she delivered tickets for me from the box office—for nothing. She was theatre-bitten. Alas! I didn't know her then.

Before leaving for Nashville I engaged a young lady who lived nearby, in a suburb of Des Moines, to go with us as the second-business woman. She was pretty, witty and had experience. But when we arrived in Nashville, Miss Eloise Taylor didn't show up. When the matter was investigated, she said she had no intention of appearing. She said she was going to Cleveland to marry the leading man in the stock company there, a fellow by the name of Pat O'Brien.

I appealed to Equity and we made a big case of it. But who can fight love?

I finally relented, sympathetically, and Eloise and Pat were married. And they still are, after forty-nine years. How foolish I was to think I could prevent that.

Neither of the two Nashville newspapers had a drama critic. There was a young reporter named Frank Waldrop, who was elevated (I like to think) to that job on the Nashville *Tennessean* and who later became managing editor of the Washington *Times-Herald*. The critic on the *Banner* was the sportswriter, Ralph McGill, who later became managing editor of the Atlanta *Constitution*. One of the great newspapermen of the country. They both became good friends.

One night Frank Waldrop came backstage after the performance and said, "How do you feel about a drink?" He was good company and I thought that was a good idea. We set out to get a bottle of aged Tennessee moonshine corn, than which there is no better whiskey.

Our supply depot was an upstairs men's hostelry on the capitol square, appropriately called the Senate Hotel. There were twelve or fifteen residents sitting around the lobby, some of whom obviously had been sipping the illegal mountain elixir. We made our need known at the desk and were told to wait while the clerk/owner went downstairs somewhere to the cache.

Presently four men with shotguns came up the stairs and ordered everyone against the wall. We were frisked and told to go downstairs. It was the law. A raid. We went down to the street, where the four guardians of the Eighteenth Amendment scrambled into an open Ford, with their guns still on us. We were told to march on the sidewalk toward the jail and they low-geared ominously alongside us, still pointing their hardware.

As our band of marching sons of Bacchus proceeded toward the jail, it occurred to me that if an account of this parade reached the papers the local stock company would have to pull down its final curtain and go back up North, even though our prescription at the Senate Hotel hadn't been filled. We could have been visiting a friend at the hotel, but probably no one would have believed that.

Almost everyone in Nashville drank, I think, but no self-respecting person talked about where he got his liquor, or where you got yours. Prohibition was the law of the land. Tennessee was dry before the United States was dry, and revenue men were social outcasts. So, too, were people who had public traffic with them. And if this wasn't public traffic, what was?

I expressed my apprehension to Frank and he managed to get around to the other side of our Model T escort. After a moment he returned with instructions to drop to the back of the pack and, when we reached the next corner, turn left as the rest of the suspects continued straight ahead.

This was a magnificent demonstration of the power of the press and the humanity of the law. And Frank Waldrop may have saved me from theatrical oblivion.

We had two successful seasons in Nashville, interspersed with a short season in Evanston, Illinois, next to Wilmette, at the theatre where I had seen *Little Lord Fauntleroy* and *Buster Brown* with my mother and father when I was seven or eight years old.

After signing the contract for the Evanston theatre, I found that the previous manager had left debts all over town, including an $1800 phone bill. The telephone company wouldn't connect the phone until the bill was paid, and I was told I'd have to have eleven stagehands, the same number as the members of the cast. There was nothing to do but pay the debts and make the best of it. I determined to stick it out until we recovered the debt payments and go back to Nashville, which we eventually did.

I was happy enough to leave Evanston, under the stench of the preceding management, and maybe with some reference to "a profit in his home town." But at least I was able to renew my acquaintance with some old New Trier friends.

Walter Kerr, the dean of American theatre critics, was a student at Northwestern University and a regular patron of the

Evanston Theatre. I asked him recently if he'd be so kind as to make an estimate of those days. Here it is:

"Stock of course had nothing to do with 'summer stock' of later years. It was mostly a wintertime operation, so that the acting company really lived in the community and to a degree became a part of it for the entire theatrical season, it was also a matter of using the same basic group of actors for *every* play (the bill changing weekly). No package touring or anything like that.

"Do I think it was valuable theatrical training for these actors? Yes and no. It depended on the individual performer. Obviously the speed with which plays were mounted (one in rehearsal while the other was in performance) meant that there wasn't much time for digging into characterization; the solution very often was to resort to tricks of personality or easy, superficial approximations of the characters as written. And because the number of actors to a company was necessarily limited by the economics of the operation, certain basic types were cast. There was a standard heavy, a standard comic, leading man, leading woman, character ditto, general utility, and so on—with each actor pretty much in the same role, or same kind of role, each week. This tended strongly toward stereotyping, of course, even though it was simultaneously making the actors quick-witted and instantly adaptable within a limited range. I'd say that the actor who sank into his 'type' and just took his paycheck could have been hurt by stock."

[I include the following three paragraphs with, I hope, excusable pride, considering the source.—R.B.]

"But there were always the exceptions, yourself among them. This is not flattery; in my eight or nine years of watching stock in Evanston, you were the only performer who ever surprised us by altering character radically from play to play. Since you were the leading man, and therefore expected to turn up strictly in romantic/dramatic roles, the surprise was all the greater. But I can remember my own delight (I was impressed as hell) watching you do the Reverend Davidson in *Rain* one week and a goofy detective in a comic murder mystery (was it *The Ghost Train?*) the very next. [It was *The Rear Car.*—R.B.] The shift was startling, and it was evident you weren't going to settle for anything like routine practice. I knew routine practice quite well because during the twenties, certainly through my high school years, I saw the Karl Way Players at the same house week after week, along with several other companies that took up residence for single seasons when Way was elsewhere. In all of that, I never saw anyone else do what you did, forcing us to accept you in totally altered character (*not* done with make-up, as the character men might) from Monday to Monday. I think your company played only one season, or at the most two, in Evanston; but for me it was the high point of my youthful theatregoing. The only other performer who ever lighted a particular fire there was a very pert ingénue named Joan Peers (originally with the Way company, I think); she was sassy and cute and was occasionally even starred by producer Clyde Elliott (he owned the house); she also made it to Hollywood, appearing as Joe Cook's leading lady in his only feature film, *Rain or Shine*. But no range. She was strictly ingénue, cute as she was, and couldn't seem to build a further career. I also liked a character comedian in your company named William A. Lee.

"But once again, he worked a very narrow vein (somewhere between Eric Blore and Franklin Pangborn) and seems never to have escaped it. On the other hand, it was at once apparent that you were an actor and not a quick-study robot. So I suppose it was simply up to the individual to find his own flexibility (and thereby grow) at the same time he was acquiring the simple expertise that constant changes of bill did provide. Those who stayed with the stereotype became merely slick, and were stuck with that; the others picked up the slickness all right, but had enough imagination to reach for something more. I suppose the fact that it *was* your own company (with your father at the front of the house) enabled you to select plays that would give you freedom to try alternate styles. Anyway, it worked, and even though when you finally went into films you seemed terribly confined to your comic vein (in farces with Irene Dunne, and so on) the serious equipment was also there and of course eventually it surfaced.

"But there's another angle to the stock company practice. It had several specific values for audiences. After, and during the twenties, once a show that had originated in New York had played its various touring dates, it was over and done with. If you missed *Lightnin'* or *Seventh Heaven,* you'd missed it. Except that stock gave you an opportunity to fill in many gaps, and if you still wanted to see *Michael and Mary* or, heaven forbid, *White Cargo,* you could do it in your own home town. Stock was thus a sort of public library on which audiences could draw at will, especially since so many shows were done per season.

"And for me in particular, it was a godsend, because stock didn't simply do the shows that had finished their tours a season or so earlier, it also went back for its materials to the previous decade. Which means that I was filled in on a lot of material I couldn't possibly have seen (too young when they were first done) and I'd say I added ten to fifteen years of material to my working knowledge, catching up with *The Meanest Man in the World* and *The Bat* and God knows what else. It was as though I had been born before my time, and I was grateful to see what had delighted my elders, even if the shows had begun to date. Call it historical research or whatever you want; stock provided it.

"And then, of course, talking films (with a little help from the Depression) killed off the institution. So long as the films were silent, there was a real need for the living, spoken theatre that stock provided. It was another kind of entertainment altogether. But sound took the necessity away; it even, in its beginnings, did the same plays that stock had been doing, scarcely altered for the cameras: *The Home Towners, The Green Goddess, Jealousy, The Last Warning,* and on and on and on. And so a special kind of training ground (valuable for those who could use it wisely) and a special opportunity for audiences went by the boards. (And *that's* an unfortunate phrase; it was the 'boards' that went.)

"But no matter. The theatre's still around; it's even unexpectedly flourishing right now. And the OOB (Off-Off-Broadway) workshops, together with the resident companies across the country, are now helping to do the job for both audiences and actors. A special flavor, and a week-to-week familiarity are gone; but the training and the experience have become available again somehow."

The second season in Nashville was as successful as the first and I had many good friends there.

Nashville is a beautiful city on the Cumberland River, with its state capitol of Greek architecture, Andrew Jackson's antebellum house The Hermitage on the edge of the city and many cultural and educational institutions, the best known of which is Vanderbilt University. The popularity of country and western music hadn't blossomed yet so they had to settle for the Ralph Bellamy Players at the Orpheum Theatre. And they did. In a big way. But I got that Broadway feeling again.

I went to a hotel on West Forty-second Street in New York, but that didn't last long. In the early summer I got a job as leading man in the stock company in Freeport, Long Island, at $50 a week for six weeks. One of the plays we did was O'Neill's *Desire Under the Elms*.

Julian MacDonald came into town again and he and I lived in a cold-water flat in the upper Eighties on the East Side for a while until Julian went to Canada for his mile of fireworks scenery.

Melvyn Douglas had come in from a season with the Jessie Bonstelle Stock Company in Detroit. He was living with his mother and father on the second floor of a brownstone on West Sixty-ninth Street. He invited me to move in with them, which I happily did. We both visited the agents every day during the summer.

Melvyn's father was a brilliant pianist. He'd been in the czar's orchestra in Russia. He had enormous strength in his fingers and he used to delight in appearing in his nightshirt and brutally tapping Melvyn and me on the forehead to awaken us. It was most effective and the headache lasted for a good ten minutes while he laughed at us through his Vandyke beard.

Finally Melvyn got a contract with William A. Brady and went to work opposite Fay Bainter in *Jealousy*. I had to move out and I went to the attic of the Marseilles Hotel at 103rd and Broadway, where the night clerk was a friend I'd met at Sixty-ninth Street.

During Prohibition, it would be a fair generalization to say that the best food in New York was in speakeasies, as best typified by "21" and the Stork Club. There were many of them, of such variety that almost any pocketbook could be accommodated—if one had a pocketbook. Many people didn't. Especially toward the end of Prohibition, around the time of the stock market crash and just before the bread lines.

During this broke time, I was taken to an Italian restaurant on Third Avenue where for fifteen cents they served delectable homemade minestrone with homemade Italian bread, both made by Rose. And if my host was flush, a large glass of homemade Italian red wine, made by Rose's husband, Joe, and kept in a barrel in the hallway, was available for ten cents.

To enter this dining room, one passed through a fruit stand on Third Avenue to a narrow room in the back and sat on a bench on one side of the only table, a long one. At the end of it was a roll of wrapping paper that provided place settings. Guests simply tore off a sheet as they came in.

Most of the patrons were gentlemen of the press, who seem to have a gift for finding good and inexpensive food.

This establishment is still in existence, a block from its original fruit stand, and Rose is still in the kitchen, catering to a more affluent clientele. It's called Joe and Rose's, just as it was then.

But I'm married to the greatest cook in the world. So I don't miss any restaurant.

At the end of September I got a job in *Town Boy*, a backwoods Pennsylvania play which had the distinction of opening at the Belmont Theatre in New York on the night of October 4 and closing after the Saturday matinee on October 5.

In the twenties, every young actor was just getting by financially. Stock salaries weren't big. Even managers were not wealthy. I had only partly conquered Broadway, but the two performances of *Town Boy* did lead to a fine job as leading man in the stock company in Rochester, New York. It was operated by George Kondolf, Jr., whose partner until that season had been George Cukor, of later Hollywood fame.

One of the plays we did there was O'Neill's *Strange Interlude*, which has nine acts. We started at two-thirty, broke for dinner and resumed at eight-fifteen. On opening night, no one missed a comma, but at each succeeding performance during the week, at least one of us "went up" higher than a kite.

I also played there opposite Helen Hayes in *Coquette* that season.

Radio was beginning to come into its own now, and one of the first programs to capture the country was "Amos 'n' Andy."

There was a shop next to the Rochester stock company theatre that sold radios. Not everyone had a big set yet. Most reception was through earphones connected to crystal sets.

(The first deep impression I had of radio, after the crystal sets, happened on an election night at the Majestic Theatre, back with Melvyn's stock company in Madison. A large oblong box about four feet by one and a half feet by one and a half feet arrived backstage and when it was hooked up, it produced the election returns in a clear voice, to the amazement and pleasure of the audience. Precedent for this, I guess, was the instance in 1922–23 season when John Barrymore appeared in costume before the curtain during an intermission of his record-breaking run of *Hamlet* on Broadway to announce the Dempsey-Carpentier prize-fight decision, which he had heard over the radio in his dressing room.)

The shop in Rochester had a loudspeaker that faced the sidewalk, and each evening about seven o'clock, when "Amos 'n' Andy" came on, there was a crowd gathered in front of the store, amused and chuckling.

Freeman Gosden, who was "Amos," is an old friend of mine, and I asked him if he'd go back in memory and recall the early days of radio. Here's his letter:

"Dear Ralph:

"Here's a short fact sheet:

"First appearance on stage—called out of the audience as a volunteer by Thurston (great magician). Next—diving contest with Annette Kellerman. Both in Richmond.

"Amateur night once or twice, dancing with another boy (Slim O'Neil) in Richmond too. Played in several amateur shows in Richmond for 'Elks,' 'Shriners,' etc.—the last one just before World War One (I was in the Navy—Naval Reserve for two years and one week). I was asked by director if I would like a job directing amateur shows around the country and I accepted.

Went to Durham, N.C., to meet a director with the company (Joe Breen Production Co., Chicago). This guy was playing the piano and trying to teach sixteen girls a dance routine. I introduced myself—'Freeman Gosden' and he said, 'Charlie Correll.' That's how we met. He asked me if I knew the routine—which I had just watched in the show at Richmond. I got out in front of the kids. He played and we taught them the routine. He gave me what I came for—the music for the show. I went to Elizabeth City, N.C., to put on my first show. Went back for three years for shows there. Met Correll in Chicago. We sang together (summer vacation), first in our apartment, then on WEBH—free. Then WGN, the Chicago *Tribune* station, offered us a job with pay. We sang for a year or so and made a few Victor records until the Rhythm Boys hit (Bing Crosby and his two partners), and that was the end of our record business. The *Tribune* asked us to do 'The Gumps' (comic strip) on the air but we asked to do two black characters (Sam 'n' Henry), which we did for two years. We were only on WGN and wanted to go national, but the *Tribune* wanted us to stay on WGN only. We quit and when we went to WMA we called ourselves 'Amos 'n' Andy.' First we had about forty stations on record and then NBC signed us coast to coast on their network and we signed up with Pepsodent for the first nine or ten years."

A bit of nostalgia from *Good Evening, Everybody—From Cripple Creek to Samarkand,* Lowell Thomas' promised autobiography, belongs here.

Lowell Thomas followed "Amos 'n' Andy" on the radio, with the news.

The first time we heard his "Good evening, everybody" was over CBS in August 1930.

His instruction from William Paley of CBS was, "When you hear the buzzer, start talking. Talk fifteen minutes—I don't care about what. Then stop."

Later that year he was on both CBS and NBC, replacing Floyd Gibbons on the latter.

In 1946 he went solely to CBS, where he's been ever since— "the longest-running daily program in the annals of broadcasting," with his familiar "So long until tomorrow."

And of course many of us remember him as the voice of *Fox Movietone News*, beginning in 1932.

He reports an anecdote from his adventures with Allenby and Lawrence in the Holy Land: "A homesick Tommy wrote his mother in England, 'I am in Bethlehem where Christ was born. I wish to Christ I was in Wigan where I was born.'"

Which brings to mind a story told to me by correspondents who followed Mark Clark during the Italian campaign of World War II: After a press conference, he was asked if he remembered any amusing censorship anecdote. He said, "Yes. A young, second-generation Italian boy began a letter to his mother: 'Dear Mom, you'd shit if you knew where I was.'"

Returning to New York City in August 1930, practically broke, I found a nicely decorated basement room in a cold-water flat on West Eleventh Street near the river. It was still customary to "make the rounds" of the agents each day, which meant a subway up to Times Square and back. The fare was a nickel then, and nickels were guarded carefully. A nickel bought things.

For instance, on hot and humid summer weekends there was a fine way to keep cool for a nickel. The Staten Island ferry terminals had rails dividing incoming and outgoing passengers. Once inside the nickel turnstiles, it was possible to slip under the dividing rail at the end of each trip, as one was leaving the ferry, and join the outgoing passengers. It made a very pleasant New York summer day in the ocean breezes, if one took a sandwich.

One hot August morning the coin phone rang on the main floor of my basement residence. I ran up, as always, to answer it. It was for me. It was Chamberlain Brown, the biggest Broadway agent.

"Get right over to Arthur Hopkins' office," he said. "There's a part Walter Huston was going to play, but he's going to Hollywood."

Arthur Hopkins was one of the most highly regarded producers, by critics, actors, playwrights and the public.

"What's the part?" I asked Brown, wanting to present myself as nearly as I could to what was called for.

"Never mind," he replied. "Just get over there quick."

With pounding heart I ran to the subway and fifteen minutes

later hustled up the stairs of the Plymouth Theatre to Arthur Hopkins' tiny office. It was just big enough to contain his desk and chair and one other chair.

Hopkins was one of the most human of all producers, to which any actor who knew him will testify. He was short, round, gentle, big-eyed and red-faced (from an occasional, but controlled, drop of Prohibition spirit, maybe). He took me down to the stage and asked me to read a few speeches from a script "in an Oklahoma drawl."

"Fine," was his monosyllabic reaction when I'd finished. There was a frightening silence as he seemed to look me up and down. Then: "This character has to lift a man by the scruff of his neck with one hand. He's a little man, but he has to be lifted with one hand."

"I can do it," I said. I'd have lifted the man with my little finger. I was broke and in debt.

"Let me think about it," Hopkins mumbled. "Come back at two o'clock."

And we parted, he to his office upstairs and I back to West Eleventh Street.

It was plain that this character was strong and muscular. I put on a pull-over sweater and the vest to the suit I was wearing, hoping to appear more robust when I returned to the Plymouth Theatre. This was before World War II, when they stopped making vests to conserve cloth. So, dripping wet from perspiration, I returned at two o'clock and got the part of Texas in *Roadside*, Lynn Riggs's first play on Broadway. A few months later the Theatre Guild produced his second, *Green Grow the Lilacs*, which afterward, in its musical version, became *Oklahoma!*

Texas was a magnificent star part, and the opening night at the Longacre Theatre in New York was like an actor's dream. At the end of the performance, and after several company curtain calls to a literally standing and cheering ovation, Arthur Hopkins led me out alone to more ovation. He said something but I didn't hear it. I think my whole past appeared before me during that moment, as they say it does to a drowning person. It was the moment I'd hoped for and fantasized about since *The Shepherd of the Hills* and before.

The curtain came down and I was prepared for a run of a season or two, when Hopkins said, "I'm glad we did it, anyway. Aren't you?"

"You mean it's not a hit?" I asked.

"No, I'm afraid not," he answered.

I was stupefied.

After eleven performances we closed. But I had contract offers from M-G-M, Paramount, United Artists and Fox. Hopkins asked me to take the United Artists offer (which was the least attractive financially) because Joseph Schenck, the head of United Artists, was a good friend of his. What could I do?

Sound had forced Hollywood to go to the only source it knew which could provide actors who could learn and speak lines, and lest I do injustice to many actors who had come to Hollywood before sound, I hasten to say Hollywood needed more just as good. Earlier thespians who had invaded Hollywood included William and Dustin Farnum, Mary and Jack Pickford, Dorothy and Lillian Gish, Cecil B. DeMille, William S. Hart, Marie Dressler, Bert Lytell, Conrad Nagel, Lewis Stone, Wallace Beery, Warner Baxter and Marguerite Clarke, all considered infidels by their legitimate theatre brethren. But there were many without theatre background.

During the heyday of the legitimate theatre, and during silent picture days, it was not considered *comme il faut* for a "legitimate" actor to "defame" himself by "going into pictures." That's why the first studio in the United States was built by Thomas Edison in 1904 at Decatur and Webster avenues in the Bronx, which was then way out in the country. Casting would be accomplished surreptitiously at the Lambs Club in Times Square and the actors spirited to the hideaway in the Bronx at five dollars a day, regardless of the length or importance of the part.

Probably the first negotiated salary increase in pictures above five dollars was achieved by Frank McGlynn at the Lambs Club. They needed someone who could ride a horse up at the Edison studio and McGlynn was the only Lamb who could perform this feat. He asked for, and got, ten dollars.

Incidentally, all silent pictures were originally made for New York and shown in storefronts called "nickelodeons," because of the five-cent admission. This way, one's fellow actors didn't know about the sin, and the silent picture audience hopefully would not recognize the legitimate theatre actor. This attitude persisted until the thirties.

It was necessary to change trains in Chicago when traveling from New York to Hollywood. I was changing to the Santa Fe Chief in Chicago on my way to fulfill my contract with Joseph Schenck. My friend Frank Morgan, who was playing in *Topaze* in Chicago, came to the Santa Fe station to see me off with the most vituperative language, including calling me a prostitute, selling out for money. Six months later, at the end of the road tour of *Topaze*, Frank was in Hollywood, under contract to M-G-M.

On my trip to California I had a drawing room, supplied by Schenck, but I had no money for meals. The salary from *Roadside* had paid my debts but left me broke again. Hopkins discovered my predicament and insisted on lending me money so that I could arrive in Hollywood with some kind of dignity.

Incidentally, although *Roadside* wasn't too well received by the critics, I came off pretty well, and David Belasco, whom I'd never met, sent for me.

He and his general manager, Burke Symond, and I met in the lobby of the Belasco Theatre about seven-thirty one evening before my performance of *Roadside*. Belasco was in his familiar uniform: black suit, clerical collar and locks of white hair over his brow. He was smiling and cordial. We chatted, and he said, "Look at him, Burke! Isn't he wonderful?"

I mention this only because the same words had been used on an earlier occasion when I managed to get out to Jamaica, Long Island, for an interview with Mae West, who was playing the "Subway Circuit," to talk about the replacement of the young Salvation Army man in *Diamond Lil*.

It was after her matinee, in her dressing room with her manager, Jim Timmony, a portly, fastidious fellow with spats and a "stick."

We chatted, and she said, "Walk away a couple of steps and turn around." I was broke enough to do it. And she said, "Look at him, Jim! Isn't he wonderful?"

I was never offered a part by Belasco or Mae West.

PART VII

First-class travel between New York and Los Angeles began
with the Twentieth Century Limited or the Broadway Limited
from New York, changing in Chicago to The Chief, the elaborate
extra-fare Santa Fe train that crossed the prairies, the mountains
and the desert, floating into Los Angeles like a magic carpet.
One of these trains has had to discontinue service because of
modern economics. The Twentieth Century Limited no longer
exists.

Airplanes are fast and comfortable. They're cheaper than
trains, too. No meals to buy, no porters to tip. But that bygone
luxury of three and a half days of anonymity, Fred Harvey food,
good books, the hypnotic clickety-clack of the rails and the rolling panorama out the window is not to be equaled today, even
on a long sea cruise.

I arrived in Los Angeles on a Saturday in November 1930 with
Arthur Hopkins' money in my pocket. I moved into the Holly-
wood Knickerbocker Hotel, which was fairly fashionable then.
It's now a home for senior citizens.

It was a hot November, and my first venture onto Hollywood
Boulevard, just a few steps from the hotel, made an impression
that quickly confirmed my presence in the land of make-believe.
The sidewalks were crowded with Californians facing the center
of the street in anticipation. We were all in summer apparel. I
was wearing white flannel slacks.

Presently up the street it came. In the blazing sun, to the tunes
of Christmas carols, came a procession led by a truck pulling a
large propeller, which faced backward, and into which a man

was feeding white confetti that blew onto a following float bearing three teams of plastic reindeer hitched to a sleigh, in which sat Santa Claus, who was waving to us. This was followed, amid the fluttering confetti, by a truck carrying the musicians, in some kind of folk costumes. Then came many open cars with stars sitting on the collapsed tops, their feet on the back seats. And Western actors on horses, and clowns, and cars. We spectators were fairly well covered with confetti too, and perspiration from the glaring heat of the sun made it stick in our ears and noses.

The following Monday I met Mr. Schenck, to whom I was under contract for thirty out of fifty-two weeks. He was a quiet, severe-looking man. I got the impression, as he looked me over, that he felt he'd made a mistake.

I never saw much of him, except to draw a little money from time to time later on, after the Arthur Hopkins loan was exhausted. He sent me to see Irving Thalberg at M-G-M. In retrospect, I think he was hoping Thalberg would take me off his hands, at any price. I never did make a picture for Schenck.

Thalberg did put me in an M-G-M picture on loan from Schenck in December 1930. It was *The Secret Six*, which went into production almost immediately. It was based on a true story of six Chicago citizens who secretly and anonymously undertook to cope with Chicago mobsters.

The cast, incidentally, included Wallace Beery, Jean Harlow, Clark Gable, John Miljan, John Mack Brown, Paul Hurst, Lewis Stone, Marjorie Rambeau—all dead now.

Gable, who had come up through stock too, got his contract with M-G-M on his performance in this film.

I was the "baby-faced killer," with a scar on my chin that I still have. The make-up man used the wrong kind of collodion over a painted abrasion. The second day, and for the rest of the picture, I didn't need the painted abrasion. The collodion had made a perfect scar and scab. The scab's gone now, but I still have a memento of my first picture.

During the filming of *The Secret Six*, I was dining alone one night at Henry's Restaurant, owned by Charlie Chaplin. Gable came in and sat with me. After he had ordered, he asked, "What do you think of all this out here?"

"I don't know yet," I answered. "I haven't been here long enough to form an opinion."

"I just got eleven thousand dollars for playing a heavy in a Bill Boyd Western," he exclaimed. *"Eleven thousand dollars!"* he went on, almost in disbelief. "No actor's worth that. This can't last. I've got myself a room at the Castle Argyll [an inexpensive hostelry at the top of Vine Street] and a secondhand Ford. I'm socking away everything I can and I'm not buying anything I can't put on The Chief. This just can't last."

With the advent of sound, the studios had to seek new finances to convert their theatre projection equipment and meet the new production procedures to accommodate this innovation. It meant having to acquire many millions in new money.

Each studio had its list of stars, directors, writers, etc. under long-term contract. They were developed, nurtured and publicized. They were the studios' greatest assets. They were principal collateral (along with pictures they might have just completed) when it came time to borrow from the banks for production each year.

John Gilbert was probably *the* number-one box-office draw in silent pictures, and his contract with M-G-M was drawing to its termination.

M-G-M, in need of new money for sound, quickly signed Gilbert to a new contract at three million dollars for two years and got the new money.

But when Gilbert appeared in his first picture under the new contract they found that his voice recorded at a high pitch and sounded effeminate. They tried to get him to terminate the contract, but he wouldn't. They put him in mediocre pictures, hoping he'd refuse to appear and thus break the contract, but he didn't.

I was in a picture with him at this time called *West of Broadway*—a very mediocre one. He told me the story I've just related and while we were shooting he said to me, "I'll work out the contract cleaning spittoons, if they make me, for that kind of money." My second picture was with him.

West of Broadway was the story of an eastern playboy who comes West to the ranch he's inherited, resulting in his redemption, and he finds a good clean girl whom he marries and becomes the upstanding fellow we always knew John Gilbert to be.

I was the ranch foreman. In the segment of Gilbert's arrival from the East, I've shown him over the ranch and we're returning on horseback to the hitching post in front of the ranch house. We ride up, dismount, tie our horses and walk toward the house. No dialogue.

I had learned to ride on a Wellington saddle with a colonel friend at Fort Des Moines, Iowa, and I was a pretty good rider. I could even jump a little. But I'd never before sat in a western saddle. I took the reins, one in each hand, as our two horses were led to the hitching post for the cameraman to light us.

The director, Harry Beaumont, then told us to go out the gate and around the corner, out of sight, and await the cue to come in. Gilbert turned his horse and left. I tried first one rein, then the other, attempting to turn my horse, but it seemed only to confuse him. He was a picture horse, though, and he'd got the idea from the director. So, on his own, he turned and we followed Gilbert through the gate and around the corner.

But now we were on a narrow cow path on the side of a rather steep hill, which meant we had to turn around on the spot. I was viciously pulling on one rein, trying to turn my horse, which was nose to nose with Gilbert's horse, which had already turned. Gilbert was roaring with laughter as we heard, back at the ranch house, the clapping of the sticks in front of the camera which ensured synchronization of picture and sound just before the action was photographed.

My horse, being an old pro, recognized the clappers and remembered the director's orders. The next thing I knew I was at the hitching post, with both feet out of the stirrups and both hands on the pommel. My ten-gallon hat had been knocked off coming under the bough of a tree.

Now I know about neck-reining, and I'm a fair western rider.

I wouldn't have felt so embarrassed at the time if I'd been aware of others' difficulties in their early experiences in pictures.

For instance, my good friend Harry Morgan was in a Western with Jimmy Stewart in one of his first pictures. It contained the classic "good guys" and "bad guys." Harry was one of three bad guys. They'd been abusive and troublesome in many ways and they were unwanted in the town.

At one point Jimmy, a good guy, was leading several hundred townspeople to the saloon, where Harry and his cohorts were relaxing. He ordered them out onto the boardwalk in front of the saloon and, saying he represented the assembly behind him, he admonished the three bad guys to "Get out of town, or stay and fight."

The three bad guys looked over the multitude of townfolk, shrugged, went to their horses at the hitching post and were supposed to ride out of town.

Harry's two cronies mounted and rode away, while Harry struggled with his shying, frisky horse and couldn't mount. He couldn't even get his foot in the stirrup. And Anthony Mann, the director, said, "Cut."

They tried again—and again—and again. Still Harry couldn't mount.

Tempers were shortening and Harry said to his pals, "Why don't you wait till I get on my horse before you ride out?!"

They tried again.

The other desperadoes mounted and waited.

Harry fought his horse, who would still have nothing to do with him, and the two of them went round and round.

Finally Harry said, in disgusted defeat, "Ahhh, the hell with it. Let's stay and fight 'em."

There was a tragedy—a real one—connected with *West of Broadway*.

Lois Moran was the leading lady. One hot, sultry morning she and I were picked up at our houses by a studio limousine, to be driven to a location in the hills north of the San Fernando Valley.

It was blistering hot and all the windows were open as we started our steep, winding ascent after crossing the valley. I recall a slight feeling of nausea as we climbed the circuitous, weather-beaten road.

The road was rutted gravel, and we had to go slowly around the sharp curves. We were silent as the driver avoided possible drop-offs from the open side of the road.

We finally reached a flat area on our left that sloped to a sheer drop-off some five hundred yards away. This was our location.

As we made the left turn I noticed that the driver used only one hand. And now we were headed for the drop-off.

We gathered momentum as we bounced over the hard, dry ground toward a live oak tree in our path.

The driver seemed to make no effort to control the car.

Something was obviously amiss.

I opened a door and pushed Lois out, then jumped myself.

In a matter of seconds, a bough of the live oak tree caught the windshield and went through the three open windows and held the car as it stuck in the rear window.

The driver got out and dropped dead.

He'd had a heart attack—for how long, no one knows—and he had been trying to hold on against hope.

If it hadn't been for the live oak, the car would have fallen hundreds of feet.

My contract with Schenck guaranteed thirty weeks out of fifty-two, allowing him to lay me off twenty-two weeks out of fifty-two—which he did, after *West of Broadway*. All twenty-two of them, in succession. My funds didn't last long. Neither of my first two jobs had taken more than two or three weeks to complete.

I repaid Arthur Hopkins and moved from the Hollywood Knickerbocker Hotel to a house that Frank Conroy, an actor friend from New York, and I rented for a hundred and forty dollars a month. Designed by Frank Lloyd Wright's son, it contained a swimming pool and built-in furniture.

The living room had a picture window on one wall, opposite a copper fireplace, and all four walls had bookshelves from floor to ceiling. We measured the shelves and made a deal with a secondhand-book dealer for seventy-five dollars for so many feet of books. That was fine, and really interesting. Most of the books weren't much, but some were quite worth having and reading. All this for seventy dollars a month apiece.

But we'd overlooked two niches, opposite each other, in the walls that didn't accommodate the fireplace and picture window. They were perpendicular niches about four feet high and about two feet wide.

In a junk yard we found two automobile crankshafts and two shot-puts, all very rusty. We had them cleaned and chromed and placed a shot-put on top of a crankshaft in each niche. We had a lot of fun double-talking to our friends about the sculptor until we finally described what our art work was and where it came from. I think it cost around eleven dollars for both "sculptures."

During these twenty-two weeks I had to make regular trips to Mr. Schenck's office to draw money to buy a car, which is necessary in Hollywood, and to get money to live on. Finally I came to. One must have an agent in pictures and I didn't have one. So I quickly took care of that and we persuaded Mr. Schenck to release me from my contract, for which he paid me a small sum and canceled the money I'd drawn.

The matter of agents in Hollywood is a very considerable one. Everyone has an agent who guides his professional affairs. Each agent has several or many clients.

On Broadway and in stock and road companies, etc., unless one has a personal agent, which few do, the commission on a job is, in general, 5 per cent of the first ten weeks' salary. All agents handle all actors, and all actors who are "at liberty" visit all agents' offices every day—"Anything for me today?" New York agents are more like casting offices. A producer usually works with one agent's office. In Hollywood a producer works with many offices on all productions.

In Hollywood one signs an exclusive management agreement with an agent for three years at 10 per cent of his salary. If no work is forthcoming for ninety-one days in pictures or television, or a hundred and twenty days in the theatre, the actor can terminate the agreement by notifying the agent by registered mail.

In the early days of "talkies" the studios had their rosters of contract players who were built and maintained by their publicity departments through the terms and renewals of the players' contracts.

Before the studios were forced to abandon their contract personnel with the loss, by government decree, of their theatre chains, they held the strong hand. There was almost an animosity between the agents and the studios. As an example there's a story which bears credibility, that Mike Levee, who was an important agent with popular clients, got into an argument with

Jack Warner and was barred from the Warner Brothers' lot. Mike, who already had several Warner Brothers' players under managerial contract, offered to handle Errol Flynn, who was Warners' top draw, and Olivia de Havilland, who was also under contract to Warner Brothers, for nothing. Errol accepted. Then Mike made Warners so uncomfortable with demands for all his Warner clients that they opened the gate for him. I think that, and another story that seems valid enough, concerning M-G-M, might have been the beginning of agents' clout.

The other story goes that many years ago Lewis J. Selznick was forced out of the combine that became Metro-Goldwyn-Mayer by Louis B. Mayer and they became enemies. Selznick's son Myron formed an agency with Frank Joyce, an ex-vaudevillian. Joyce and Selznick became a powerful agency, acquiring as clients the top stars, directors and producers at M-G-M. Then Myron put the screws on as Mike Levee did at Warners. His sole object, the story goes, was to avenge his father. This was probably the beginning of astronomically high superstars' salaries. Incidentally, Lewis' other son, David O. Selznick, produced *Gone with the Wind*.

Now the studios are principally concerned with renting space to independent producers of both feature and television programs, with partial financing and distribution. This places the agents in the position of forming "packages" with their actor, writer, director, and producer clients, since very few studios have such contract personnel any longer. Or if a producer wants a star, his agent can make it a condition that other clients of his be cast in the same project, or he can force up salaries or demand script approval and various working conditions. These are pretty much the circumstances today when most production is done by independents, renting space in the old studios.

Most everyone in Hollywood has had more than one agent. I've had six.

There have always been big agencies and small ones. The big ones seem to be breaking up. The smaller ones seem to be thriving. There's an advantage both ways to being with the smaller agency: the agent gives more personal attention and works harder for his clients, for obvious reasons of commission if nothing else, and the client prospers because of it. The larger agencies have "leg men" who visit offices with lists of clients almost saying, "Anything for any of these today?" just as it was back on Broadway when we did it for ourselves. Except for superstars.

This is all an oversimplification, but fairly accurate.

But, to get back to my story, in a matter of days I had a job at Paramount.

The Magnificent Lie, opposite Ruth Chatterton, was my third picture (1931).

I have two recollections of it that stay with me.

First, I have a separation between my two upper front teeth, which is not uncommon, but isn't particularly becoming in front of a camera.

I had a paper-thin plastic shell cap, made in one piece, that I placed over my separated teeth, secured with false-teeth powder.

It worked fine, except for *s*'s and *f*'s. There was no escape for the forced breath needed to execute those letters, so I had to be careful and gentle with them.

I was playing a blind fellow, and in a two-shot scene with Ruth, my eyes raised, vacantly focused on nothing, I was suddenly aware that my cap wasn't there. I'd obviously overlooked an *f* or an *s*. I stopped the scene and all of us, cast and crew, cautiously searched for the missing cap. In the midst of our bent-over quest, Ruth looked up and I saw my two front teeth stuck to her forehead.

The other recollection is music. As soon as a scene was finished and the director, Berthold Viertel, said, "Print," we heard a violin and portable organ. This, I was told, was designed to keep a calm and harmonious atmosphere on the set. The beginning of Muzak, maybe?

Solly Baiano played the violin. Solly was an extraordinary left-handed tennis player and later became a scout in the casting department at Warner Brothers. A fine Italian friend. And his music did much to inspire performances and maintain "happy" sets.

"Happy" was a big word in those days of contract players, writers, actors and directors. Every effort was made to keep everybody happy.

My fourth picture was *Surrender* at Fox (now Twentieth Century-Fox), with Warner Baxter and Leila Hyams. It was an adaptation of a World War I German prison camp novel. I was the German officer in charge of the camp. I wore a full German uniform, had a black patch over one side of my face and eye, a great Dane the size of a pony which I led around on a chain, and a Prussian haircut.

My agent persuaded Fox that the haircut would keep me out of work for some time after the shooting was finished. They saw his point and gave me fifteen hundred dollars for having my hair cut. It looked as if Hollywood was going to provide a decent living.

On the same picture we had a fantastic set requiring two stages, for a scene of the prison camp at night.

There were mounds of earth, barbed wire, moving searchlights, horses, many extras, much shouting of commands and confusion. In the midst of all this a bit player came into the foreground of a shot including everything and read a hysterical speech about a page long. He had nothing else in the picture.

This is one of the hardest things to do. There's no continuity to help the actor. There's no give-and-take with other actors. There's no character development. The actor just has to come on and do it. All alone.

We lined up the prisoners, guards, soldiers and horses. We started the fog effect, which was sprayed Nujol, blown lightly by slowly revolving airplane propellers. And we tried a "take." Everything and everybody on two stages were moving. The little bit player came forward to his chalk mark, started his speech and began releasing the dramatics of his hysteria when he "went up."

We turned on the house lights, opened the doors to air out the Nujol and backed up the horses. The prisoners, the guards and the soldiers returned to their starting places, and after an hour or so we tried again. And the bit player "blew" again.

We broke for an early lunch and began again afterward with everyone fresh. The director, William K. Howard, said encouragingly, "All right, everyone. This is the one. Make it a good one."

All the action started, the bit player came forward and it was going fine. Then—again—he was gone. He looked at Bill Howard and said, "God damn it, Mr. Howard, I'll get it if it takes a thousand years." But that was too long. He didn't get another chance. The poor fellow!

Incidentally, *Surrender* started at the old Fox lot at Western Avenue and Sunset Boulevard in Hollywood. It finished at Fox Hills, which is now Twentieth Century-Fox. Ours might have been the first picture made there.

At one point in a picture at Fox with Sally Eilers called *Second Hand Wife* (a real soap opera story, by Kathleen Norris, I believe), we were in an elaborate hotel bedroom on our honeymoon. We were about to retire when a phone call came with word of an accident to my little daughter by my first marriage. I quickly left to go to her and, quite late at night, returned to find Sally in an enticing nightgown, sound asleep on top of one of the twin beds. I was in pajamas.

The direction then was: you get into the other bed and turn out the light—fade-out.

I told the director, Hamilton MacFadden, "If I do that it'll be the biggest laugh in the picture. It's our wedding night! I have to do something besides get into another bed and go to sleep, no matter how late it is or how tired I might be."

This was during the days of the Hays Office and rigid adherence to an industry-wide code of moral "don'ts." MacFadden agreed but he said he was helpless. He had orders to shoot the script the way it was written.

At that moment the producer, Sol Wurtzel, walked onto the stage and sat in a director's chair. He was a gruff-appearing fellow with toric-lensed glasses. He wore a white cap and he was smoking a cigar.

With MacFadden's approval, I squatted beside Wurtzel's chair and repeated my opinion. He listened sympathetically, occasionally spreading open his lips over his very white teeth, which were clamping the cigar—a habit that many people mistook for smiling, and they'd smile back at him. But he wasn't smiling.

He heard me out and said, "Yeah! I think you're right. I come home late at night sometimes and I find my wife asleep with a book in her lap and the lights on. I think any guy coming home late like that and finding his wife asleep like that would wake her up, kiss her good night, put out the lights, be a little bit salacious toward her."

It's been said that a man isn't a man till he's had his first fist fight. In my first two tries, I failed at both.

In pictures, when a punch is delivered, the punch thrower usually stands with his back to the camera and throws his fist across the face of the victim, who snaps his head in the same direction as the fist. The sound of contact is dubbed in. The fist needn't come closer than two or three inches from the actor's face.

I had a scene with Pat O'Brien in *Air Mail*, one of the first big air pictures. I was the manager of the airport and Pat was a reckless, daredevil flier from World War I who was one of the original airmail pilots. He caused great anxiety around the airport with his wild stunts, not the least of which was a ten-thousand-foot dive through a single-plane hangar.

The scene of moment was in his quarters, where I'd come to let him know that I wasn't going to stand for any more of his antics. He, of course, talked back and laughed at me. He was standing beside his cot with his back to it. I was facing him. After a bit of vituperative dialogue, I was to hit him, knocking him backward and sideways onto the cot.

I still have a little trouble throwing punches in pictures because I've never had a real fist fight. When I throw a punch it looks as if I'm reaching up on the shelf for the jam.

We rehearsed the shot with the camera over my shoulder facing Pat. I threw my fist across his face and he snapped his head and fell onto the cot.

Jack Ford, the director, said, "Follow through with the punch and hit his shoulder just beyond his chin. It'll jar him and it'll look better."

"I don't want to do that, Jack," I said. "I'd hit him in the clavicle. Not only would it hurt, but it's a slender bone and it could crack."

Ford was a perfectionist. He was also rugged. And he was Irish. He moved Pat to one side and took his place in front of me. "Throw the punch at me and hit my shoulder," he directed.

"I don't want to, Jack," I repeated. "I'll hurt you."

"I'm telling you to do it!" he said.

I threw the punch and hit his shoulder. He gasped as he grabbed it with both hands, lost his balance and fell onto the cot. "Do it your way!" he directed as he walked away clutching his shoulder.

I had a scene with Jim Cagney in *Picture Snatcher* in which I, as the managing editor, was reprimanding Jim, the photographer, for some unethical journalist behavior, and he was responding in classic East Side New York jargon. I was to hit him in the jaw. In rehearsal I threw a fist across his face in a close shot over my shoulder, just showing the back of my head and his full face.

Jim has done quite a bit of boxing. He said, "Aim at my chin right here." And he pointed to the left side of his chin. "Don't worry," he continued. "I'll ride the punch. I'll be out of your way. You won't touch me."

We did a take. I aimed at his chin, hit the side of his face and broke a tooth. We're close friends now, for some reason or other.

I claim two firsts at Columbia Studio.

In my early Hollywood days I had a handshake deal, without an agent, with Harry Cohn, the head of Columbia, and his chief adviser Sam Briskin, to do a Frank Capra picture opposite Barbara Stanwyck called *Forbidden*.

This was to be a big picture, a bid to turn Columbia into a major studio, to take it out of the category of "quickie" productions, typified by Tim McCoy Westerns that were made in four or five days, and less than "B" pictures, made about one a week. (A week's work was six or even seven days in those days before Screen Actors Guild.) Many of these were made by Jack Holt, who was a qualified holdover from silent pictures because he could work with sound.

A day or two later, Dan Kelly, Columbia's casting director, called me at home and said, "Mr. Cohn says if you're going to do *Forbidden*, you have to do another one first with Fay Wray."

"I thought we had a deal on *Forbidden*," I said, "but it's entirely possible that one with Fay Wray can be done first. Let's see the script."

He sent me the script and called me again the next day for my answer.

"The picture with Fay Wray is a tough one physically and it goes to sea on location for a week," I told him. "It's water and night shots. It finishes one day before *Forbidden* starts, and I'm in nearly every shot of that one, growing older in the part, over a span of many years. I'd have to have a stand-in if I did both."

There was a pause and Dan mumbled, "We've never had a stand-in at Columbia."

"Well, I'd have to have one if I do both pictures," I replied, and he said he'd call me back. He did, with the message that Harry Cohn would like to see me.

"What the hell is this?" was my icy greeting from Mr. Cohn in his office. "You New York actors! A stand-in! We never had a stand-in on the Columbia lot and we never will have one!"

I repeated the answer I'd given Dan Kelly and continued, "I'd have to have one to do justice to the two parts and to you and to myself."

"Well, you're not going to have one!" he declared with what he thought was finality.

"In that case," I countered, "let's forget both pictures and maybe we'll find something else to do later on."

You weren't supposed to do that to Harry Cohn, and he wasn't expecting it. But he wasn't shaken. He directed a diatribe at me concerning "New York actors" in general, and me in particular, forgetting that "New York actors" were in Hollywood at the behest of the studios, with the advent of sound, because they were trained to read lines, which most silent actors couldn't do.

After listening to him for a few minutes, I rose to make a polite departure, but he said, "Wait a minute!" I sat again and he said, calmly but with desperation in his voice, "All right, God damn it, you can have a stand-in—on one condition: don't tell Jack Holt!"

"I don't know Jack Holt," I replied, "but if I met him I don't think I'd be inclined to say, 'I have a stand-in and you haven't.'"

"Don't get fresh!" he ordered. "Just get out, and do the two parts."

I did the two pictures and, after a year under contract with Fox, I signed a five-year contract with Columbia.

The business was booming and it was the day of the double features. The industry was turning out some five hundred pictures a year. During the early part of my contract I was in almost every picture Columbia made, and we worked six days a week from early morning till late at night, and sometimes all night Saturday, until the leading lady fainted Sunday noon, or some such obstacle.

Through all this, Jack Holt was still turning out about one a week.

The Screen Actors Guild had not yet been formed and there were no restrictions on hours and conditions. Some of my friends were arbitrarily quitting work at six o'clock, and since I was giving my all to Columbia I thought I had a right to do this—and I did.

At five-thirty each evening I would alert the assistant director not to let the director get into a setup that included me after six o'clock because I wasn't going to be there. A week or so went by and a boy came onto the set one day with a message for me. It was a note from Harry Cohn, summoning me to his office "when I finished work."

A few minutes after six I was in his office and he blurted out, "What the hell is this? Walking off a set!"

By this time I knew Harry well. I understood his bluff manner and I liked him. I knew that if you gave him as good as he gave you, he liked it. And if you didn't, he had little respect for you.

"What the hell do you want for a day's wages?" I said. "I'm here almost every day and I'm in almost every picture you make. I can't stand the hours!"

"You're under contract to me," he bellowed. "You'll do what I tell you to do. And you'll stay on the set until you're dismissed!"

"In that case," I said, "let's tear up the contract, because I can't work every week, seven days a week like that."

Again, you weren't supposed to do that to Harry. He carried on again, as before, for a few minutes and stopped, glaring at me across his desk.

"All right, God damn it," he practically cried, "you can quit at six o'clock—on one condition." He pointed a threatening finger at me. "Don't tell Jack Holt!"

I never did meet Jack Holt.

Shortly after this the Screen Actors Guild was formed and I was on the first board of directors. Hours and conditions, minimums, pension and welfare have gradually and with difficulty been achieved by this magnificent organization.

Forbidden was my first chance at a really fine part, and one of my biggest professional mistakes was not being more selective after that. It was a lesson that stood me in good stead in my ensuing excursions back to Broadway.

Barbara Stanwyck, Adolphe Menjou and I were starred in *Forbidden*, and Frank Capra was on the verge of attaining the greatness with which his name and pictures are now associated. And Barbara was on her way to one of the longest and still-continuing careers of stardom in the history of motion pictures. Two magnificently warm, talented and human people.

Frank says in his book *The Name Before the Title* that the picture wasn't especially meritorious. I disagree, to the extent that in its day it was the type of human drama audiences craved. It was an absorbing story, written by Jo Swerling, whose son is now a successful producer, and it was a money-maker. There was music on the set again—the violin, played by Solly Baiano, and portable organ.

Frank used the music for inspirational background in rehearsal preparation for the upcoming scene. I remember his clearing the stage of cast and crew while rehearsing, except for those involved in the scene; then, in a quiet and intelligent voice, discussing the requirements and moods to be achieved in this honest tearjerker, with the soft music in the background. I've never heard it used that way since and now, of course, not at all. I wonder why? It was a good idea. *Forbidden*, with Frank and Barbara and 'Dolph, is a fond memory.

I asked Frank if he had anything he might be willing to add to this and he sent me a warm letter from which the following is an excerpt:

"I remember one scene well . . . Barbara Stanwyck, with a pistol in her hand, was standing behind a closed door that Bellamy, a tough editor, was trying to break down to get Stanwyck (his present wife) to verify a scandalous story about Stanwyck he was running down; a story about Stanwyck and his archen-emy—Adolphe Menjou, who was now running for governor.

"The scandal was that Stanwyck had had a secret lifelong affair with Menjou, who was married all that time. A child had been born to Stanwyck—Menjou's child.

"Stanwyck warns Bellamy not to break down the door. As the door begins to splinter, Stanwyck raises her pistol and fires three shots through the door.

"Then we take the camera to Bellamy's side of the door. Bellamy is not seen. The door opens quietly, revealing Stanwyck looking down at the presumably dead Bellamy. I shall never forget the wild look on her contorted face as she stood there quivering with hate, the gun still smoking. She had killed for her lover! Pride and hate bursting from wide-open eyes. I go to Stanwyck's side, take her quivering arm, and escort her to her dressing room. She was making incoherent noises. I had just witnessed a murder. A real murder. Shaking like a leaf, I leave her to return to our set. And lo and behold—there is the dead Bellamy walking around talking to other actors. Was he a ghost? It took minutes for me to adjust my bearings. Yes, of course. Sure. We had just shot a scene for a movie, that's all."

Harry Cohn used to sell mink-dyed rabbit skins for real mink in upstate New York. They were sent to him from New York City by Nate Spingold, who was later vice-president of Columbia Pictures. Also, in his early days, Harry sang to slides in silent picture houses.

After time passed, he did a fine job of running Columbia Studio and he was proud of it. He brought it from a less than second-rate "quickie" studio featuring the Hall Room Boys and later Colonel Tim McCoy in Westerns, and Ralph Graves and Jack Holt in adventure pictures until it gradually evolved to "B" pictures and finally to a major studio.

Harry ran the production end of Columbia from the studio in Hollywood at the corner of Sunset Boulevard and Gower Street, known as "Gower Gulch," because that's where the cowboy ex-tras gathered, hoping for work in Harry's pictures, which for a while were mostly Westerns.

Harry's brother Jack ran the New York office, which handled distribution and some financing.

The brothers got along fine as long as they commanded separate coasts. But, reportedly, face-to-face confrontations were calamitous.

The following story was told to me by an eye-and-ear witness while I was under contract to Harry Cohn:

Unhappily, the two brothers found themselves sitting opposite each other in Harry's office in Hollywood. After unsuccessful attempts at conversation and a considerable pause, Jack said, "Harry, why don't we make a Bible story?"

"A *Bible* story!" said Harry. "For Christ sake, why?"

"Well," Jack said, "they're like Foreign Legion stories and Westerns. They always seem to make money. And besides, there's no royalty or anything."

Harry could hardly contain his pique as he said to his brother, "You run the East Coast and let me make the pictures. And anyway, what the hell do you know about the Bible? I bet you don't even know the Lord's Prayer."

"I do too," Jack replied.

"For fifty dollars you don't know the Lord's Prayer," Harry sneered as he put a fifty-dollar bill on his desk.

"I do too," Jack repeated, hurt. And he matched Harry's fifty-dollar bet with his own bill.

"Let me hear you say it!" Harry commanded.

With chin and eyes raised, Jack chanted, "Now I lay me down to sleep—"

But Harry interrupted, saying, "All right, that's enough. I didn't think you knew it. Take the goddamned money."

And Jack did.

The Awful Truth has become a classic. But its origins would provide Mel Brooks and Larry Gelbart with material for a satire on how pictures are made.

My experience with it began with a telephone call from Dan Kelly, the studio manager at Columbia, who said, "Mr. Cohn is sending you by motorcycle a script called *The Awful Truth*. It's an adaptation of a stage play. He wants you to read it for the part of the Englishman, which was written for Roland Young, but don't pay any attention to it."

"If I'm not to pay any attention to it, why should I read it?" I said. "And anyway, I wouldn't attempt to play an Englishman."

"I don't know anything except what Mr. Cohn said, and the guy's on his way over with the script," Dan droned.

The next day, Dan called and said, "Mr. Cohn wants to see you about *The Awful Truth*."

When I'd made the long walk from Cohn's office door to his desk, he said, "What'd you think?"

"I think it's a very funny script," I told him, "and I think Roland Young is perfect for the Englishman."

"He's not going to be an Englishman, he's going to be from the West," said Cohn. And that was about the substance of that meeting.

A few days went by and I had a call from Mary McCall, Jr., one of Hollywood's best writers. "Are you a good friend of mine, Ralph?" she asked.

"Sure," I assured her.

"Well," she said, "I'm trying to make a Westerner out of an Englishman and you're going to play him."

"Oh," I said. "*The Awful Truth*."

"That's right. And I'm not getting anywhere. Would you come to my office and see if you can help me get some ideas, since you're going to play it?"

I spent a couple of hours with Mary and we got some crazy idea of a strange Western character making an entrance down a fire escape and through a window. And that was that.

Time passed, and Dwight Taylor, another top Hollywood writer, called and said, "Ralph, I'm having a bad time trying to make a Westerner out of an Englishman in *The Awful Truth*. Have you any ideas?"

"Are you working with Mary McCall, Jr.?" I asked.

"No, I'm on it alone, but I can't seem to get anywhere with it."

I don't know whether I mentioned Mary McCall again, but I did say I was familiar with the script and the difficulty and that I thought Roland Young would be great as the Englishman the way the original script read, and Dwight agreed.

Again time passed, and I saw Dorothy Parker and Alan Campbell at a cocktail party. Dottie said, "Isn't it great that we're going to work together?"

"Really?" I said. "What's it about?"

"*The Awful Truth,*" she replied, "with Irene Dunne and Cary Grant, and Leo McCarey's directing."

"Oh, that'll be great," I said. "When does it go?"

"As soon as we can get the script out," Dottie said. And again, that was that.

Then, one Friday, Dan Kelly called and said, "You start *The Awful Truth* on Monday."

"To play what?" I asked. "Where's the script?"

"There's no script yet. Just report Monday morning."

"What kind of clothes?" I asked.

"I don't know. Just bring a lot of clothes."

I went to the studio to see Harry Cohn, to see if I could find out what was going on. He was uncommunicative, beyond saying that Leo McCarey was on top of it and that he had no idea how the story had developed and that he had complete confidence in Leo. Leo had that kind of respect and record in the business. I asked Harry if he'd object if I went to Leo's house to talk to him about it and he said, "Go ahead."

When I went to Leo's house, he met me with his perpetual gleeful grin and dancing eyes. He wasn't helpful at all. He said nothing much about the story or the part. He just joshed and said not to worry—we'd have lots of fun, but there wasn't any script. I suggested, again, that Roland play the part as originally written and let me out. Leo grinned more deeply, as if he had a secret, and with flashing eyes and teeth he said, "You'll see. I'll see you Monday morning."

Monday morning I came on the set made up, and with an armful of clothes. Irene was sitting at a grand piano, trying to read the sheet music of "Home on the Range." Leo came toward me, grinning, and I, with arms loaded with clothes and madder than hell, said, "I don't know what I'm playing. They told me to bring a lot of clothes."

"What have you got on?" he asked.

"Odd jacket and slacks, the way I came to the studio," I sneered.

"Just what I want," he said. "Can you sing?"

"I can't get from one note to another," I grumbled as I unloaded the clothes.

"Great!" he said. "Do you know the words to 'Home on the Range'?"

"Yes," I said, "but I can't sing it."

"Great!" he repeated as he took me by the arm to the piano, where Irene was struggling with the sheet music. "Irene, play it just the way you're doing it now. And Ralph, you belt it out with loud Oklahoma pride. It's a comedy, you know."

The camera was set up to shoot over the grand piano at the two of us and Leo said, "Roll it," and "Action!" and Irene hammered out the sheet music as I threw back my head and slaughtered "Home on the Range."

We finished and no one said, "Cut!"

Irene and I looked up and Leo was under the camera, so doubled up with laughter that he couldn't speak. Finally he said, "Print it!"

After several similar episodes in which dialogue was by Leo, seemingly out of the air, we finished the day.

Cary Grant didn't have much to do that day, but he went to Harry Cohn and suggested that he play my part as it was written for Roland and I play his part, or let him out of the picture and he'd do another. Irene was in tears, begging to be let out, and I was still trying to find out what I was playing.

Cohn would have no traffic with us. He left it all to Leo.

There never was a script. Each morning Leo would appear with a small piece of brown wrapping paper more often than not, and throw us lines and business. After a few days we saw what was happening. Despite Mary McCall, Jr., Dwight Taylor and Dottie Parker and Alan Campbell, Leo knew all the time what he wanted. And he got it. We were quickly won over to him and had the fun he'd promised. And we made the film in six weeks, a record for that kind of picture.

And I got an Academy Award nomination.

I asked Irene and Cary if they would jot down any recollections they had of *The Awful Truth*. Irene wrote me the following in part:

"—And, yes, I remember our rendition of 'Home on the Range' and your line about the little brown hen.

"One of the things I remember about *The Awful Truth* was Cary Grant's attitude at the beginning of the film. He could not understand Leo's improvising as he went along. I really think if Cary could have gotten out of the film at that time he would have done so.

"Also my inability to do a 'bump,' which I still can't do. When I came to the part in the song 'My Dreams Are Gone with the Wind' where I was supposed to do the 'bump' he (Leo) said, 'Just say, "Never could do that."' Also the part in the film where I impersonated Cary's sister.

"The dialogue was written over the weekend and handed to me on Monday morning. I always thought it a choice comedy bit. Also, as I recall, the writer (Leo McCarey) did not know how to end the film, and the story goes that a member of the crew got the bright idea of having the boy on the cuckoo clock follow the girl into her little door. I thought it was brilliant."

Cary said he would try to jot down something. But he told me on the telephone, "I'm no writer—I don't know."

I guess he's no writer because that's the last I've heard from him.

But he's a hell of an actor.

This is as good a place as any to relate the nature and scope of my vocality; some years later in New York I was offered the lead role in a musical. I would have loved to be in a musical, but alas —I was forced to reveal the sad fact that I couldn't sing.

I was told there was a marvelous coach on Central Park West who could awaken latent vocal talents in anyone. He'd coached Bob Preston for *The Music Man*.

An appointment was made with this genius, whose name I can't remember.

His apartment was on the second floor overlooking the park. It was a warm sunny day and the windows were open.

"Open your collar and face the park and sing 'My Country, 'Tis of Thee' out the open window as loud as you can," he said. "Never mind the key—I'll find it and accompany you. Belt it out."

I did as directed. But when I got to "Land where my fathers died" he stopped playing and interrupted me.

"Mr. Bellamy," he said, "it is my solemn duty to tell you you cannot sing."

I knew this before I went to see him. I'd proven it in *The Awful Truth*.

I like to think of myself as being more or less versatile. I've played parts of all kinds and all ages. Whether or not they were all palatable I have to leave to unbiased judges. And I'm not one. I can't stand myself on the screen.

But in *His Girl Friday* I had to meet a new challenge. I played the leading lady.

His Girl Friday is a rearrangement, or perhaps *de*rangement would be a more appropriate word, of *The Front Page*.

In *The Front Page* Hildy Johnson, the reporter, was played by Lee Tracy on the stage and by Pat O'Brien in the motion picture. In the play Hildy's fiancée was played by Frances Fuller and in the picture by Mary Brian. In *His Girl Friday* Rosalind Russell played Hildy and her affianced was played by me. Cary Grant was the editor, Walter Burns.

This was the idea concocted by Howard Hawks, the director, who sold it to Harry Cohn.

One day I wasn't working, and I hadn't worked the day before, but I went to the studio just to watch what was going on. Harry Cohn got wind that I was there and sent for me to watch the previous day's rushes with him in his private projection room. We were on the best of terms at this time.

The scene we were watching was between Roz and Cary in Cary's office, in which he had persuaded Roz (Hildy) to postpone her honeymoon with me so she could cover the story of an escaped criminal. I was waiting for Roz, with bags, raincoat and umbrella, at the entrance to the railroad station.

Our planned honeymoon had been derailed several times by Walter Burns, and now he was doing it again.

Burns (Cary) was on the phone with a hoodlum, directing him to kidnap me. He told the hood where I was waiting and was asked for a description. Cary turned to Roz and asked, "What does he look like?"

"Ralph Bellamy," Roz replied (new line by Hawks), and Cary

said over the phone, "He looks like that fellow in pictures." Turning to Roz: "What's his name?"

"Ralph Bellamy," Roz repeated, and Cary said into the phone again, "Yeah, Ralph Bellamy."

Cohn hit the ceiling, but he got over it. And the line always gets a laugh.

Speaking of Harry Cohn and phones, he loaned me to Warner Brothers for a picture with Carole Lombard, *Fools for Scandal* (my second with her; the first was *Hands Across the Table*). Working with Carole was a delight. There was continuous laughter off-camera and great energy and performance on-camera. Mervyn LeRoy was the director.

On a Monday morning the phone rang on the set on the assistant director's portable table. It was for me. It was Cohn. He said, "What the hell have you been saying about me around town?"

"I don't know," I said. "What did you hear?"

"You said I put on a rough front but underneath I'm a sentimentalist."

"Oh," I said. "You must have seen Mervyn LeRoy over the weekend. I did say something like that to him."

"Well," he replied, "you're under contract to me and I'm ordering you not to say things like that. You'll ruin my image around town." And he slammed down the receiver.

He behaved as if he was mad. But I think he liked it.

During my bondage to Harry Cohn and Columbia Pictures, I was in New York one time for a vacation. I checked into the Columbia office to say hello and overheard a conversation about a xylophone player Frank Capra wanted tested for his upcoming production of *You Can't Take It with You*. The stage version was still playing on Broadway. Frank and I had become friends. Also I'd always thought I'd like to direct pictures. I mentioned this to the New York staff and said I'd like to direct the test. They thought it was a fine idea.

I went to see the play and I liked the xylophone player. His real wife was to be the off-camera wife, Essie, for the test. I looked forward to it.

I got to the Tenth Avenue studio early, to see what scenery was available so that I could show the young xylophone player to best advantage. And, of course, to show my directorial talent at its proper level.

The set they'd provided consisted of a wall with a fireplace in its center, joined at a right angle to another wall that had an arch at the far side from the fireplace wall. The arch had a backing which led offstage. There was an upholstered settee with its back to the fireplace. Nothing else.

My plan was to place the xylophone parallel to, and opposite from, the wall with the arch, as if it were against a third wall that joined the fireplace wall. I would have the camera shooting over the xylophone, with the hopeful musician entering through the arch so that we could get a full-figure view of him. He would walk forward to the xylophone, pick up the hammers and play a few bars. Then he would look up and off one side of the camera, still playing, and call, "Oh, Essie," and I'd cut and place the camera at another angle. That was to be the beginning of the test.

The xylophone player and his wife arrived. But he wasn't the one from the play. He played club dates, bar mitzvahs and banquets. They were a charming couple, and it was obvious that the young lady was from the deep, deep South.

I had some intuitive misgivings about their ability to read lines. I asked them to run through what they'd learned and they proved my intuition valid. Furthermore, since Essie was to be off-camera, and since she had this Alabama cottonfield accent, it could be taken that we were suggesting miscegenation. And society had not yet, at that time, achieved an enlightened, receptive attitude on this point. Not even our courts. We were still somewhat WASPish and segregationist.

I now had myself to think about in the test—not only professionally but philosophically. The titles and credits would read "Test for *You Can't Take It with You*. Xylophone player. Director, Ralph Bellamy."

This test would go beyond Columbia Studio, to other studios. I could become known in the industry as an advocate of mixed marriage, using an unknown xylophone player, an unknown black girl and Frank Capra as a device.

This was before the McCarthy era, but we know what happened to people in the moving picture business then. I might even have been dubbed "The Hollywood One." But I was committed to make the test.

I left the crew to light the set and retired to the dressing room of my potential stars to do a little rehearsing.

The boy just couldn't read lines at all. And the girl sang them like a southern mammy.

There's only so much time and money allocated to a test, and the pressure was on. We had to be through by noon. It got to the place where I was saying, "Listen to me, and read it exactly as I do!" Any professional actor would have a few emotionally inspired words to say to any director who said that and then he would be gone, like a flash of lackopodium.* But they were grateful.

Finally, when we were on the set rehearsing for the cameraman, the boy practically ran through the arch to the instrument in the foreground. I explained that it should be a leisurely stroll so that we could see him full-figure. The next time, he came through all arms and hands, elbows bent out. I recognized his amateur lack of ease and poise.

"Take your coat half off before you enter," I said. "Then when I say 'Action,' come in completing the removal of your coat, throw it on the settee as you approach the xylophone, pick up the sticks and play."

We tried a take. As he came through the arch with both arms in back of him in his half-emptied sleeves, trying to take off his coat, he tripped on the flat floor-iron in the archway and fell forward on his chin.

We picked him up, dusted him off and calmed him down. Up, off and down. That's what they should have called this test.

We tried it once more. This time the mechanics were perfect. He came in taking off his coat, threw it on the settee and, strolling leisurely, picked up the hammers and played. And played, and played.

"Cut!" I called out, after too many bars of the beautiful xylophone melody. "I can't use the shot until you look up and call 'Essie,' " I told him.

* A white magnesium-based powder spread in a horizontal metal trough at the end of a handle for producing light in photography. You'll see it still in old movies in which reporters take photos.

"I forgot to tell you," he said, apologetic and embarrassed. "I can't play and talk at the same time."

The poor fellow didn't get the part in Capra's picture.

Anyone who remembers, or watches old Westerns on TV, will have noticed that the extras in the background of exterior scenes are almost always paired into couples. The man cavalierly clutches the woman's arm as they traverse the boardwalk or whatever and are passed by similar couples moving in the opposite direction, all cued by the assistant director off-camera on the sidelines. This was true of other pictures too but was most noticeable in Westerns. Apparently someone in the front office noticed this and issued an order. Ever since, extras have appeared on streets in much the same way as people do in large movements and mostly one at a time.

At the beginning of this innovation I was making a picture with Fay Wray which sent us to sea for a week on a freighter. Our director, Al Rogell, knew his business, having come up through the Mack Sennett and scriptless and "silent" days. He was short, muscular, mildly profane and husky-voiced. On location he continually shouted orders through a short megaphone, and he usually lost his voice before the picture was finished.

Our first shot at sea was to be from the bow of the ship, shooting back to see the winches working under the guidance of the engineers posted at their controls, the hatches being buckled down by the crew and the captain shouting orders from the bridge. A busy freight ship. We were waiting for land to disappear in the background before taking this shot.

Our property man, George Rhein, had tied a bandana over his nose and mouth to avoid nausea from the stench of the garbage he'd gathered in large cans and which he was scattering by handfuls from the stern to keep the seagulls in the background of the opening shot.

Rogell decided the time had come and after directing much movement, standing at the bow beside the camera, he called through his megaphone, "Action!"

Everything on the ship moved—captain, crew, engines, winches, extras, gulls et al.

After a few seconds Rogell called through his megaphone, "Cut! Send those goddamned gulls through one at a time!"

Rhein, green at the gills and close to vomiting, threw the garbage, cans and all, overboard. And we never saw the gulls again.

Later, on the same picture, I was to go overboard and under water in a diving bell suspended from a winch. I was ready to enter the chamber and have the door bolted from the outside so they could hoist me and the bell into the air and then lower me beneath the water, on-camera.

Just as I moved to enter the bell, my friend George Rhein passed behind me and whispered, "Don't get in it. I saw it made!"

I hesitated and then said to Rogell, "Put it over and down empty first. Just as a precaution."

They did. But after it was submerged, the winch stuck and they couldn't get it up for an hour or so.

When it was finally brought up to the deck, it was full of water to the top.

My friend George Rhein had saved my life.

While I was at Columbia Harry Cohn asked me one day if I'd show a young actor around the studio. Cohn had just signed him. He said the boy had made only one picture and didn't know anyone in Hollywood except the people he'd just been working with.

The boy was William Holden and the picture he'd just made was *Golden Boy*. Cohn was splitting his seventy-five-dollars-a-week contract with Paramount, which was signed before he made *Golden Boy*.

Bill was charming and somewhat awed by it all. His chief concern was that he lived in Pasadena and was afraid his run-down secondhand car might fail him and keep him from getting to work at the studio.

I tried to reassure him, in light of his success in his first effort, that if the car wouldn't start or if it broke down, the studio would happily provide him with transportation (especially at his salary, which I didn't mention to him).

When we parted, I had the feeling that he had some skepticism about this and that he was apprehensive about his whole future.

But everything seems to have worked out all right.

Myles Connolly, a handsome, talented, six-foot Irish writer, gave me a capsule account of his career in pictures, leading up to the fate of the "original" story that he considered his masterpiece.

He said his record revealed a series of sales of his works to studios, with the provision that he also produce them. But during preparation for each production he crossed with the studio heads. His Irish temper led to fist fights and he was fired, leaving production to someone else.

He sold his masterpiece to Harry Cohn of Columbia, with whom it was easy to have an argument. As usual, this deal called for him to produce, and he was determined to keep control of himself—which he did.

At that "point in time" in Hollywood, Gable, Grant, Stewart, Tracy, Colbert and Dunne were at their peaks in romantic roles. Most casting of important pictures began with "penciling in" and hoping to get a couple of them.

Frank Capra was under contract to Columbia and he was also at his peak with *Mr. Smith Goes to Washington* and *It Happened One Night*.

But for various reasons they couldn't get any of them.

The pressure was on, however, to get into production—the sets had been built, the exterior locations secured and minor parts set. After combing Hollywood for appropriate star talent, they settled for a "B" picture cast and a gravel-voiced, vociferous, "quickie" contract director named D. Ross Lederman. He had great technical knowledge and experience with ten-day pictures but not much more than a modicum of taste or sensitivity. And I say this without unkindness, because I liked him.

Through all the painful preparation and casting and the assignment of the director (largely dictated by Harry Cohn), Myles kept control of himself and vowed not to let go.

In those days we worked six days a week. And on Saturday afternoons, although the sound stages were busy, most everyone in the front offices (producers, writers and unassigned directors) managed to go to the race track during the spring meet. At Columbia, incidentally, this meant sneaking out because Harry Cohn, demanding and getting a full day's work, had all contract people signed in and out.

The Saturday before shooting was to start was a warm, sunny spring day. A birds, bees and flowers day. Windows were open and all was quiet at the studio except the sound stages. Virtually no one was in the front offices but Harry Cohn and his secretaries. Myles had made a date for that afternoon to meet the gravel-throated Lederman in his cubbyhole office, to make a final desperate pitch for his masterpiece.

Lederman's office had just enough room to accommodate a desk and chair, with its back to an opened window, and a chair opposite the desk for a visitor. In this case, a hamstrung producer.

Myles began his plea. He said the story was largely autobiographical. It meant more to him than anything he'd ever written. He referred to a heart-rending scene between the leading man and the character woman (Myles's mother in real life), a moving scene between the leading man and the character man (Myles's father in real life) and a scene between the leading man and the leading lady (Myles's wife in real life)—all of them personal, intimate and touching.

Lederman was obviously affected and he'd risen from his chair spellbound, leaning forward, supporting himself with his hands on the desk.

Myles thought to himself, "I'll go on a bit more and see if I've really got to him." He continued until he saw a tear in the director's eye.

All choked up, Lederman said in his gravel voice, "Myles, I'll kick the shit out of it!"

Myles said that's exactly what he eventually did.

In the mid-thirties in Hollywood, a group of friends from the theatre days in New York got into the habit of meeting for dinner each Thursday evening, sometimes at a restaurant and sometimes at the home of one of the group.

Pat O'Brien brought me into this intimate little gathering, which eventually included Pat, Jim Cagney, Lynne Overman, Frank McHugh, Frank Morgan, Spence Tracy and me.

There was no particular point to these friendly feasts except that we liked each other. We took turns as host and we laughingly referred to ourselves as "The Boys' Club." As Frank

McHugh says, "It was the renewal of friendship, not the beginning."

The dinners usually were either at Chasen's, Romanoff's, Lucey's or La Maze restaurants and they continued into the fifties. But, alas, they ceased because Lynne Overman and Frank Morgan died, Frank McHugh moved East and from the mid and late forties until 1961 I did several plays, many radio and TV shows and a TV series in New York.

Of his return to New York, Frank says, "About 1950 the time 'between pictures' seemed to be lengthening for me. Live television was burgeoning in New York. I had speculated in going to Hollywood in 1929, without a contract, and as I later learned, I was set for a job at Warner Brothers before I had passed San Bernardino. Perhaps history would repeat.

"There was the New York stage too. If a picture did come up I could always commute to California, as Stanley Ridges and so many other actors did.

"That it didn't work out that way is only one circumstance in a long theatrical experience. Risks always have to be taken in this precarious business we have chosen for ourselves."

My own departure came about as the result of a visit to an old friend, Mark Hellinger, at his Warner Brothers office.

As we chatted, his phone rang and I was left seated opposite to him at his desk. There was a script facing me, the top page of which had a character-cast list on the left side and a description of the character on the right side, obviously for assistance in casting the parts.

I wasn't snooping, but I couldn't help reading the list and the descriptions. I came to one description that read, "A charming but naïve fellow from the Southwest. A typical Ralph Bellamy part."

I had played *The Awful Truth* and *His Girl Friday* and *Carefree* and I was typed.

Then and there I decided to go to New York and try to find a play. I did. I found *Tomorrow the World*.

I asked Frank McHugh if he remembered the origin of The Boys' Club and here it is:

"According to my memory this is the way 'The Boys' Club' started. I had been sent four blank pages from an autograph book from Hartford, with the request to have Spence, Pat, Jim and me sign them. They were to be auctioned at a church benefit.

"Pat and Jim, being at Warners, were easy targets. Spence was at M-G-M and I did not know his home address or phone. So I sent a letter (to the studio) and the blank page to him and asked him to sign. He did, and enclosed a letter in return to the effect that he thought it was rather sad that old friends living in the same town had to communicate by mail, and suggested that the four of us get together for dinner.

"In the meantime Jim and Spence had dinner together and talked it over and decided that the four of us should get together regularly and talk and dine. That is, Spence, Jim, Pat and myself. Which we did.

"We would decide at the present dinner where we were to meet for the next. I suppose I was the 'secretary,' for I would make the reminder phone calls.

"Lynne Overman was our first added member. I do not recall who came next, you or Frank Morgan.

"The true purpose was just to get together for conversation and laughs. Generally the conversational subject was 'wine, women and song.' Once in a while it would be an exchange of opinions of a picture or a part.

"Once when Spence was considering *Dr. Jekyll and Mr. Hyde* he asked the group if he should do it. Lynne advised against it. Spence asked why, and Lynne replied, 'You wouldn't be good in it!' Spence, with indignation, asked, 'Why wouldn't I be good in it?' Lynne replied in his quiet, matchless way, 'Nobody ever is.'

"Most of us were at different studios and would get out of touch. From each other we learned about the pictures and trends, and most of all we kept our friendship alive. And had a lot of fun in the bargain."

One evening at Romanoff's a grim-faced U.S. senator came up to our table and introduced himself. He asked why we were meeting each week and what we talked about, what our purpose was. We answered much as Frank's letter indicates above. The senator replied to the effect that he didn't believe us and said he was going to make it his business to find out about us. A Senate investigation, no less. We restrained ourselves and laughed it off as the self-righteous fury of an elected do-gooder in search of evil.

Obviously the good senator was disappointed, because we were never summoned before a Senate select committee and we never hit the political columns or Walter Winchell or the Washington *Post* or New York *Times*.

On another evening at Romanoff's, Jim and I were the first to arrive at a large booth in the rear. Pat was next, and he ordered his usual "double Cutty Sark and water in a tall glass."

The two Franks and Lynne came and we all ordered dinner. Pat ordered a seafood cocktail and "another Cutty Sark and water in a tall glass."

As our dinner and talk progressed, Jim nudged me and said, "Look at Pat!" Pat looked as if he'd been shot with a hypodermic needle of dynamite.

"Let me out," Jim said. "I'm going to call my brother Harry." Two of his brothers, Harry and Ed, were doctors.

After a few minutes Jim returned, and as he crawled into the booth Pat excused himself and left.

"What'd Harry say?" I asked.

Jim said, "Harry asked, 'Are his eyes glazed?' I said, 'Yes.' Then he asked, 'Is his tongue thick? Is his breathing labored?' To which I answered, 'Yes, yes! And there's a line across his forehead and his face is all red below and all white above! What does it mean?' And Harry quite calmly said, 'In a minute he'll excuse himself and go to the men's room and throw up and then he'll be all right.'"

As predicted by Harry, Pat was soon back, looking hale and hearty. He summoned the waiter and said, "Another Cutty Sark and water in a tall glass," and went on with his meal. I guess seafood and fresh water don't mix.

Today Pat mostly has just "water in a tall glass," and lots of seafood. His body chemistry must have changed, because he's never had that kind of trouble again. It just goes to show you that, with increasing years, moderation in all things pays off.

I asked Pat for some comments about The Boys' Club and he obliged with the following:

"Frank Morgan, Lynne Overman and myself were seated in old Romanoff's awaiting arrival of Bellamy, Cagney, McHugh and Tracy.

"Morgan and O'Brien were doing a little 'grog sampling,' as Lynne was 'up the pole' [on the wagon]. A shadow fell across the table. Zachary Scott with one earring. He queried, 'How do you get to join this "Irish Mafia"?' Frank's acid reply: 'You don't *get* to, you are *asked*.' And then Overman with the *coup de grâce:* 'We have run out of "asks."'" Exit gypsy.

"On another occasion Jim had completed *Yankee Doodle Dandy* and with a piece of the action acquired a bob or two. Jim began thinking out loud.

"'We are all in a precarious business—profession, if you will. I wonder if, God forbid, some unforeseen tragedy arose, how would you go about gaining admission to the Motion Picture Country Home?'

"At this point there was a lengthy McReady (in the parlance of Thespis) pause.

"Then Tracy leaned across the table and with a King Lear whisper replied: 'Buy it, you bum, and we'll all get in.'

"Then there was the time Jim, Bill [Jim's wife], Eloise [Pat's wife] and I attended the Oscars. Jim had been nominated for *Angels with Dirty Faces*. White tie and tails. When we departed the Biltmore [hotel], he got *my* hat (top hat, of course), and I got *his*. He looked like Ben Welch in burlesque. I looked like pin-head bug in a Ringling sideshow."

Frank Morgan was one of the happiest men I've ever known. He led a life of fun and pleasure. A true hedonist. He did have very strong opinions and, if crossed, he could become momentarily angry. But whatever the conflict he always ended it with a laugh. Except on one subject: Franklin Delano Roosevelt.

If you wanted an evening's exhibition of wrathful histrionics and verbal abuse that was so intense and loud it was reminiscent of a second-act curtain speech, all you had to do was say that Franklin Delano Roosevelt had again done something great. Frank would turn apoplectic. His neck veins would swell. He'd turn red in the face. It was a wonderful, intuitive performance. It was a shame to take advantage of him, but it was such a good show, and he never got wise to the fact that he was being had.

I had been in the East starring in *State of the Union* and guest-starring on TV in all the new shows originating from New York. The play closed and I came to Hollywood for a picture. On a day off I visited Frank and his wife, Alma, at their house and stayed for dinner. I went to my hotel at a respectable time and returned the next day (also an off day) at about two in the afternoon for a swim.

Frank and Alma were in their upstairs bedroom. Alma was in bed, where she spent a good deal of time because of a spine and leg injury incurred some years before when she was thrown from a horse. Two o'clock was always the daytime receiving hour in their elaborate Louis XIV bedroom.

Frank was sitting at a coffee table facing the foot of the bed, in the top of his pajamas, eating bacon and eggs. There was a pair of crutches tilted beside him and one leg was in a brace. With his touched-up moustache and his white hair falling over his forehead into his eyes, he looked not unlike Spence Tracy as Mr. Hyde.

When I had left the Morgans the night before, Frank was in fine shape. "What happened to you?" I asked.

"Ohhhhh," he whined in that high-pitched voice he sometimes assumed. "After you left last night, someone called and said, 'Come on down to Romanoff's for a drink, there's a bunch of us down here having some laughs.' It seemed like a good idea so I went down. We had plenty of laughs until Mike (Romanoff) closed the restaurant. Then we thought it would be a good idea to play basketball, so we broke a window at the Beverly Hills High School, climbed in and played basketball, and I broke the Achilles' tendon in my heel." And he laughed.

"Isn't that silly?" said Alma, and she laughed.

I agreed, and I laughed.

After a bit Frank said, "Let's go for a swim." He rose and in only his pajama top fixed himself on his crutches, and off he and I started for the pool, where Alma would join us later. We were passing the head of the stairs, Frank in quest of his swimming shorts in his dressing room, when he hesitated and said, "I forgot. I've got to take care of a little business first." He shouted the name of his secretary.

She answered and came running up the stairs with notebook and pencil. About halfway up she stopped, as if stricken, at the sight of Frank at the top of the stairs in his pajama top and on crutches. She turned away and obediently stood there with pencil poised.

"Take a letter, dear," Frank said. "'Dear'—I forget his name. Call Miss Cherry [his business manager] and she'll tell you the name of the man who's building my boat in Maine. And say, 'Dear Mr.'—whatever it is. Well, let's see— Ask Miss Cherry what it is I'm supposed to say and write it up and I'll sign it.

"And then write to the people who're going to see the boat through the canal when it comes. I forget their name. Ask Miss Cherry and she'll tell you. And say, 'Dear'—whatever it is—well, I forget what I'm supposed to tell them. Ask Miss Cherry and then write it up and I'll sign it. I guess that's all."

And the secretary was gone, like a puff of steam, without an upward glance.

After this business had been concluded Frank hiked himself to his dressing room and put on trunks and a beach jacket and we descended the winding stairway to the lower hallway, where he stopped.

"Would you like a little drink?" he asked.

"I don't think so. It's a little early. Maybe after the swim," I said.

"Well, I need one," he said as he clumsily descended one step from the hall to the sunken Louis XIV drawing room, removed a pillow from the settee, uncorked a bottle secreted there and drew a substantial quaff. He replaced the bottle and covered it with the pillow. "I have to do this," he explained, "to keep it away from Alma and George (his son). There's too much drinking around here. I even keep the keys in my pocket." He showed them to me.

He didn't know, as everyone else did, that if Alma or George wanted a bottle they took the pin-hinges off the storeroom door, opened it and helped themselves.

We proceeded down a long flight of marble stairs in back of the house to the pool and got in the water, Frank with some difficulty.

After a dip we were lying on the grass in the sun, listening to the birds in the quiet summer afternoon, when Alma appeared at the top of the marble stairs, assisted by a servant. Under one arm she had a towel, into which there was obviously rolled a bottle.

Alma went into the ladies' room to doff some raiment and came out to stretch on a chaise. She and I chatted, and after a few minutes Frank was napping.

"Would you like a little drink?" Alma mumbled softly.

"No thanks. It's a little early," I answered.

"If you do," she added, "it's behind the mirror in the ladies' dressing room."

Suddenly there was a piercing Tarzan-like howl from the top of the marble stairs. There stood George in swimming trunks, beating his breast.

Frank, startled from his nap, looked up and shouted, "Ohhhhh —youuu—there he is!" Then to me, still shouting: "Came home at eight o'clock this morning, made a pass at the maid and she quit!" To George: "Ohhhhh youuuu—"

"Oh, Dad, leave me alone," George interrupted. "I've got an awful headache." And he tumbled down the stairs and into the pool.

After he'd splashed and gulped and done three or four laps he stretched out on the grass. Presently he rolled over to where I was lying in the sun and said, "Would you like a little drink?"

"No thanks," I said, "it's a little early."

"Well, I just had one. I needed it." He groaned. "If you feel like one, there's a bottle back of the books on the third shelf in the study."

I'd known Frank for a long time, and very well. We'd been friends back in New York. I'd sailed with him on several of his boats. I'd spent much time with him over the years. He was always spirited, animated and spry—very much alive.

I was a pallbearer at his funeral in Brooklyn. I helped lower him into his family-plot grave. But for some time afterward I had an experience that I'm sure is not uncommon to those who've been close to someone who was always so alive but who has died. I'd find myself going to the phone to call Frank, momentarily forgetting he was no longer with us.

He was a man to remember.

Jim Cagney was raised a city boy on New York City's Upper East Side, where the code was survival of the fittest. He played stickball, street ball and later amateur baseball, and he boxed. In between all this he'd had occasional fist fights.

His first job in the theatre was as a female impersonator in a vaudeville act.

He became a hoofer and taught dancing to keep himself and his wife Bill in groceries between small-time vaudeville jobs. Subsequently he got into the legitimate theatre, and in *Penny Arcade* with Joan Blondell he was noticed by Warner Brothers and brought to Hollywood.

All through his early period he'd developed a love of the country and animals. Today he has a farm in New York where he raises horses and cattle. And for years he's been a conservationist, lending his name and effort to the cause. He paints and writes amusing and philosophic verse.

When Jim's position in pictures was secure, he bought a sizable piece of property in a canyon adjacent to Beverly Hills. He built a house and fenced the property, making provision for horses, chickens, ducks, goats and a dog. He wanted a bit of the country practically in the city.

The house was finished and ready to be occupied. The livestock had been moved into its new quarters. Jim went up the canyon to inspect his new paradise. The bewildered horses' heads projected over the top halves of their stable doors, the goats were grazing the canyon hillside, the ducks were wallowing in their pond and the chickens seemed content in chicken-wire garden and coop.

On his return round Jim stopped at the chicken yard, where he thought something seemed amiss. He watched the pecking fowl for some time before realizing that there were twenty-six hens and only four roosters.

This new Eden was to be Happy Valley, where every creature had an even break. So he went into town and brought back twenty-two roosters, so that none of the hens would feel they were wallflowers or left out of the best things in life.

In no time at all the twenty-six roosters were flying at the twenty-six hens, which were huddled in distress on top of their coop. It was a feathered holocaust. In fact, the canyon was clouded with feathers until a wiser farmer, one of Jim's "hired hands," removed twenty-two roosters and took them back to town.

Here are a couple of samples of Jim's verse. The first was included in a note he sent me one time.

"A Belfast newsman wrote a piece entitled 'The Irish Should Grow Up,'" his note said. "I know one day there will have to be a settlement, but I wrote this to an Irish friend who wanted a comment:

> "The men of Tyrone and all the six counties
> (Intransigent seems to describe them)
> Supply all the bounties from all of those counties
> So England continues to bribe them.
>
> Elizabeth I, the queen called virgin,
> Set up the haves and have-nots
> By usurping the lands of the old Irish clans
> And gave them to Anglos and Scots.
>
> Essex and Raleigh and Cromwell,
> All Englishmen of distinction,
> Had an overall plan for the old Irish clans
> And the overall plan was extinction.
>
> So you want us to take them to our hearts
> And treat them as brother to brother.
> A poor foolish dream and futile, my friend,
> For they're not Irish, they're 'other'."

The second one, "Podap," was written for his son, Jim Jr., and the epilogue was appended some time afterward. Here they are:

PODAP

> Mayhap you have heard of Podap; tremendous fellow he,
> Height two or three inches, not feet, weight-nothing complete.
> Of prodigious strength, he'll jump his length
> Quicker than you can see.

Uproot a blade of grass with ease,
And tear a dandelion asunder.
Will bring a beetle to his knees
With grunts and growls that sound like thunder.

A needle he'll toss as any javelin
And pierce the bee's wing thru and thru,
Causing the busy bumbler to travel in
Circles eccentric, his flying askew.

Will throw a thorn a yard, yea two,
Can lift a leaf thrice o'er his head.
Now these are truths you well may lay to,
So help me, may I drown in bed.

Pleasureful pastime he'll find in most anything
Requiring great brawn accompanied by a slyness;
Just on a dare he'll do any zany thing—
Like drowning a prawn to show off his spryness.

With an acid contempt for things orthodoxical
He is quite often found lacking in tact.
Podap's views may be held paradoxical—
Brought on, no doubt, by his love for a fact.

When his attitude's most presuming
Their presence alone can insure his quiet;
For his passion for fact is all-consuming,
Since they compose his entire diet.

That he eats what he loves may prove disquieting
To any or all who are choosy of food,
But to eat what one hates merely proves that one's dieting,
Since rarely will one eat a jot 'less it's good.

Some may hold Podap cruel;
Cruel he is, and makes no pretense
Of being else, which no doubt you'll
Grant is far his best defense.

Time will come, and time will tell
That he serves an end, both yours and mine,
And serves it most exceeding well
When facts are gone and left no sign.

Happy we'll be in healthy confusion
With nobody holding this right or that,
When none are impelled to bestow a contusion
On a good friend's head in a factive spat.

So let's not sit in condemnation
Of a meaningful chap with a purposeful bent;
Just lend a moment to contemplation
And review in quiet what the Gods have sent.

So here's to his pleasure, his strength and his honor,
Let's toast him standing and wish him well;
Where the great man walks every fact is a goner,
May our ears ever ring to Podap's dinner bell.

EPILOGUE

Upon a time, as he looked in search of a sweet
To end a repast that had suited him fine,
He chanced on a fact that came right to his feet
Then moved not, nor spoke, but lay there supine.
It was fluffy and white, and gave at the touch
Like a lovely meringue, which he liked oh so much.

He viewed with delight this precious comestible
But he found when he gulped it, 'twas most indigestible.
With much heaving and retching he tried then to throw up
The treacherous goody that laughingly mocked
From within all his efforts to get it to show up;
But all went for naught as he felt his throat locked.

His thoughts all went back to the days of his daring;
For up until then there was nothing that daunted him,
When he gobbled up facts without looking or caring,
And in his last waning hours the taste of them haunted him.
He might have saved all of us, given the time,
This bravest of chaps who'd embarked on a mission;

Now our chance for survival's not worth a plugged dime,
For the fact that ate *him* was nuclear fission.

Jim and his wife Bill and my wife and I cruised the Mediter-
ranean on freight ships. We'd put into France and Spain. We

stayed for a week or so in Santa Margherita, Italy. Each day Jim and I walked through this lovely fishing village. We were on a bowing and smiling acquaintance with the villagers. On one of our strolls, after a silence, Jim said, "Do you want to hear one?"

"Sure," I said.

He recited:

> "In Italy, France and Spain
> To the tourist 'tis most plain
> That the masses and classes
> Are well endowed with tits and asses."

Another verse of Jim's, one of my favorites, is:

> A phrase too long neglected,
> Three words on which to grow—
> Great philosophies have been erected
> On the little-used "I don't know."

The following is from a tape Jim gave me for use in this record. I'm reproducing it with understandable pride.

"There are times when things do happen that one remembers forever. Ralph Bellamy and I are now old friends—forty-odd years. One of those times that I recall was when I was sitting in the lunchroom at Warner Brothers. The phone rang and the waitress said as she brought it to me, 'It's for you, Mr. Cagney.' I said hello to the other end and it was Dennis Morgan. Now Morgan had had a couple of drinks apparently and he said that Ralph was not well and would I get over to his (Denny's) dressing room fast. I dropped my fork and ran. Well now, the run from where I was down to Denny's dressing room I made in nothing flat. It's over a quarter of a mile. When I got there I said to Ralph, 'What's the matter? How are you?' He said, 'I'm fine.' He didn't know what I was talking about. He didn't know that Denny had called me.

"All that Denny wanted was to have me and Ralph and himself sit down and cut up a few touches and have a drink or two or so. I said, 'You Swedish so-and-so!' and he laughed, and then Bellamy saw that I was very upset, because Denny had told me that he was bleeding at the mouth, which wasn't true at all.

"I stayed awhile and then left. I saw Ralph later and he said, 'That was damn nice of you, Jim, to be so concerned.' I said, 'Well, Ralph, why not?'"

One evening Jim's wife, Bill (really Frances, but her parents wanted a boy and they nicknamed her "Bill," which stuck), said to their daughter, Casey (a contraction of the first letters of Kathleen Cagney), who was approaching her teens: "Casey, come into the library with me. I want to have a girl talk with you."

Bill explained the facts of life in detail to the straight-faced, silent Casey.

Then, after she'd covered the subject thoroughly, she said: "Now, Casey, if you ever have any questions I want you to bring them to me. I don't want you talking about all this at school with your girl friends. Remember! Ask me anything and I'll tell you the truth. I promise. Now run along."

The still silent Casey moved to the door, opened it, turned back to her mother and asked: "Mother, how do they make cardboard?"

One night after I'd gone to bed, the doorbell rang.

I threw on something and ran downstairs. I put on the hall lights and outside front-door lights and opened the door.

It was Spence Tracy, who said, "Put out the lights! Let me in!"

I obeyed, and there he stood with a beaten, wild-eyed, frightened look. "What's the matter?" I asked.

"I'm through in pictures!" he blurted out as I moved him into the living room.

"What do you mean? What's happened?"

"I just saw a preview of *Dr. Jekyll and Mr. Hyde*. I'm through in pictures!" he repeated.

Granted there was some merit to his reaction to the picture (we've all been in bad pictures and seen ourselves in performances we'd like to forget), Spence had made enough good ones and created enough great performances to be allowed that one. And maybe Lynne Overman's sage remark at The Boys' Club dinner a while back had merit.

In our early Hollywood days, Spence and I often dined at each other's homes and saw a great deal of each other when we were both under contract to Fox. We made two pictures together, *Young America* and *Disorderly Conduct*, in which Dickie Moore, then about four or five years old, also appeared.

Spence was always the great actor he was later recognized to be. He also was neurotic to the extent that he had guilt feelings about his son John, who was born deaf and dumb (but who has developed hearing and speech) and in whose name Louise, Spence's wife, founded the John Tracy Clinic. He was also neurotic about his marriage difficulties.

I'm not being disloyal when I say his neuroticism led him, intermittently, to alcohol. It was a fairly well-known affliction and it interfered with his work at times. He'd disappear.

I covered for him several times at Fox, where we were both under contract. And I had a doctor friend who was helpful with "diagnoses" and alibis.

In the first year or so of these "attacks," after he had disappeared for several days, he'd ring my bell. There he stood, an apparition, more often than not in an overcoat with a bottle in every pocket, with a beard, unkempt hair and no hat, and he'd say, "Gimme some bacon and eggs." That meant he was coming back to reality. Eventually he got this tragic psychosis under control and became a teetotaler.

I was answering some mail one day after having recently seen *Judgment at Nuremberg*. I thought Spence gave a remarkably penetrating performance as the judge. As I remember it now, he was away from behind the bench only once or twice. But when the picture was over you knew all about that judge, even though practically all you'd seen of him was his head and shoulders and arms and hands. But how expressive!

I dropped him a note in the midst of my correspondence, saying I thought it was one of the greatest performances I'd ever seen. A couple of days later I received the following wire, which I still have:

"Dear Ralph: Wish I could express my feelings after getting your message. As you must know it means much more than just an ordinary message, as nice as that might be. It reminds me of the time you saved me way back when so that I could carry on all this time. Deepest gratitude and love always—Spence."

Lynne Overman was one of the wisest, wittiest and gentlest companions I've ever known. He had a keen sense of good taste for the excellent but simple things of life. He had a brilliant career on the stage as a light comedian. In his Hollywood days, raising orchids was his hobby. Then came food and drink, though he was a teetotaler by the time he reached Hollywood.

You might also add ladies to his list of pastimes. Lynne loved women in general and on frequent occasions, one in particular.

One of his favorite meals at our gatherings was a minute steak and two orders of lyonnaise potatoes.

When asked why two orders, Lynne explained, "When the lyonnaise potatoes are served, someone invariably inquires, 'What are those?' I reply, 'Lyonnaise potatoes.' And almost without fail they say, 'lyonnaise potatoes! I haven't seen those in years. Do you mind if I have a forkful?' So I pass the plate and he helps himself and passes it to the companion next to him, who helps himself, and so on. When the plate's returned to me most of the lyonnaise potatoes are gone. So I ask for two orders of lyonnaise potatoes—one for me and one to pass around the table."

Lynne called me "St. Elmo," the romantic title role in a popular play of a previous era.

Frank McHugh probably has the most impressive theatrical background of any American actor, with the possible exception of Eddie Foy, Jr.—Frank in every area of the legitimate theatre and Eddie in vaudeville and musical comedy. But if they were to make comparisons it would probably be a draw.

Frank was practically "born in a trunk," as the old theatrical term went. His mother, father, two brothers and he were the nucleus of a traveling repertoire company, playing the small towns in the East for one-week stands. Frank's father's nickname was "Cutie," so the company had its beginnings as "Cutie McHugh's Big Five Minstrels."

Frank will be remembered for his many pictures at Warner Brothers, where he played so often with Jim, Pat, Alan Hale, Guy

Kibbee, Joan Blondell, Humphrey Bogart, Allen Jenkins, Priscilla Lane, Errol Flynn and George Brent. They were known in the industry as "The Warner Brothers Stock Company," because for a while they were all—or many of them—in almost every Warner Brothers picture. And, of course, Frank made famous that triumphantly insulting "Haaaa-haaaa-haaaaaa."

In response to a request for recollections of Boys' Club nights, Frank contributes the following:

"Were you present the night Frank Morgan, after having partaken of a few gills of the demon rum, sounded off vociferously about certain actors changing their family names to better and more pleasantly sounding names for the stage? Principally, Edward G. Robinson (Rabinowitch) and John Garfield (Garfinkel). He stressed that their family names were old, respectable and historical names that they should be proud of.

"I paused long enough to let Frank be completely satisfied with his oration, then I leaned forward and said, very quietly, 'Frank, what's your real name?' His educated eyebrows shot up to his hair line, his eyes blazed, he stammered, he stuttered and finally shouted, 'Goddamn you, Frankie, you're a—you're a—' Then he simmered down and came out with the old reliable stage laugh. But he never told me what he thought I was. Frank Morgan's family name was Wuppermann.

"From time to time we were visited at our table by most of the leading stars of the day, from Clark Gable on down the list. Celebrity was not necessary, but one did have to be able to say a thing or two. Bert Lahr was a frequent invited guest. Lou Calhern was always welcome.

"When we wanted to be private we had dinner at one of the members' homes.

"Remember the time at La Maze Restaurant on the Strip, when the out-of-town girl, with a slight load aboard, came demurely to our table and asked for our autographs? We politely gave them to her. Then she deliberately tore the paper into small pieces and tossed it in the air so that it came down on our table like confetti.

"One night, after Lynne's death, Pat arrived at the appointed restaurant quite some time ahead of the rest of us, and whiled away his loneliness at the bar with his very good friend Cutty Sark. By the time the gathering had assembled Pat had allowed his friend Cutty Sark to influence him into a deep mood of sentimental emotion. At the table, Pat asked for two orders of lyonnaise potatoes in honor of the late departed Lynne. When they were served, they were passed around as a sort of culinary toast to Lynne.

"Most of the diners participated but when the lyonnaise potatoes were offered to me, I declined. Pat said, 'What's the matter with you, Frankie? These potatoes are a toast to Lynne. Take some!' Again I declined. 'That's disloyal!' said Pat, almost in tears. 'These are Lynne's potatoes. You ought to be ashamed of yourself. Didn't you love Lynne?' 'Yes, Pat,' I said. 'I loved Lynn. I loved him dearly. But I do not want to join him.'"

Frank finishes off saying, "During several discussions at dinner of the Boys' Club it was concluded that the picture business, as we knew it, was on the wane. Which, of course, later proved to be true. The government divorcement of theatre chains and studios seemed to be the death knell."

I'm not too sure about the "death knell," but working in pictures isn't what it used to be. I think Frank is right about "the divorcement of theatre chains from studios," but I think with that went the glamour of the whole picture-making process: the rosters of stars and writers and directors at each studio, publicized by the publicity departments, which created a mystique around the stars and the whole procedure. The studios couldn't gamble that investment without their guaranteed outlets.

Also, the public is now invited to witness all the tricks and special effects of the business, destroying the illusions, as opposed to the time when stars and picture-making were kept from the public, inside an aura. Then when TV became a reality, the biggest efforts of everyone in the industry turned in that direction. And this requires time and budget considerations which produce enormous pressures. Some of the fun is gone. And that fun (I don't mean comedy—I mean the fun of making pictures, shared by cast, crew and producers) photographed. It got on the screen some way.

One of the geniuses of the picture business—of whom there haven't been too many—is Fred Astaire, still going strong at eighty.

I did *Carefree* with Fred and Ginger Rogers, directed by Mark Sandrich. There was one of those familiar scenes in which Fred dances over settees, chairs, tables and stairs, usually while singing. In *Carefree,* it started on the terrace of a large house or club and ended on a golf course.

We went to a golf course in Pasadena for the finish, in which he picked up a golf club while dancing, jumped over a low exterior dividing wall and approached eight golf balls lined up about four feet apart. Still in time to the dance beat, he hit the balls in rhythm and danced out of the shot.

When the property man went out on the fairway to recover the balls, they were within eight feet of each other.

It was around this time that I made the first Ellery Queen series with Margaret Lindsay and Charles Grapewin. We only made four, but there's an impression that it was a lengthy series.

I was in one of those horror pictures that included the Frankenstein Monster, the Wolf Man, Bela Lugosi and most of the actors in Hollywood. The director was a little fellow. I've forgotten his name, but he had all the mannerisms and characteristics of the little man. He wore riding britches, puttees, a Norfolk jacket and a large scarf. While working he communicated through a megaphone that was almost as tall as he was. But he was a nice little fellow. He had a tall thin female secretary who followed him everywhere. She always wore a hat.

We finished a scene and the director said to Cedric Hardwicke and me: "Why don't you gentlemen sit here on the stage and wait for us. I have to get a silent shot of Evelyn Ankers on the Notre Dame stairway down on the back lot."

The Notre Dame stairway was an elaborate grand stairway built originally for *The Hunchback of Notre Dame,* with Lon Chaney, Sr., and left standing for use in other pictures.

Cedric and I were old friends and we chatted for an hour or so, all alone on the huge stage. Then, after another hour or so, we thought we'd take a walk to the back lot to see what was keeping the company so long. A silent shot is comparatively simple, since it doesn't have to accommodate microphones with their shadows and threats of getting into the picture.

The set was covered with tarpaulins over a high frame that had catwalks under it on which large lamps were anchored and focused on the stairway. The cameraman was shouting to the men on the catwalks, directing the lighting of the set, and there was a general hubbub of activity on the ground in preparation for the shot. Cedric and I found a couple of director's chairs and sat watching the confusion.

Presently the assistant director approached the director, who was sitting in a director's chair with his secretary on one side of him and his megaphone at eye level on the other. "Ready, sir," the assistant said.

The little director lifted his megaphone and, aiming it at the assistant director beside him, ordered, "Get Miss Ankers on the stairway!"

In a minute or so, the assistant director bellowed, "Quiet! Qui-et, everybody!"

And in the ensuing silence the little director rose, clutching his megaphone, and advanced to the foot of the stairway. Evelyn Ankers was standing in the center of it, halfway up, in an evening gown.

The scene was a geography shot of Evelyn coming downstairs, to let the audience know that the action was now going to be downstairs instead of upstairs in the castle.

The little director, in his puttees and Norfolk, was now pacing back and forth at the foot of the stairs, saying to Evelyn, through his megaphone:

"Now, Evelyn, your mother's been carried away by the Frankenstein Monster—your father's been killed by the Wolf Man—your lover's being chased across the moors by the dogs—the servants have fled, and you're all alone in this ancient, dank, slimy castle, and it's four o'clock in the morning. Now I want to get the feeling from you—when you come down these stairs—that you're fed up with it all."

I had worked with Gregory (Grisha) Ratoff as an actor and now he was directing. He told me the following story of how he became a director:

He had promoted the production of a cheap circus picture in London and he'd run out of money in the midst of it. He heard that Darryl Zanuck was in London at the Dorchester Hotel. He tried unsuccessfully to get an appointment with Zanuck, who had been alerted. So Grisha sat in the lobby every day, hoping for an encounter. But Zanuck, not wanting to be associated with a cheap picture and not feeling obliged to get the animals, acrobats and clowns out of the London streets, used the freight elevator.

After a few days, Zanuck left for Monte Carlo. Grisha was apprised of this and followed him. He hounded Zanuck even into the gaming rooms, and Zanuck finally said, "What's the problem?"

"No problem," said Grisha, "but, Darryl, I got a story that's just for you." (Not the circus story.)

In desperation, Zanuck took him into a corner and said, "Let me hear it."

Ratoff told him a story and, again in desperation, Zanuck said, "I'll buy it."

"I need five thousand dollars," Grisha said. "Now! Adwance!"

"Give him five thousand dollars," Zanuck told an aide.

Grisha used the money to finish his London epic and turned the menagerie loose.

Months later in Hollywood, Zanuck said to an aide, "I bought a story from Ratoff in Monte Carlo. Find him and get the story."

Ratoff was traced to Europe and he replied that he wanted a contract to write the screenplay of the story and plane fare to Hollywood. He then found himself on salary with an office and a secretary, under contract to write the story—which he'd forgotten.

But he invented and wrote *The Man Who Broke the Bank at Monte Carlo*, which Zanuck couldn't use and sold to Samuel Goldwyn, who eventually made it with Ronald Colman.

But Grisha was broke again.

He got himself into a fifty-cents-a-point gin rummy game with Zanuck, Joseph Schenck and Phil Berg and deliberately lost thousands of dollars to Zanuck.

Then he went to Zanuck's office and told him he didn't have the money to pay his debt and the only way he could see to work it out would be for Zanuck to put him under contract as a director and take $1,000 a week out of his salary. And that's what happened, according to Grisha.

Somewhere about this time I was crossing from England to France on the Dover-Calais ferry. I struck up an acquaintance with the deck steward, who was a charming, energetic and loquacious Cockney. He was a little fellow, slight, with fair hair and blue eyes that really took you in with a discerning appraisal. He wore his white cap and jacket with an air of authority. He obviously liked his job and his clients. He had friends all over the world, he said. We talked of many things and people.

A few weeks later I returned to England aboard the same ferry and renewed my friendship with my Cockney mate. He was interested in my anecdotes and impressions of France. Really interested. He'd never been farther into France than the Calais docks. And he was a good listener. I'm sure he was comparing my observations with the hundreds of others he'd had reported over the years. He asked questions that indicated he had a fair image of the picturesque French cities and provinces, though he'd never seen them.

Soon, as we leaned side by side on the rail, talking while we gazed at the water and the dim horizon, the White Cliffs of Dover appeared through the mist and we fell silent.

The cliffs began to take form and grow larger, and after a few minutes my friend said, in that plaintive, melodic Cockney that almost always ends with an upward intonation, "Mr. Bellamy."

"Yes," I said.

"D'yew very much mind if I ahsk yew a question?"

"Of course not," I replied.

"Mr. Bellamy," he went on, with that almost forlorn upward intonation, as if he might break into tears, "would yew very much mind if I wrote t'yew w'en yew get back to the Stites?"

"I'd like that," I said. "Please do."

There was a pause after this exchange while we again gave our complete attention to the ever looming, larger white cliffs. Presently he almost lamented, "Mr. Bellamy."

"Yes," I said.

"W'en I wroite t'yew, would yew wroite t'mae?" And with that ascending note that was almost desperation, he could have added, "Fer Gawd's syke?"

"Yes," I replied. "I think it would be very nice to have a correspondence with you. Yes, I think that'd be fine."

Now there was a long, long lapse, while the awesome, historic and overwhelming cliffs became quite distinct and we were rapidly approaching our slip.

Finally my little Cockney drew a deep breath and emitted a pent-up sigh. "Mr. Bellamy," he said again in that submissive, pathetic tone.

"Yes," I replied.

"W'en I wroite t'yew, w'at sh'll I saye?"

In the June before Pearl Harbor, Errol Flynn, Fred MacMurray and I were making *Dive Bomber*, part of which was shot at sea on the U.S.S. *Enterprise*. The whole world was queasy and the *Enterprise* was not happy about our being aboard. In fact, they had denied our initial request, but an appeal to Washington by a studio "fixer" put us out to sea for a week.

I wouldn't care to publicly suggest that the officers and crew were bent on reprisal because we went over their heads. But every evening, after shooting all day in somewhat turbulent waters, we'd be ready for bed (or bunk) right after dinner, when we'd suddenly be plunged into blackest darkness. All lights were cut off and the *Enterprise* held night battle practice until dawn. That included the continuous firing of every explosive on the ship.

We were shooting again at 7:30 A.M. with our eyes in our cheeks.

The director of this fine movie was Michael Curtiz, whose greatest effectiveness was the manipulation of people en masse, in panorama, and then singling out individuals for punctuation. He also had a Hungarian accent that sounded like the low comdian in a 1910 musical comedy. He was tall, straight, commanding in appearance and voice. He wore his hair crew-cut and he played polo—viciously.

Mike had further alienated the officers by such acts as pulling the sleeves of high-ranking gentlemen with yards of gold braid, pounds of stars and several feet of decorations and citations and giving them a push into a scene, saying, "Be good fella! Chust valk tru back dere!"

It didn't endear him. In fact, it could be that the decline in movie theatre patronage dates from that summer of 1941. Maybe moving pictures were put off limits to the United States Navy.

We got all the long shots and medium shots called for in the script during our week at sea, but Mike saved the close-ups to shoot against the superstructure of the *Enterprise* while we were returning to its San Diego base. This was good planning. It allowed us to get all the medium and long shots without rushing and then shoot the close-ups against the ship.

As we steamed into San Diego Harbor, we were frantically shooting close-ups, even up to the time we could see our dock. Mike was furiously shooting close-ups from scenes we had done days before. He had a public address hookup and, in his disjointed, excited, self-styled English, he was desperately trying to get all the close-ups before we had to disembark.

As we came closer to the dock, in the midst of the confusion and strange city sounds that were intruding, huge billows of smoke floated comfortably through our scenes before the camera. Obviously the *Enterprise* was preparing to stop.

In his own special dialect Mike went to pieces. He lost all control of himself. He exploded over the public address system to the assistant director, wherever he was, "Art! Tell de captain to blow de smoke de udder vay!"

There are many stories about Mike and they're all part of the classic Hollywood heyday—such as his exploding to a property man who had brought him something other than what he'd ordered: "De next time I send some dumb sonofabitch to get something, I go myself!"

And the time, on location, during the lunch break (box lunches then; a ham and cheese sandwich, an apple and a piece of cake), when he mounted a twenty-foot-high parallel (platform) anchored in an empty concrete pool. He hated actors because they ate lunch. He didn't. That lost an hour's shooting time. So Mike was using this lost hour to examine possible camera setups. He squatted down and looked through the detached camera-finder (lens) in all directions. In the midst of his search he called down to his assistant, "Hey, Art! T'row me up a bottle-a-milk!" (This was before cartons.) The milk was thrown aloft. Mike drank it down and put the empty bottle out of his way.

There was an extra, dressed as a monk, sitting and leaning against the footing of the parallel, basking in the sun and enjoying his box lunch. As Mike shifted around with the finder he backed into the milk bottle, sending it over the side onto the head of the monk, who was rendered unconscious.

Mike, still on his haunches, finder in hands, peered down at the monk, now lying on his back, and shouted down, "Quit fuckin' around!"

The monk was carried away on a stretcher. He's probably in some other line of work now.

But I was in on the *Enterprise* episode.

World War II united the country to the greatest degree in our history. Roosevelt had much to do with it with his constant "fireside chats" over radio. He kept us informed about the threats to our coasts and our ships at sea and he kept our will and spirit alive. Everyone made some contribution. Gas rationing, food shortages, changes in diet, travel restrictions, blackouts were all accepted with enthusiasm.

The picture business formed the Hollywood Victory Committee. Its function was to visit troops at home and overseas, to entertain, to assist bond sales, to rouse rallies of any sort aimed at the war effort.

And we had air raid wardens, comparable in a way to the home guard of World War I. Their responsibility was to patrol neighborhoods during blackouts, rehearsing for or anticipating enemy air strikes. They were charged with monitoring absolute adherence to the blackouts, persuading pedestrians to leave the streets, reporting any infractions or ominous incidents and, if necessary, ministering first aid.

The air raid warden was the most dedicated, resolute and comic defender of the United States against Germany, Italy and Japan.

I know. I was an air raid warden.

We were instructed at weekly meetings in the areas of responsible patrol behavior in our assigned districts and the ministration of first aid. The patrol requirements were simple to grasp:

order the immediate extinction of all lights, empty the streets of pedestrians, report offenders and, in case of attack or any incident at all—if you survived—be polite.

But the first aid was rather involved. It was a kind of crash course in elemental medicine, lifesaving, surgery and therapy, crammed into six weekly meetings and a final examination. All I can say is, it's fortunate that the United States was never subjected to enemy attack. The air raid wardens would have taken more lives than the enemy.

We were a well-outfitted defense arm too. My habiliment was a trench coat with an arm band about six inches wide on the upper left sleeve reading in large letters, "Air Raid Warden"; a round button about five inches in diameter pinned over my heart reading "Air Raid Warden"; a medicament container resembling a cartridge belt about my waist; a flashlight "long enough and heavy enough to be used as a weapon if necessary," the instructor said; a whistle to summon aid from a nearby warden in case of assault from a non-conformist, which we were told might occur; a pencil and notebook; a gas mask over my shoulder; and of course a helmet.

Proof of my vigilance was the provision I'd made for call to duty. I lived in a two-story house. My trench coat, with button and arm band, was hanging at the top of the stairs. The notebook, pencil and whistle were in the pockets. The first aid belt was hanging at the foot of the stairs. The flashlight, helmet and gas mask were at the front door. I could get out of bed when the siren sounded, pull on shorts, trousers, socks, shoes, shirt and jacket on the way to the stairs and by the time I reached the front door be fully equipped to defend against the enemy or a non-compliant citizen.

Why we thought the enemy would attack only at night I don't know. We did have one embarrassing episode in daylight. But that was really to get used to the intricacies and delicacies of performing our night duties.

My precinct was that portion of Beverly Hills bounded by Santa Monica Boulevard on the north, Wilshire Boulevard on the south, the alley between Rodeo Drive and Camden Drive on the east and the alley between Camden and Bedford drives on the west. In other words, Camden Drive and the alleys on each side of it, for the four blocks between Santa Monica and Wilshire boulevards.

But to get back to the daylight affair: We were told in advance to appear at the fire station on Rexford Drive at noon one Saturday in full battle garb. We would then be given an address where we would find a body with a note on it indicating the simulated wounds inflicted by the enemy. We were to give the appropriate first aid and then call the fire station for an ambulance.

I drew the address of a house in the 500 block on Camden Drive near Santa Monica Boulevard. It was out of my regular domain, but I guess they quite rightly didn't want to disturb the business activity that begins in the 400 block.

I drove to the address, tumbled out of my car in full regalia and checked my gear. It was an unusually warm spring day and the trench coat, steel helmet and gas mask had the effect of a steam cabinet. The body was lying on his back on the lawn in front of the house with his eyes closed and a note on his stomach that read, "Unconscious—find broken leg—minister first aid—call ambulance." I went to work.

In those days everyone in Beverly Hills knew everyone else. It was Saturday noon and people were walking to and from the shops. Soon a small crowd gathered, curious at the sight of a trench-coated figure in a gas mask bent over what seemed to be a dead man in shirt sleeves on someone's lawn in the hot bright sun.

Suddenly someone said, "My God, it's Ralph Bellamy!" Then they saw either my air raid warden's arm band or button, or both, and all sorts of comments and advice were volunteered—none of them too respectful—as the crowd gathered.

I proceeded to apply a splint to the stranger's leg, careful not to raise his head or disturb his body for fear of aggravating possible brain damage or internal injury, as I'd been instructed. Disregard of this could have given me a demerit if the stranger had reported it.

I completed the splint and phoned from the house, where they were appalled at my appearance and request to call the fire station for an ambulance. Then I stood guard over my charge. When the ambulance left with the stranger I took off my gas mask, got into my car, to the applause of the crowd, and went home.

But we finally had one at night. And it was real.

I was working on a picture and was in bed when the siren sounded about 10 P.M. I was quickly out of bed, into my clothes and gathering my equipment as I worked my way in the dark to the front door. I lived only a few blocks from my territory and I was securing my regalia and tools as I ran down the familiar street in the pitch blackness.

I remembered everything except the curb at the first corner.

It was one of those painful spills. Both palms and wrists were scored and there were frayed holes in both trouser legs, exposing bloody knees. The helmet was down over my face. The gas mask, not yet having been mantled, was between my stomach and Carmelita Drive. My first thought was to find the flashlight, to look the situation over.

As I rose I realized I had a sprained ankle. But I had to save Beverly Hills from the Japs, so I felt around with bloody hands until I found the flashlight, pulled myself together and limped painfully to the bailiwick entrusted to me. The only good the ill wind blew was the darkness that prevented anyone from seeing the condition I was in.

The blackout lasted for an hour, as I recall, and after the all-clear sounded I sat on a curb on Camden Drive until I was able to hitch a ride home. I finished the picture the next few days with a taped ankle, trying not to limp.

The cause of the blackout, I discovered later, was that the Navy sent up a plane without notifying the Army and the Army shot it down—or vice versa. The pilot parachuted and landed on Vermont Avenue with a broken leg. That made two casualties.

I'm sure most World War II air raid wardens have similar reminiscences.

One of my excursions under the auspices of the Hollywood Victory Committee was a visit to a Marine Station in the desert. Fliers who had been through the Guadalcanal episode assembled there to learn the new Corsair plane.

I visited the hangars and "shot the breeze" with the boys all day. At dusk, just before returning to Beverly Hills, I was invited to have a drink at the Officers' Club.

I never ceased to be ruffled at finding the officers to be mostly in their twenties. One thinks of officers as being older.

A group of half a dozen or so officers and I stood at the bar chatting and enjoying a beer. One of my companions, noticing a seemingly shy fellow standing alone with his beer at one end of the semi-circular bar, called to him to join us.

"Tell Ralph about the food on Guadalcanal," he said.

The shy fellow said, sort of like Gary Cooper, "Aw—he doesn't want to hear that."

"He'll get a kick out of it," insisted my companion, with urging from the others.

There was an explanation by his brother officers that the shy boy was raised in the desert. He could be alone in the desert, far from civilization, without fear. By nightfall he'd have housing, a fire, food and water.

They persuaded him and here's his story of food on Guadalcanal:

The island was taken after the struggle we know and all was secure. There was no action except daily reconnaissance flights. Tents were arranged in rows and life was dull.

One afternoon the call for mess came at four o'clock and the desert boy didn't feel like facing the same old chow. He wandered aimlessly into the jungle to pass the time.

After he'd gone some way he was aware of muttering up high in the tropical trees. He saw what seemed to be thousands of cockatoos in nests. He squatted and watched, and concluded they were sitting on eggs. He hadn't had a real egg since San Diego, just that powdered stuff. So he shinnied up and sure enough there were eggs. He brought down a handful, buried them and started back for headquarters to get a frying pan and Crisco.

On the way he saw a native cow followed by a calf. That meant milk.

He quickly drew lengths of parasitic, stringy growth from surrounding trees, loosely braided them and lassoed the cow, tying it to a tree. Now he had to include a bucket in his trip for culinary equipment.

Having collected the frying pan and Crisco, and realizing he would have milk, he snitched some baking powder, flour and salt and returned to the jungle.

That evening he had fried cockatoo eggs, baking powder biscuits and milk.

Gradually he added other loot from the kitchen tent and boxes and crates to use as tables and chairs.

Word got around of course since he was missing at all mess calls. He couldn't take everyone to his jungle short-order retreat but he did take a few each meal.

He taught the natives how to use the crossbow and they brought him wild pigs and showed him where the French had buried their wine before fleeing.

One day the commanding officer summoned him. He was put at ease and the CO said, "I understand you've been having meals in the jungle."

"Yes sir," replied the desert boy, thinking, "I've sent up a smoke signal, alerting the enemy, and we've lost the war in the Pacific."

"What do you have to eat out there?"

"Fried cockatoo eggs, baking powder biscuits, roast pig, milk, mangoes and wine," said our boy.

The CO said, "It's now three-thirty. I'll meet you at your tent at three forty-five and have dinner with you in the jungle."

They met and enjoyed the repast, sitting on crates.

Time passed and the beer ran out. So our friend confiscated some copper pots and copper air-speed indicators from the wings of the planes. Putting them together, he ran large cans of fruit juice through his copper distillery.

Having collected empty illegal whiskey bottles that had been smuggled in, he wrote to his sister to send him, V-Mail, bourbon extract and caramel coloring, which he mixed with the distillate, and filled the bottles.

Word got around again and he entertained as before, a few at a time.

Presently the CO sent for him again.

"This time," he thought, "it'll be court-martial."

The CO said, "I understand you have liquor on the base."

"Yes sir."

"What have you got?"

"Bourbon, sir."

"There's a visiting general stopping by here tomorrow on his way up north," said the CO. "If I could produce a bottle of Bourbon it'd be the greatest thing in the Pacific war to date."

"It would be my pleasure," said the genius.

"I'll meet you at your tent in fifteen minutes," said the CO.

The boy stood at attention in front of his tent fifteen minutes later. "At ease!" said the CO.

They entered the tent and the distiller raised the overhanging blanket of his cot, revealing a row of I. W. Harper, Jim Beam, Old Crow, Jack Daniel's et al.

"Jack Daniel's!" cooed the CO. "My favorite! Could I have that?"

"With pleasure."

"Could I just take a Jim Beam too? Just in case?"

"Be my guest."

The next day the CO and the visiting general held a loud and joyous conference. And the jungle restaurateur had anything he wanted after that with no questions asked.

I returned to Beverly Hills feeling I'd been more entertained than entertaining that day.

Actors went to Canada during World War II to help in the sale of Canadian war bonds, just as we did here in our own war bond drives. I had the pleasure of joining the Canadians in all their bond drives.

It was a particular source of pleasure to me because my mother was born in Hamilton, Ontario. She had attended Moulton Ladies' College in Toronto and on one of my junkets up there she asked me to see if the college was still there and, if so, to bring her back a maple leaf from the grounds. I found Moulton Ladies' College on a cold fall day. It was a single large early-Victorian building, set back on about three beautifully landscaped acres abounding in all manner of arboreal splendor—except maple, the symbol of Canada.

I made myself known and stated my mission. The headmistress, in long skirt and ruffled blouse and with hair piled high, was cordial and she regretted the absence of maple trees. She asked me if I'd meet the lady collegians.

A bell rang somewhere as we advanced through wide halls

lined with tall oak doors and an occasional potted palm tree, until we came to the auditorium. It was not large for an auditorium and it had a small stage at one end, framed by tied-back velvet curtains. We mounted it up steps at one side. In the corners of the auditorium were more potted palms, taller than those in the halls, and the room was neatly arrayed with rows of folding chairs.

Presently there was a sound like a stampede from the halls and through the doors came a horde of scampering, chattering teen-age girls in old-fashioned full bloomers, sailor blouses and ties. The Moulton ladies!

I talked for a few minutes and told them my mother was an alumna. Then they asked questions and we chatted. It was very pleasant.

On the way back to my hotel with my friend and Canadian custodian, Joe Sedgwick, I found a large, beautifully colored maple leaf. I carefully transported it back to my mother, to whom I told the story of my adventure at her old alma mater. She was delighted with the maple leaf, but I didn't think it necessary to tell her there'd never been any maple trees on the Moulton Ladies' College campus. Memories play tricks!

On another Canadian bond visit I was waiting one morning in my room at the Royal York Hotel in Toronto for Joe Sedgwick to bear me off for the day's chores. In the street below one of my windows there had been a cacophony of drum bursts, bugle blasts, trombone slides and clarinet trills—obviously a preparation for something harmonious when it was directed to organized music. When Joe arrived I learned it was a band assembling to lead a parade to the Coliseum, the largest in Canada, seating 100,000 people.

The occasion was the annual Army-Navy football game, one of the biggest annual events, and the Coliseum was sold out. Joe told me I was to join the parade, sitting on the rolled-back top of a touring car. When we arrived at the Coliseum I was to chat with some wounded war veterans in wheelchairs and on stretchers below the grandstand on the fifty-yard line.

The Coliseum was packed. Excitement was high, and I was escorted to the veterans. The two teams came onto the field to a wildly emotional reception. The vets and I were chatting away when I heard a voice on the PA system say, "Ladies and gentlemen, may I have your attention! It gives me great pleasure to announce that our good neighbor from the south will kick the first ball. Ladies and gentlemen, Mr. Ralph Bellamy!" I say, humbly, that there was applause.

Suddenly I was frozen. Joe hadn't told me about this. And I hadn't kicked a football since an undistinguished athletic career at New Trier High School.

However, with 100,000 people cheering, and having been called a "good neighbor from the south," and my mother having been born in Hamilton, and keeping in mind that I was on a good-will mission to end the war, and with the newsreel cameras focused on me, and with both teams in place and waiting, there was nothing to do but run out there and kick the ball.

I was bareheaded, in a business suit and Oxford shoes. As I started onto the field, past the newsreel cameras, someone threw me a headgear. Donning it, I bravely waved to each team, wishing them luck. Then I backed about fifteen feet from a player who was lying on his stomach holding the ball at arm's length between his two first fingers (this was Canadian football), secured my headgear and ran at the ball.

Something drastic had happened to my kicking leg since high school. The ball tumbled on the ground, about sixteen feet to the left. I had kicked the ball-holder's fingers. He jumped up, flailing both hands up and down as if they'd been dipped in boiling water and referring to me and my mother, whom he described with a word denoting the canine feminine gender. The headgear was down over my face and the newsreel cameras were still running as the whistle blew.

Without a word, I left the field in shame and embarrassment, wishing I could keep running right back down south to be with the rest of the good neighbors. They started the game over with just the Army and Navy, as they should have done in the first place.

It would seem that I'd destroyed my usefulness to Canada's bond drives with that burlesque performance. But no. Another memorable visit went smoothly and productively. I was part of a troupe this time. I guess they weren't sure what I'd do alone after the football fiasco.

Our troupe was Ingrid Bergman, Patsy Kelly and Barry Wood, a very popular radio team, and me. We made appearances at factories, theatres and auditoriums in several cities and finished our tour in Toronto.

The finale, which highlighted the trip, was the performance over national radio of a two-character adaptation of Paul Gallico's *The Snow Goose* with Ingrid Bergman and me. We were accompanied by special music composed and directed by Percy Faith, who had not yet brought his orchestra to the United States.

I would like to have had commercial records cut from the master radio recording, not for financial return but because it turned out well. But Miss Bergman vetoed the proposal because by the time the idea was presented to her she'd been successful in losing her accent, which was noticeable in the recording.

I have many memories of Canada during the war, and mementos from the government. But none of the mementos mention football.

Everyone in Hollywood seemed to want to become involved in the war effort.

Lew Ayres was under contract to M-G-M. He had some difficulty with the draft board about being a conscientious objector. Eventually he became an ambulance driver.

Louis B. Mayer was head of M-G-M and, upon being told of this, allegedly said, "Lew Ayres has some kind of phobia about killing people."

PART VIII

I had met Charles Farrell in my early days at Fox. He was under contract there when Spence Tracy and I were. He and Janet Gaynor, teamed together, broke all box-office records until sound came in. Charlie suffered the same fate as John Gilbert.

In 1933 we renewed our acquaintance in Palm Springs, where we'd each rented a house because we loved the desert.

At that time, Palm Springs had a population of about two hundred. It hadn't been discovered yet.

Palm Springs is Agua Caliente Indian Reservation country, checkerboarded every other square mile by reservation land. Land for houses or shops built on reservation sites can't be bought. It's leased.

Originally the area was noted for its benefits to tuberculosis victims. Nellie Coffman, a widow from back East, had been sent to Idyllwild, atop San Jacinto Peak in the mountains just above Palm Springs, to cure her TB by sleeping on the ground among pine cones. She tired of this and went down to Palm Springs, where she found the dry desert air beneficial and started a hostelry with a row of tents which became, in time, the Desert Inn. It has since been rebuilt into its present namesake.

At the time Charlie and I were there, there were several small accommodations, but the Desert Inn in the center of town and the El Mirador, on the north edge of town, were the only hotels with tennis courts—one each. Charlie and I were tennis players. I was just learning. Naturally we had to have a court. We tried both of the hotels by jumping the fences. There weren't many players then, so the courts were fairly free. We preferred the El Mirador because the Desert Inn's court had a bad crack in it.

One day we were horseback riding cross-country and we crossed Indian Avenue, a rutted, gravel, washboard desert road running through the town and out into the desert. There was a sign about three feet by two feet on Indian Avenue that read "53 acres for sale. See Alva Hicks." We knew Alva Hicks. He was a carpenter who had walked into town with his wife to cure his TB. We called him "Uncle Alvie." He'd become the mayor and he owned the small waterworks, which was fed by wells.

We went to see Uncle Alvie out of curiosity and asked him what he wanted for the fifty-three acres. He said, "I've got to get a lot of money for that piece."

"How much?" we asked.

"Thirty-five hundred dollars," he replied.

Thirty-five hundred dollars for fifty-three acres! For no reason at all, except a gambling investment, we bought the fifty-three acres and went about the business of enjoying the desert that we both loved. Charlie has lived there ever since.

One day when we were playing tennis on the El Mirador court, a bellboy appeared with a note from Warren Pinney, the sole owner, asking us to come to his office when we had finished playing. We did so, dripping wet from the game. Warren gave us a drink and then said, "Will you fellows please stay off my tennis court? Every time guests go down to play, Bellamy and Farrell are on the court."

This was true. We were there the better part of each day. We laughed, agreed with him and left.

Outside, one of us—I don't remember which—said, "Why don't we put a court on our property?"

Well, to make a long story shorter, we did. We engaged the Davis Company, the leading tennis court builders in Los Angeles, to come down and build a court.

They brought the sand for what's now the number-one court from San Pedro, a hundred and twenty-five miles away. Sand to the desert!

The construction was the finest. As they were pouring the concrete, made of the finely sifted sand, over the three layers of three-quarter-inch construction steel that was crisscrossed every six inches, a few townspeople and visitors stood by watching. Noting this, Mr. Davis said, "If you think you'll ever need another court, now's the time to put it in while the equipment's here."

"Put in another," we said.

Then there had to be a nine-foot fence around the two courts, with four feet of stout two-inch-square construction wire on top of it.

Incidentally, a tennis court is sixty feet by a hundred and twenty feet. Mr. Davis then said, "You ought to have a three-sided shelter from the sun for observers."

"Build it," we said.

Now there was a sudden interest in tennis in the town and we brought in the utilities from the edge of civilization, a mile and a quarter away. We put in a toilet and a drinking fountain and closed the front of the three-sided shelter, which is now the main clubhouse and shop.

Since we had a lot of irrigation water rights originating from the west side of the property, we asked Mr. Davis to build us a rustic swimming pool. After many conferences, that ended up to be just short of a championship pool, with heater and filter, locker rooms and showers.

By now there was a considerable interest in tennis, and especially in our courts, by local friends and the few visitors who knew about Palm Springs.

We added up our expenditures and found that we had invested $78,000 in two tennis courts and a swimming pool. In other words, any time we happened to be in Palm Springs and felt like a bit of tennis and a dip in the pool afterward, we had a place to do that—for $78,000.

The summer following all this building, Charlie and I met in Beverly Hills at my behest. I told him I didn't have the money for that kind of self-indulgence. We talked it over and came to the conclusion that we had the nucleus of a club. We ordered two more courts and the gardener and I planted eucalyptus, Arizona cypress and tamarisk trees alternating around the whole property as a windbreak.

We had a kind of blueprint drawing of the courts, pool and trees printed on an impressive heavy white paper folder, with a map showing how to get to Palm Springs and an invitation to join "The Racquet Club." We were not especially looking to make money, we just wanted to get us off the $78,000 (plus two new courts) hook a little.

We sent the invitation to one hundred and seventy-three friends in the picture business, most of whom played a little tennis but had never heard of Palm Springs.

The fees were $50 for a single membership and $75 for a family membership, plus $9 a month dues for the seven months we were open, September to March. The opening date was September 15, 1934.

September 15, 1934, came and went and none of our one hundred and seventy-three friends had the decency to respond to the invitation, or even mention it if we met them. And we'd invested in two more courts.

We had another conference, the result of which was a notice to the same one hundred and seventy-three friends that on October 15 the initiation fee was going up from $50 single to $75. And from $75 family to $100.

We got four members—Frank Morgan, Charles Butterworth, Reginald Owen and Paul Lukas.

That was a fine club but it didn't help us financially. We gave Charlie Butterworth and Paul Lukas each a piece of property adjoining the club on which to build houses.

When the houses were completed we had an offer to sell forty of the fifty-three acres for $4,000. We quickly grabbed it. (It now sells for about $1,000 a front foot.) And Walter Marks, the purchaser, began a development.

In the meantime, using the same list, we continued raising the initiation fee $25 each month and the response was fair, but increasing.

When it got to $650 for a membership, we had a waiting list. Then our troubles began. We had added a bar, decorated in bamboo and leather by our friend Mitchell Leisen, the director from Paramount; a dining room with a dance floor; a kitchen to serve the dining room, and more members than we could accommodate if they all showed up at the same time. Six hundred and fifty was the magic number.

Louella Parsons passed the hat for a $400 clock that she felt was necessary over the bar.

We had orchestras and a portable dance floor with a bar at each end of the number-one court, under a circus tent each Saturday night during the season, with forty extra waiters from Los Angeles. Rudy Vallee and his entire orchestra were regulars on these Saturday nights.

The tents, the portable dance floors with their accommodating bars, and indeed the original kitchen and dining-room equipment and many other things would not have been possible without the assistance of our good friend Bearl Murphy, who set up the parties for the most extravagant party-givers in Hollywood—the Zanucks, the Rathbones, the Hal Roaches et al.

"Murph" was with the United Tent and Awning Company, which bought up bankrupt and abandoned large-scale projects of all kinds and then rented or sold what was wanted. Our original stove, for instance, cost twenty-five dollars. And it served many a large party until we could afford a shiny new one. The original one could well have seen service at a then-bankrupt restaurant or cruise ship.

Murph is still my good friend. He's the father of Michael Murphy of picture fame, so he doesn't have to work any more. I'm kidding. He's retired and living happily in Phoenix with Mike's mother (George—believe it or not; her parents too wanted a boy). Murph has a twin brother named Earl—Earl and Bearl.

As tennis pros we had, in succession, Keith Gledhill, Alice Marble with her teacher, Eleanor Tennant, and Lester Stoefen.

We were now big business. Charlie left the country for two years, to make pictures in England and Australia when things at the club were at their peak. We had a full list of members and a full staff working almost around the clock.

Things became uncomfortable with friends, in many ways. After the New Year's Eve party several good friends thought there was a mistake in their bills. They were sure they ordered only two bottles of champagne but the bill showed five. The signed chits had to be found and verified in their alcoholic scrawls by the celebrants.

Other friends, who were not members, wanted to join, but there was no room. So we had to establish a membership committee of members. When we had a drop-out or someone moved away, we'd notify the membership committee of the number of available openings and the list of applicants so there couldn't be any favoritism on the part of management. Indeed, no say in the matter at all. But it seemed that all Hollywood had come to Palm Springs. And today it's one of the most popular resorts in the world.

When Charlie returned I asked him to let me out for my original investment, because running a club wasn't my line and he was made for it. Charlie's a good manager and a good greeter.

Charlie and I like to think Palm Springs, as it is today, began with that horseback ride which ended with a $3,500 investment in fifty-three acres.

In those Palm Springs days I sprained an ankle learning to play tennis. It was the fifth sprain. The doctor taped it and ordered me to walk with a cane.

Walking up the street from the doctor's office, I met a friend who offered me his sympathy and asked me if I'd heard of a carpenter-healer from Hemet who was in town.

Hemet is a village reminiscent of the 1900s, with a population of a few hundred people, at the top of the steep mountain about three thousand feet directly above Palm Springs.

I said I hadn't heard of the carpenter. My friend said the carpenter laid on a hand and effected cures.

"We brought him down to see what he could do for the Duchin baby," he said. "Eddie and his wife and the baby are staying at my house and the baby's been in an incubator since he was born. Every time he's taken out to be fed or anything, he cries. Well, the carpenter took him out of the incubator this morning to see if he could find the center of the baby's ailment, so that when he laid on his hand later he'd know where to concentrate his powers. And for the first time in his life when taken from the incubator, the baby didn't cry.

"And also," my friend continued, "I have this badly walled eye and I've had a headache in the back of my neck for twenty years. Maybe he can help me too. The carpenter's staying at the house too. Why don't you come over tonight and see if he can do something for your ankle?"

"A sprained ankle is torn ligaments," I said. "The ligaments have to mend together. I know. This is my fifth. They used to have you lie in bed for a week with the sprained part raised. Now they tape it into immobility and order you to walk on it. I don't think the carpenter could help me."

"Come on over anyway," he said. "A lot of people are coming by."

About nine-thirty that evening I dropped into my friend's house to find thirty people or so dancing to records. Among them was Ray Hallor, a man who hadn't been able to stand up straight for years. He was bent in two with a painful back ailment.

Ray was dancing as perpendicularly as anyone.

I was directed to a bedroom where my host was closeted with the carpenter, who was standing beside him as he sat on the end of a twin bed with a drink in his hand.

The carpenter, tall, thin and blue-eyed with sandy hair, maybe in his late forties, stood as straight as a Hemet pine, in blue workman's shirt with open collar and heavy-soled workman's shoes. His right hand lay across the back of my host's neck and in his left hand he had a drink. My host's eyes looked at me evenly as he said, "This is the first time in twenty years I haven't had a headache."

I sat at the foot of the other twin bed. My host said, "I feel great. Let's have another drink." Drinks were called for and one came for me. After a minute or two my host said, "Let him put his hand on your ankle."

"Oh," I said, "That's a sprain. He can't do anything about that. But I saw Ray Hallor out there dancing. That's remarkable."

"I don't know what it is," said the carpenter. "But it helps people, that's all I know. And that makes me feel good."

"Okay," I said, going along with it.

The carpenter squatted, cowboy fashion, and put his hand on my ankle while we all sipped our drinks.

When someone puts a hand on you, there is always a transfer of body heat. But the heat from the carpenter's hand was like a heating pad.

We talked of many insignificant and unrelated things for ten minutes or so and the carpenter said, "Stand up on that now. See if it's any better."

I stood. There was no pain. The bandage over the swelling was shriveled and I took a few steps without the cane.

What does one say to something like that? I said, "It doesn't hurt. There's no need to limp or favor it. I don't understand it. It was a good sprain. The doctor said it would take several weeks to mend."

"Well, if it feels good, I feel good," said the carpenter.

We drained our drinks and started for the other room to join the other guests. I discreetly tried to slip a twenty-dollar bill into his hand.

"No, no!" he said. "I never take any money. If I've got a power to help people, I didn't have anything to do with it. If it was given to me, that's fine." And out he went.

I don't know what experience Peter Duchin had, and I guess he doesn't either. He was too young. But the carpenter was gone the next day. And Peter Duchin got out of the incubator and seems to be all right. I've never met him.

I went through a period of fancying myself a hunter. I'd done a little halfhearted rabbit and bird shooting in Iowa and Michigan and some friends in Los Angeles had invited me to join them on trips to duck blinds on a little lake or reservoir down below Indio in the desert. I didn't shoot any ducks but I shot *at* many of them.

During my Palm Springs days one of my friends invited me to join a group who were going to drive over the mountain one midnight to an inland area that was great quail country. We would be a group of four and would return the next afternoon.

I accepted eagerly, not realizing that I could have lain in bed and shot all the quail I wanted out the bedroom window in Palm Springs. I wasn't even sure what a quail looked like. But the four of us who were going on this safari were assured that we'd return with dozens of quail. So I invited six people for quail dinner at the Racquet Club the night of our return.

It was about 5 A.M. and still dark when we reached our hunting ground, which was the top of a gently sloping domelike hill.

Our strategy was for each of us to go down the hill in separate directions and wait for the sun to come up, at which time the quail would assemble for us in flocks. If for some reason one of us found a lot of quail and had not heard shots from the other areas, he was to fire two quick shots in the air to summon the rest of the company.

The sun came up, and I was obviously the most favored hunter. I had a half dozen or so in no time at all. Since I hadn't heard any other shots, I fired two rapid shots in the air and continued my slaughter until I had a bagful, probably a couple of dozen.

Not having heard from any of my comrades-in-arms, I trudged up the hill to see if perhaps they'd missed my signal. I presently saw all of them sitting in and around our car, way up on top of the hill. When I was about two hundred yards from the crest, lo and behold, one of my feathered quarry, bolder than the rest, glided in and perched on a tall, spearlike blade of sturdy weed. He was not at all disturbed by my moving presence. Indeed, he cased me like a New York City detective coming upon a murderer who is caught still holding the smoking weapon.

In less time than it takes to relate, I loaded, cocked and shot. One more for the overloaded bag! But this time with an audience. The audience, however, reacted in a confusing way. They were roaring with laughter as I joined them and they examined my stuffed hunting bag.

I had been shooting meadowlarks. And it was against the law to shoot meadowlarks.

We dug a hole and buried them.

This was obviously not the day of the quail. No one had even seen one. But we had to get back to Palm Springs. It was like going back from safari to Nairobi without a trophy.

I still had a little problem: six guests for quail dinner at the Racquet Club.

When we got to town I swore my game-shooting comrades to secrecy and went to a hardware store where I ordered some of their best BB shot. Then to a butcher shop, and told my butcher friend of my unfortunate predicament. I asked him to give me an odd number of squabs and to force the BB shot into them with a pick and to enclose any remaining BBs in the package in case some of his fell out. I smuggled the squabs to the chef at the

Racquet Club, told him my story, and asked him to make a heavy rich gravy and serve the squabs with mashed potatoes and gravy on individual plates.

I made sure my guests had a few drinks before dinner. The chef did a magnificent job of covering everything with gravy. We had wine with dinner, which called for toasts to the success of the shoot and the honor of the huntsmen.

I don't believe I ever would have been caught if one of the guests, Townsend Netcher, hadn't asked for another quail and more mashed potatoes. When it was served to him, the gravy had BBs in it. All over the mashed potatoes. The chef was giving it his all. And the BBs were brass. At that moment I felt like the Emperor Jones.

After that, at various times, I hunted in New York and Pennsylvania for deer, with no luck. Then, one fall at Sun Valley, Idaho, I went on trips that were sensational for a hunter. Pheasant were abundant and excellent eating. It was the end of the season. The guests had departed and the staff was preparing to close up for the winter.

The two guides, Taylor Williams and Joe Burgy, were good company. And Ernest Hemingway occasionally came in from his home in nearby Ketchum for a drink at the end of the day.

He was an enormous man with unruly hair, a beard, a stomach and a resonant voice which he used blusteringly at times and sometimes quite sensitively. But always to arresting advantage. Except when he was listening. And that he did flatteringly. I wished I could have got to know him better, and I could have if I'd been there longer. He was easy to know. An inquisitive conversationalist, avid for the possibility of something new or different in what you might say. Simpatico. He seemed to crave company.

He was a hunter too. He used to go out for birds almost every morning at sunrise and then come back to write. I got the impression that he was self-disciplined to an extreme. Frequently his pretty blond wife, Mary, was with him. They seemed extraordinarily close. The next year he was dead.

I joined a pack trip on horseback to the middle fork of the Salmon River with Taylor and Joe for deer just before the trails were closed for the winter. It was the most completely "outdoor,

Carefree with Ginger Rogers, Jack Carson, Fred Astaire and Clarence Kolb, 1938 (*Courtesy of RKO General Pictures*)

With Irene Dunne and Patric Knowles in *Lady in a Jam*, 1942 (*From the motion picture* Lady in a Jam. *Courtesy of Universal Pictures*)

With Rosalind Russell and Cary Grant in *His Girl Friday*, 1940 (*Courtesy of Columbia Pictures*)

L. to r.: Edith Angold, Skippy Homeier, me, Joyce Van Patten and Shirley Booth in *Tomorrow the World*, Barrymore Theatre, New York, 1943 (*Photo by Vandamm Studio*)

L. to r.: Me, Sir Cedric Hardwicke, Lon Chaney, Jr., and Lionel Atwill in *Ghost of Frankenstein* (*From the motion picture* Ghost of Frankenstein. *Courtesy of Universal Pictures*)

Ruth Hussey and me in *State of the Union*, Hudson Theatre, New York, 1945

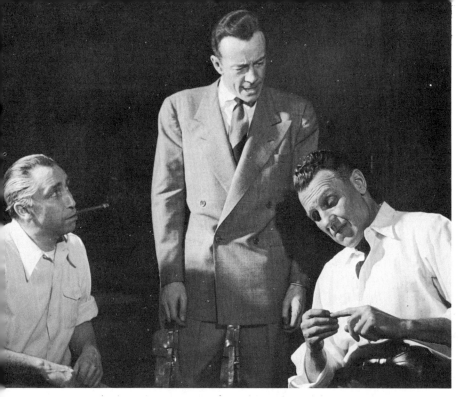

Detective Story, Hudson Theatre, New York, 1949, l. to r.: Horace MacMahon, Les Tremayne and me (*Photo by John Swope*)

With Elizabeth Montgomery in *The Court-Martial of Billy Mitchell*, 1956 (*Courtesy of Warner Bros., Inc.*)

With George Meany, president of the American Federation of Labor,
when I was president of the Actors Equity Association

In front of Actors Equity in New York

Why I gave up hunting

back to nature" experience I've ever had. It was the land of the Nez Percé Indians before they fled to Canada. The river was wild. It could be navigated, perilously, but only one way. At that time probably not more than fifty to a hundred humans a year got in there.

We were on horseback, on a trail that followed the river, and it snowed most of the time. In addition to Taylor and Joe from Sun Valley, who were out for their deer at the end of the season, there were two Salmon River guides in our party—Bill and Joe, who were brothers. We had two Joes in the party. It was cold. We slept in sleeping bags in an abandoned shack that we used for headquarters. First thing in the morning and at the end of the day, the fire in the broken-down stove was a wonderful and welcome comfort.

I dislike fat of any kind. I even prefer non-fat milk. But such idiosyncrasies are forgotten in the stimulation that comes from riding up and down slopes on a cold gray day, dismounting and stalking in the wind and snow, and then riding again.

Joe, the Salmon River guide, was the cook. I remember, with revulsion now, Joe sitting on a high stool between the dilapidated wood stove and a head-high shelf on the wall behind him, where he'd stored some of the utensils and foodstuffs we'd packed in. He could handle everything on the stove and reach back to the shelf without leaving the stool.

On each of the three nights we spent there, he began preparation for the evening repast by slicing raw potatoes into a huge skillet greased with lard. Then he greased another skillet with lard and put pieces of venison in it. After that there was nothing to do but watch it all and nurse it. This consisted of frequently shaking the potato skillet, reaching back to the shelf without turning his head, dipping his hand into the lard bucket and not too gracefully slopping another gob of lard onto the potatoes. The eventual decision to return to civilization could well have been because we'd run out of lard. But the meals were relished as if they'd been prepared by Escoffier. We gorged ourselves each night until there was nothing left in the skillets.

Taylor and Joe Burgy had their deer and I got my eight-point buck on the fourth day in a heavy snowstorm. He was about four hundred yards away down a slope, pursuing a doe that was walking through some trees. At the sound of the shot our party assembled for the ritual which followed, and which I'd never before witnessed.

First the hind feet and then the fore feet were tied together and the deer was hung about four feet from the ground on a stripped branch that was supported at each end by forks in adjoining trees. The stomach was slit down the middle and he was relieved of all his entrails. It was bloody. I didn't think of it at the time, but it was the result of love for a female.

We cleaned him up and tied him over the back of a pack mule and went back to the shack. The next day we started back to Sun Valley.

The Sun Valley chef butchered my deer and cut him into pieces that he wrapped, marked and refrigerated. The frozen pieces, in a canvas sack, were part of my baggage when I took a plane for New York.

At La Guardia Field, I approached the baggage claim area with a porter. I saw my sack before he did. It was dripping blood. I fully expected that I'd be sent to join Winnie Ruth Judd in Arizona. I gave the porter my claim checks and told him I'd meet him at the taxi stand, wondering if *he'd* meet me or a United States marshal. When the porter came with his cart I mumbled something about Idaho and hunting. He believed me, fortunately, and I took my deer to the refrigerator room at my hotel.

Some time afterward, I received a picture of my deer and me, taken after the kill and our return to Sun Valley. By then the buck had been devoured by my friends and me in New York, each meal accompanied by the romantic story of the pack trip, the meals in the shack, the kill and my anxiety at the airport. But not the sordid details that followed immediately after the kill. The snapshot now brought all that back to mind, and I even wondered about the doe.

I've hunted since, for deer in New Jersey and New York and for ducks in Haiti. But those are other stories and the hunting was unsuccessful, except in Haiti. Soon after, I gave it up and disposed of my guns. I found that I couldn't aim a gun at anything because of the memory of the Salmon River incident, and because the picture of my Idaho deer haunted me. Every time I see the picture now it seems to say to me, "How would you like it if you were . . . ?"

But what I learned about hunting has been useful on safari, or handling a rifle or stalking a quarry in pictures.

Gary Cooper was a hunter and expert marksman.

I ran into him up in Sun Valley. He was there with a photographer from *Look* magazine who was to record Gary's feat of shooting wild turkeys in the neck with a .22 rifle.

He was unsuccessful because there were no wild turkeys that season. But we chatted and recalled a couple of pictures I'd made with him—*The Wedding Night* and *The Court-Martial of Billy Mitchell.*

Working with Gary was as fascinating as watching his pictures. When he played a scene with you he'd look you in the eye while speaking—straight in the eye—for a second, then he'd drop his head and stare at the floor almost as if apologizing for having intruded.

In an exterior scene—mostly Westerns, of which he did so many—he'd contemplate the ground instead of the floor and kick one boot, then the other, at the dirt in the street while he spoke. This earned him, in the business, the title of "the shit kicker."

Gary was one of the few actors who had as strong a following of men as he had of the ladies.

I never missed one of his pictures.

PART IX

It was the fall of 1942 that the incident in Mark Hellinger's office, referred to earlier, took me to New York again and, in early 1943, to *Tomorrow the World*.

The cast included Shirley Booth, one of our best actresses and a delight to work with, and two promising child actors, Joyce Van Patten and Skippy Homeier.

The play concerned a true incident of the effort by America to rehabilitate Nazi youths by bringing them over here into American homes.

In reality, the effort upon which the play was based was unsuccessful and the people who'd "adopted" the Nazi boy sent him back to Germany. The Nazi indoctrination had penetrated too deep.

But in the play we're left with the suggestion of the boy's dawning realization of the propaganda with which he'd been instilled. Skippy and Joyce were brilliant natural actors, as they've repeatedly proven since. And of course Shirley goes on and on so magnificently.

Dorothy Sands played my sister in the play. We had many scenes together and she too was a delight to work with.

We opened the second act together and at each performance I noticed that there were tears in her eyes and running down her cheeks. I was fond of Dorothy and I pictured her between acts, barricading herself in her dressing room, torn with a wracking grief that she was keeping to herself in true trouper fashion.

I finally told her I didn't want to intrude into her personal life but that I'd noticed the apparent result of an emotional surge as she appeared for the second act, and I asked if I could be of help.

She said, with a grateful chuckle, that I wasn't intruding at all and that she had no grief and needed no help. She was just getting used to new contact lenses, which were just coming into use, and some of the wetting solution leaked out when she took them off and put them on again between acts. She thanked me for my concern and we had a good laugh.

Radio was now a fixed habit of our life, though we were used to some mechanical and technical difficulties at times. It fed the masses as television does today. There were three networks: the Red Network, the Blue Network (both NBC—the Blue later becoming ABC) and Mutual.

At the end of 1943 the Blue Network acquired a new president by the name of Nolan. They produced an elaborate New Year's Day program from New York, representing all phases of our society and culture and peering into 1944. I was on the program because I was in *Tomorrow the World*.

The program started with an address by Mr. Nolan. He was to be followed by the columnist and radio commentator Drew Pearson, who made a series of predictions on each of his shows, preceding each with, "I predict—"

After Nolan's address, he said, "Now, since we're looking ahead into 1944, what could be more appropriate than to turn the proceedings over to the man who is famous for his predictions—Mr. Drew Pearson!"

Pearson made fifteen predictions, including the invasion of Italy and the downfall of Mussolini. Then he said, "And now to Seattle, Washington, for an address from Eric Johnston! Take it away, Seattle!"

There followed a loud, persistent, static scratching, and a voice came on saying, "Just this morning George Bernard Shaw said, 'Not even I can predict anything for 1944.'"

They had incorrectly tuned in to what should have been a relay station but they got mixed up with a local news broadcast from Burbank, California.

The static came on again and someone said, "Due to circumstances beyond our control, we are unable to reach Seattle. Mr. Johnston's speech will be read from our New York studio."

Someone then read an emergency, protection copy of Johnston's speech.

After that, John L. Lewis was to speak from Miami, Florida. When he was introduced ("Take it away, Miami!"), the static returned and someone read *his* speech from the studio. It was a two-hour show and it went seven minutes over.

I did six or eight radio plays opposite Gertrude Lawrence on her own show.

Before each show, which was done before an audience in a large studio, Gertie would go in front of the curtain and do what we used to call a "warm-up." It's still done on TV for some live-tape-audience shows. It's a talk, with jokes and charm, to get the audience in a comfortable, receptive mood. Gertie would finish by introducing the guest star, who would come out and say a few words, and then get on with the play.

One night I was standing back of the curtain, which opened in the center, waiting for Gertie to introduce me when I heard out front, "And now, ladies and gentlemen, it's my pleasure to welcome once again a favorite of ours who'll be with us again tonight, Mr. Frank Bellamy."

I had to step out. And I had to say something. I said, "It's always a pleasure to be on the Sarah Lawrence show."

I also did several guest star appearances opposite Helen Hayes on her radio show.

There were many weekly anthology radio shows going: "Studio One," "The Theatre Guild on the Air," "The United States Steel Hour," "Armstrong Theatre of the Air," "Suspense," "Philip Morris Playhouse," "Radio Reader's Digest," "The Theatre of Romance" (the last two directed by my brother-in-law, Marx Loeb) and many others. I guest-starred on all of them. It was radio's heyday.

Sylvester Weaver, known by all his friends as "Pat," should be properly introduced here. He began his communications career in radio and later became president of NBC. He was a large figure in the early radio and early TV scene, most notably remembered for his many innovations. I asked him for a résumé, which follows:

"When I started in radio in the early thirties at the CBS station in Los Angeles, no recordings were allowed, and our tiny group of workers could be found writing, directing, acting, singing, announcing and even selling. Yet, the magic of the medium was so great that the audiences attended our meager efforts in vast numbers. It quickly became apparent that this magic rested in the capacity of taking people to places they would like to be, even though they remained comfortably at home.

"This was even more true when TV added sight to sound. With television we could now all be in the studio audience of a Bob Hope or Jack Benny and see everything, instead of just hearing it. And of course, we could attend the theatre and movies and sports too. And our show forms followed this. Indeed, in radio we devised many more new forms than we needed in television. Because TV, to this day almost, has as its greatest appeal, and reaches its biggest audiences, when it takes us to an event and covers it. In early television, we used this magic by building shows that were in Broadway theatres, and originated there, like 'Your Show of Shows' or Fred Coe's 'Philco Playhouse.' Later we were able to afford putting almost complete Broadway attractions on at full length, as in Mary Martin's *Peter Pan* or the Bogart-Bacall-Fonda *Petrified Forest* in 'Producers' Showcase.' We also tried to push into new theatre areas, as with the musical based on Thornton Wilder's *Our Town,* starring Frank Sinatra with Paul Newman and Joanne Woodward, music by Sammy Cahn and Jimmy Van Heusen, from which "Love and Marriage" emerged. All these all live, performed once, and in most cases without even a decent recording, or kinescope, of the performance.

"I did try in those early days to complement the great coverage power of the medium to take us everywhere with new forms that TV could use for greater viewer enrichment. 'The Today Show' was to cover what was new across many interests each morning. And 'Tonight' was started as a lighthearted comedy coverage show of the day we had lived thru. The power of TV to go beyond the limitations of films and radio was also being explored in those early years by 'Wide Wide World,' 'Home,' and of course 'Matinee Theatre,' where with five hours of product a week, all night-time quality in planning, we could do novels, try new kinds of drama, and experiment widely. And so much more! Exciting times."

I guess everyone in the country knows Steve Allen.

He was one of the originators of radio humor and talk shows.

He's also a very involved gentleman, in many areas. I remember having the pleasure of presenting him with an award for unusual efforts in behalf of the American Civil Liberties Union. He's a man of good will as well as good humor. The following is his reply to a request for a word or two about early radio:

"When I went to work for KNX Hollywood (CBS) in 1948 my instructions were simple, but I made it my business to disobey them at the earliest opportunity. 'Just play records,' my new employers told me, 'and in between do a little light chatter. We'd like somebody who'll handle the show with a humorous approach.'

"Perceiving at once that by playing a great many records I would be performing an estimable service for Bing Crosby, Frank Sinatra, Dinah Shore, et al., but doing very little for myself, I decided to make music on the new program secondary in importance. Therefore I wrote a seven- or eight-page script each evening, read it in an offhand conversational manner to create the impression that I was speaking extemporaneously, and played a bit less music than instructed.

"The reaction, from listeners, was immediate and encouraging. For all its impact I don't think television will ever be able to establish the kind of personal contact between speaker and listener that was possible in the pre-TV days of radio. This continued for about two months until one day I received a memo from a member of the KNX program department. 'We hired you to play records,' the directive said in substance, 'not to do a comedy program.'

"Here was a formidable obstacle to my plans, vague as they were. I solved the dilemma by the expedient of reading the executive memo on the air. Listeners came at once to the rescue. In the following two days I received over four hundred letters, all of which stated the case precisely as I perceived it myself. 'If we want to hear music, there are a dozen other stations in Los Angeles playing it night and day. The reason we listen to this particular program is that it offers us something different.'

"The following day, carrying a large box full of mail, I walked into the office of Hal Hudson, the man who had written the memo. 'I think you'll be interested in these letters,' I said.

"After he had sampled the contents of the box he at once reversed his former position. 'Well,' he said, 'you win. Go ahead and talk. But play a *little* music, okay?'

"Within a few months our studio audience had swelled to over a hundred. One night my scheduled guest was Doris Day. Fortunately she never showed up. I say 'fortunately' because if she had I might still be doing that same radio program. The press agent who had promised that Doris would appear had evidently neglected to communicate this information to her, and at eleven-thirty on this particular evening I was suddenly faced with twenty-five minutes of dead air.

"I suddenly heard myself saying, 'Well, Doris Day evidently isn't going to show up. But no matter; I'll just take this microphone and interview some of the ladies and gentlemen who *did* arrive this evening.' So saying, I picked up a heavy floor microphone, and carrying it around like an unwieldy broomstick began chatting with people in the audience. I don't recollect what was said during the next twenty-five minutes but I do know that I had never gotten such laughs before.

"The KNX program lasted for almost three years: 1948, 1949, and 1950.

"But now in 1953–54 things began looking up. The ABC television station in New York at this time had a five-nights-a-week variety program on the air from about 11 P.M. to midnight. In format it was reminiscent of Jerry Lester's old 'Broadway Open House.'

"A regular visitor was the ever-popular 'Mrs. Miller,' Miss Dorothy Miller, who got her 'start' in my audiences at KNX in Los Angeles and then followed me to New York. She came to our show almost every night, by train from Philadelphia, where she worked. She later spent years in the audiences of Jack Paar, Merv Griffin, Joey Bishop, and Johnny Carson."

During the run of *Tomorrow the World* I did RCA Victor recordings of Walt Whitman's *Leaves of Grass* and *The Rubáiyát of Omar Khayyám* and guest-starred on many radio programs.

The play ran for a year and a half but I left it after a year to produce (with Jack Moses, a New Trier classmate and producer of "Information, Please!") and direct Claiborne Foster's *Pretty Little Parlor* on Broadway. The cast featured Stella Adler, who brought her psychiatrist to rehearsal each day. There were also Sidney Blackmer, Ed Begley and Paul Parks. The play wasn't successful but Burns Mantle cited Stella for one of the "ten best performances" in his annual edition of *The Best Plays*.

Then I went back to Hollywood under contract to Hunt Stromberg for a year to do *Guest in the House* with Anne Baxter and Ruth Warrick, directed by Lewis Milestone—a magnificent director and a fine gentleman—and *Lady on a Train* with Deanna Durbin. Before *Lady on a Train* was finished, I was sent the script of what eventually became *State of the Union*.

State of the Union, originally called *I'd Rather Be Left*, was a rare experience in the theatre for several reasons.

First, it was a privilege and a delight to work with the authors, Howard Lindsay and Russel Crouse, two of the theatre's best craftsmen. (Incidentally, they did most of their collaborating by telephone.)

Howard was also an actor. He played opposite Margaret Anglin in classics for several seasons, as well as in many other productions, and he co-authored several successful plays and musicals with Russel "Buck" Crouse, including *Life with Father*, in which he played Father. And afterward, *Life with Mother*.

Howard was something of a hypochondriac. I wrote in a magazine article that one should never greet him with "How are you?" because he would answer at more than considerable length. Howard was amused at my comment about him, which proved that he had a sense of humor that included himself.

One evening while I was making up for Grant Matthews in *State of the Union*, Howard dropped into my dressing room to chat. I was sitting at my make-up shelf before a mirror that extended the length of the shelf, some eight feet or so, covering the entire wall above the shelf on that side of the room. Howard sat in a large overstuffed chair next to me and back from the shelf, so that we could see each other in the mirror as we talked.

I'd been suffering from a winter cold and laryngitis and I was taking anything anyone suggested to relieve it: tablets, sprays, syrups, patent medicaments of all kinds, and they were lined up against the mirror to my left so that Howard was in a position to survey the lot. As we chatted, I was suddenly aware of Howard reaching forward, opening a bottle of pills and swallowing one.

"Howard!" I said. "What are you taking?"

"I don't know," he replied. "It's something I've never had before."

The cast of *State of the Union* included Ruth Hussey, Myron McCormick, Minor Watson and Kay Johnson.

"Buck" Crouse was a very intelligent, wiry, witty, nervous, lovable little fellow. He'd been a newspaperman until he met Howard. Buck was extraordinary at coming up with a needed line with what seemed like no effort or hesitation. We needed a curtain line for a heated political argument in the prologue which set the scene and background for the play in a smoke-filled, behind-the-scenes political headquarters in the process of plotting strategy, tactics and plans for my presidential campaign.

We worried about it at rehearsal until one day Howard said to Buck and the director, Bretaigne Windust, "We have to have a strong curtain line there. Come up with something, Crouse!"

In no time at all, after a walk up one aisle and down the other, Buck suggested that at the height of the emotional argument someone mention "the difference between the two parties." Minor Watson, who was playing the king-maker and caucus leader, replied, "The only difference between the two parties is: they're in and we're out!" And we had our curtain line.

Buck was superstitious in one small but important habit. Before it was necessary for authors to appear in dinner jackets at openings, he'd found by accident that he'd inadvertently worn the same four-in-hand tie at several successful openings of his and Howard's plays. So under his dinner jacket shirt he wore the lucky four-in-hand. He showed it to me before the New York opening of *State of the Union* and there must have been something to it. We ran almost two years. And received the Pulitzer Prize.

After Churchill's Fulton, Missouri, speech that introduced the "iron curtain" term anent Stalin's Russia and after his rebuttal to Stalin's reply at the Waldorf Astoria Hotel in New York, he came to see *State of the Union*. The theatre was combed by Scotland Yard, the FBI and the New York City police.

It was a thrilling evening. At one point in the play my wife (Ruth Hussey) and I were alone on the stage in my hotel suite just before going downstairs to deliver what was calculated to be the final and winning speech before the presidential election. To avoid having to suffer another banquet meal we'd ordered a martini and a hamburger apiece from room service. As we were waiting for them to arrive I was reading the late newspaper and I had to read aloud to Ruth a headline that seemed important or amusing or whatever, but something actually timely. It was my job to find a line that was topical and different each night. I used to arrive at the theatre early with the evening papers and turn on my radio to try to catch a last-minute, appropriate line.

But with Churchill in the audience, and the audience aware of it, the line should have some reference to him. And it had to be not too politically slanted, and in good taste. So I said, "Listen, Mary! 'After two strenuous weeks, Churchill relaxes in New York seeing plays.'" I understand he loved it. I know the audience did.

The next day at the gangplank of his returning ship, the press asked him what he thought of *State of the Union*. He thought a moment and then said, "I don't know what kind of speech a man could make on a hamburger and only one martini."

I was invited to Fay and Reggie Venable's New York apartment for cocktails. Fay was Fay Bainter, an attractive woman and of course one of our best-known and most talented actresses. Also she had been the leading lady in the stock company in Des Moines some years before I had my company there. Reggie had been captain of a World War II escort ship. He'd been court-martialed during the early days of the war for taking his ship off course in the middle of the Atlantic to wave to Fay, who was crossing on a passenger liner. Very romantic.

During the afternoon at the cocktail party a sadly self-conscious young man arrived, blushed a greeting to Fay and slunk around the walls surrounding the numerous guests for a half hour or so. Then, back at the door, he awkwardly said his adieus to Fay and Reggie. As Fay closed the door she said to Reggie, with compassion, "A Consterpalian!" And they both chuckled.

I asked Fay what a Consterpalian was, and she told the following story:

Their pre-teen-age son, Reggie Jr., was attending the Montessori School up the Hudson River. A great part of the Montessori theory and program is to let the very young people ostensibly alone with each other so that they develop not only their own inclinations and make their own tests but also find a social consciousness that will help them make easy, though rival, contact with one another through life.

Well, one day at luncheon, they were seated eight or ten to a table. There was no apparent surveillance, though there were "lookouts" concealed behind the potted palms ready to intervene if anyone started throwing bread or silver or otherwise disturbed the expected decorum of well-bred young people of good family.

A lookout reported to the Venables that one of the diners at Reggie's table, during a brief discussion on religion, said, "I'm a Congregationalist." Another said, "I'm a Presbyterian." And so it went around the table, "Catholic," "Baptist," "Episcopalian," etc., until it came to Reggie, who unfortunately had never even been to Sunday school. But he wanted the security of belonging, and after a pause, while with bent head he busied himself with the food on his plate, he looked up and said, "I'm a Consterpalian!" Not a bad word.

I guess the fear of non-conformity is a part of puberty, and it takes some of us a long time to evolve from early conformity to teen-age rebellion to serene reason. Some of us never make it.

Graham Greene is one of the most disciplined and prolific of writers. He writes at least four hundred words every day and then reviews the previous day's work.

He spends a good deal of time in pubs and saloons because he says people are without inhibitions and more nearly themselves while imbibing, and his deep interest is people. He told me he didn't want to live beyond fifty-five. We're the same age, and Graham didn't make it. He's still around and as prolific as ever.

He came over here to do an adaptation of his book *The Heart of the Matter* for the stage, with me. I had contracted for the rights. We holed up at the Tuscany Hotel in New York and in something like two or three weeks we had a play. My first interest was in playing it. But as we progressed, I quickly realized that the play was so British that I had to eliminate myself. I wouldn't dare play an Englishman.

But working with Graham was an inspiration. The nimbleness of his mind and his perception of human behavior and his deftness with words all were awe-inspiring. We turned the play over to Dick Rodgers and Oscar Hammerstein, who cast it with English actors living in this country. They brought Basil Dean over from England to direct it. It opened and closed in Boston. Too bad.

I saw Graham a couple of years later in Chicago, where I was on the road with *Oh, Men! Oh, Women!* He and Irene Selznick came to talk about my doing his new play, *The Complaisant Lover,* which Irene was producing in New York. Michael Redgrave did it, but it didn't have much of a run. Again, too bad. With all those talented people. Which proves that no one can consistently tell a hit from a flop.

I had been doing well financially in New York in radio and TV, but in 1949 my daughter had enormous, continuing doctor bills, my parents depended solely upon me and I'd just been through a divorce that left me almost penniless.

Out of the blue, at my lowest ebb, I was offered *Detective Story.*

It was a great play, in my opinion at least equal to *Death of a Salesman,* which won the New York Drama Critics Circle Award that season. And a great part: Detective McLeod, a man who took it upon himself to be judge, jury and hangman, a man who was wrong trying to be right. Also it was a highly intellectual experience, working with the author and director, Sidney Kingsley, one of the finest craftsmen in the modern theatre. Altogether, it remains one of the highlights of my experience in the theatre.

During the rehearsal period I lived on the dregs of my decimated finances, and when we got to Philadelphia for the road tryout I was so flat broke for the first week that I had to have all my meals at the Warwicke Hotel, where I could sign for them until the first payday.

But the theatre is food and drink to a dedicated actor and I didn't suffer.

There were two moments and a decision at rehearsal which I think characterize Sidney Kingsley as an impatient perfectionist, a fine human being and a man with a self-understood and intellectually well-balanced ego.

One day at rehearsal an actor, script in hand and seated at a table center stage, said to Sidney over the footlight trough on the bare stage with its one overhanging work light, "Mr. Kingsley, it says here I rise and cross down right. What's my motivation for this?"

Sidney has a well-controlled temper, he's a perfectionist, he's probing, discerning and compassionate. But when his gall rises his blood pressure does too, and his breathing seems to be affected, so that whatever words come out give the impression of a stammer. So, in this case, his answer to the young actor, as he came down the aisle of the dark auditorium, was, "Y-y-you jus-just d-do it, and then g-g-go home tonight and figure out the reason why."

As fine a lesson in acting as has ever been advanced.

Another time at rehearsal, he said, from the dark auditorium to all of us onstage, "Come on! Let me see a performance here!"

It happened that we were into a scene that had never been blocked. I guess *my* gall rose at this seeming injustice under the pressure of rehearsal and creation, and I shouted back over the footlight trough, "Give us some direction and we'll give you a performance!"

There was a pause and he said, "Take five, everyone." And he came up on the stage, put his arm around my shoulder and said, "I beg your pardon, I didn't realize. Let's go next door to the Palace Bar and Grill and have a cup of coffee."

You have to have a deep affection for a man like that. And I have.

The third, and most professionally revealing, memory of that period was when we found we were about fifteen minutes too long.

Sidney had an intellectual rivalry running through the play

between McLeod and the press reporter. McLeod was a Catholic from Fordham and the reporter was from CCNY. They frequently challenged each other with exchanges in Latin or Greek, which was made clear to any non-academics in the audience in further short exchanges in English. It was unusual and amusing and revealing of character.

After combing the script for cuts to reduce the time, Sidney struck out this entire running intellectual show-off—amusing and valuable though it was—and shaved the time to an acceptable limit.

I can't think of another writer who would be willing to delete such a unique and choice device from his own play. Someone else's, maybe. But not his own.

Sidney is truly a man of the theatre, as his record shows. How about another one, Sidney? Before it's too late for both of us.

Everyone in the rather imposing cast has later become well ensconced in Hollywood: Edward Binns, Joan Copeland, Lee Grant, Lou Gilbert, Horace MacMahon, Patrick McVey, Meg Mundy, Alexander Scourby, Maureen Stapleton, Warren Stevens, Robert Strauss, Michael Strong, Les Tremayne, James Westerfield, Joseph Wiseman and Harry Worth—to name those who have stayed.

I gave Sidney my account of *Detective Story* and asked if he'd care to add anything. Here's part of his reply:

"Strange the tricks memory plays on one! I don't recall the episode you mentioned about your asking for more direction. What I do recall are the occasions when I had so thoroughly blocked out the act, particularly when everyone was on the stage, that some of the actors complained the blocking was much too detailed. You will recall the stage was small, and there were moments when fractions of an inch were important in moving all the actors about the stage. At any rate, I trust your memory of that episode, and I see no objection to your using it. In fact, I'm touched by your account of the episode."

In preparation for *Detective Story* I spent six weeks, all night, every night, visiting New York City detective squad rooms. During this experience I developed a high regard for these men. Of course in any large group of any kind there are the odd ones, like the fellow I was about to portray on the stage. And I must say I saw a little, but very little, unbecoming behavior among the guardians of the law upon which to draw my characterization. There was such a preponderance to the contrary that there was an impression sometimes of sentimentality, of sympathy for the lawbreaker. Many times I saw detectives send out for coffee and Danish for their prisoners and pay for it from their own pockets while their prisoners were being booked.

This is not to say they can't meet physical resistance in a most efficient way if necessary. They're trained for it, and their reflexes are fine-tuned. My impression was that they weren't looking for trouble, but if they found it they handled it quickly and judiciously, often giving the offender a break if they thought a warning could serve as effectively as a charge.

I have many memories of those squad room nights, but two of them are special. Both incidents involved the 30th Precinct detective squad room upstairs at 151st Street and Amsterdam Avenue, where I found the most action that would be applicable and useful for my research with respect to the play.

In the first place, the precinct included some of the old Riverside Drive neighborhood that housed a few of what was left of the New York aristocracy of the turn of the century. Riverside Drive was fashionable and lavishly situated, in its heyday, with parks, cloisters, monuments and private piers, all commanding a view of the Jersey Palisades across the Hudson. The precinct also contained some of Columbia Medical School and its faculty and students, a great many medical people connected with Columbia Presbyterian Medical Center and a section of Harlem. There was always activity in the 30th Precinct squad room, activity concerning all ethnic, social, economic and intellectual groups.

One night there was a lull in the activity, upstairs in the old 30th Precinct building, as most squad rooms in New York seemed to be. One of the detectives, who'd been tracking a stolen fur coat for some time, had a hunch, based on information in another case, that he might get lucky by visiting an address in Harlem. He and his partner and I took off for a typical Harlem flat building, a brownstone with ten or twelve steps up to a stoop.

Inside the vestibule there must have been thirty or more mailboxes with bell buttons and name plates under them. It was late at night and the inside vestibule door was locked. Knowing that all Harlem residents protect each other in our precarious society, the detective in search of the coat rang several bells, hoping someone would release the electric door catch. He'd left his partner in our car. There were just the two of us.

Presently a man opened the door a crack. He appeared to be the superintendent. On his head he was wearing a woman's stocking cut in half and tied at the top. The detective put his foot in the crack of the opened door, showed his badge and asked for one of the residents by name. The super reluctantly said the man was on the fifth floor. We started down the hallway to climb the stairs. There was no elevator. As we proceeded, heads peered through cracks of partially opened doors. They were all wearing women's stockings cut in half and tied at the top. We arrived at the door of our suspect and knocked.

A voice from within said, "Who's there?"

"Police!" my friend called. "Open up!"

The door was quickly opened to reveal a young man in the top of his pajamas and half a woman's stocking on his head. The detective and I walked in as the fellow, whose single room we'd illegally entered, backed up to the double bed and sat. Behind him, in bed, was a large, annoyed, naked woman with half a stocking on her head, quite rightly and legally demanding, "Who is it? They got no right to come in here!"

Meanwhile, my detective friend was looking over the chest of drawers for a pawn ticket and asking questions.

Finding no evidence, he sat on the bed beside the poor fellow whose home we'd desecrated and asked more questions, which evoked innocent answers. Finally he inquired, with a movement of his head toward the woman behind them, "Your wife?"

"No sir," the poor fellow replied.

"Girl friend?" asked the detective.

"Yeah."

"Why don't you get married?" he asked.

"Because," smiled the fellow whose whole life we were now molesting, "every time I can pass the test, she can't. And every time she can, I can't."

After *Detective Story* had opened I took William Wyler up to the 30th Precinct. He was going to direct the picture with Kirk Douglas and he wanted to examine some authentic New York squad room atmosphere. There was no better example than the 30th.

Later, Chester Morris was going to head a road company of the play and I took him up to my favorite squad room about midnight, after the evening's performance. We arrived in the midst of a bit of drama. It was a mild spring night and the windows were open. Several people were waiting on a bench inside the upstairs door, separated from the five detectives' desks by a low, spindled rail with a swinging gate. It was quiet in the rather large room, except for the sound of a couple of detectives typing "squeals." Slouched at two of the detectives' desks were young men, one of whom seemed to be asleep with his head on his folded arms. The other was leaning his head on his hand, his elbow on the desk. The detectives were absorbed in their work and merely nodded a greeting, which heightened the sense of permeating drama.

In the lieutenant's room, just off the squad room, we could see an enormous man sitting in the chair opposite the lieutenant's swivel chair. We moved to the room and stood in the doorway. The lieutenant wasn't there but Kitty Barry, the only woman member of the narcotics division and the only policewoman who had ever dropped a man in line of duty up to that time, was standing with her hat pushed back, trying to persuade the man in the chair to make a statement in exchange for an effort to get the D.A. to go easy. But the big fellow wouldn't talk. On the desk in front of him were brown paper bags of marijuana, heroin and cocaine. Kitty's eyes, as she stood, were on a level with his, as he sat.

Kitty had masterminded the apprehension of a whole gang by spending many hours in what appeared to be an old *Herald Tribune* truck, equipped inside with two-way radio and parked in the center of a stake-out. The address was known, but she waited until the whole gang and the evidence were all assembled, including a current-year Cadillac with South Carolina plates and over 150,000 miles on the odometer. Then she gave the signal.

As Chester and I stood in the doorway watching Kitty work on the drug runner and listening to the typewriters tap away, there was suddenly a disturbance in the squad room. A bat had flown in, from the Jersey Palisades across the Hudson, no doubt, and everyone inside the rail was on his feet, officers and prisoners alike. In a body they chased the bat back and forth across the room as in a ballet.

A detective drew his gun, but he was stopped by his partner, who said, "Don't be a goddamned fool, you'll kill someone!"

After a few more passes by the corps de ballet, someone said, "Get a broom!"

One of them squashed the bat against the wall with the broom and a detective finished him off with a blackjack. It fell to the floor and everyone stood over it, looking down at it.

There was a moment of complete silence. Then from the lieutenant's room we heard, "Just a simple statement and I'll do what I can for you with the D.A."

That roused one of the detectives, who looked up and, taking in the situation, said to the prisoners, "All right, you guys! Sit down!"

They'd met their common enemy and destroyed him. They were back to cops and robbers.

Everyone in the theatre, pictures and TV knew Horace Mac-Mahon. And probably every law officer in the country knew him, too. Horace was a cop "buff" who paled all those who support their local lawmen. He played the police lieutenant in *Detective Story*. It was brilliant casting, and so was his performance. Horace was the old-line, honest, dedicated cop who lived and breathed his job.

We had a scene together in the lieutenant's office, just the two of us. Horace was in his T-shirt, in the midst of shaving. He'd entered the scene with a brush in one hand, a razor in the other, his face lathered with soap and his hair down over his forehead. It was a dramatic scene and we were both venting emotions.

We'd been in the play a year or so, and actors who've had the luck to be in that kind of a hit know that more concentration is required with each succeeding performance. There can be a tendency to ride the pattern that was formulated during the rehearsal period and followed from one performance to another. It's like doing routine daily exercises, sometimes without thinking. If one does this, even for a fleeting fraction of a second, what's just been said can go unnoted, so that what follows is lost, and you're "up." It has happened to every actor who's been in a long run.

I went up in a long speech of my own one night. When I realized it, I remember thinking, "This will hold until I catch up with myself and the situation." But being face to face with Horace, I could see, through the soap and the hair, a wild panic in his eyes. Then, as I stood there in terrible silence, Horace bellowed, apropos of nothing at all and at the top of his leather lungs, "Keep your goddamned mouth shut!"

There was a cast party the closing night of *Detective Story*.

Alice, my wife, and I had made a date to visit Lila and Lester Degenstein in Southampton for a few days beginning that Saturday night. So we left the party a little early, about 1 A.M.

It was pouring rain as we sped along the Jericho Turnpike.

After an hour or so Alice asked me to stop at a gas station that would have a rest room.

Everything was closed.

Alice's condition worsened and the rain got heavier. Finally in desperation she asked me to stop at the next gas station even if it were closed. There would be a chance that the rest room doors would be open.

I stopped at the next station.

Alice was wearing a tight-skirted red suit and had trouble hurrying with short steps through the rain to one side of the station in the dark.

There was apparently no rest room on that side. And I saw her pitty-pat to the other side, which was wooded.

Presently I heard screams, and around the station came my wife, her skirt around her waist and clutching her girdle with both hands as it was binding her ankles. She was hopping along, like a jack rabbit, bent double in an effort to pull up the girdle to run faster to escape from a barking bloodhound the size of a pony, snapping at her behind.

~ 203 ~

I have never laughed so hard as I got her into the car. And we took care of her distress behind a tree a quarter mile down the road.

On the subject of moving vehicles, there's an abundance of stories about New York taxi drivers. And they're all true. A weird one involved my wife. Here it is in Alice's words:

TAXI, TAXI

It was a steamy day in June. Ralph was working and I had a sad afternoon before me. To attend the funeral services of our dear friend, Roland Young, at the home of Cornelia Otis Skinner and Alden Blodget somewhere in the East Sixties. The solemnity of the occasion called for proper attire. I dressed in a navy-blue silk dress, hat with veil, stockings and white gloves. When the service was over I had planned to spend the remainder of the afternoon and evening at my sister's house in the East Nineties. I walked up Lexington Avenue and at Eighty-fifth Street, to cheer myself, I stopped at Baur's Bakery to buy cakes and cookies and candies for my sister's family and for us. Laden with packages I continued my walk to her house. The temperature kept rising and I arrived there in a state of near collapse. One look at me and she ran to her closet and gave me a backless sun dress and a pair of sandals to put on and told me to take a shower and change.

About eleven forty-five that night I decided to go home to meet Ralph and have supper with him. The temperature was still around a hundred degrees. So I packed my still slightly damp clothes, kept on the sun dress and sandals and left. When I reached the lobby of her apartment the doorman had retired or gone to the bar on the corner. I waited in vain and finally walked to First Avenue loaded down with my clothes and parcels. I walked a few blocks until I was able to hail a cab. Once settled in the cab I gave the driver the address, Fifty-seventh Street and Seventh Avenue, the old Osborne Apartments where we had lived for many years. The short way home was to work your way west, enter Central Park at Seventy-second Street and Fifth Avenue, cross the park diagonally and make your exit at Fifty-ninth Street and Seventh Avenue. After driving a few blocks, however, I glanced at the back of the driver's head. He was a huge man with a neck that resembled a column of lard, peppered with black hairs. I became a bit apprehensive and in my most authoritative voice told him to stay on First Avenue and make a right turn into Fifty-seventh Street. I figured it would be safer, though longer, to remain on lighted streets where there might be an occasional pedestrian, than risk driving through the dark and isolated park with this gorilla-like creature, considering my scanty garb and general attractiveness (?), and where muggings were the least that could happen to one. He said, "Why, lady?" I replied that I did not want him to cut through the park as I had hay fever and was allergic to trees. He said, "Hay fever, you got rose fever. Ya get hay fever in August." I said, "Oh, I didn't know that, but please stay on First Avenue." We drove in silence for a while and suddenly he said, "Do ya ever think you're gonna rupture yaself?" Me: "No, why?" He: "Ya know, when you start coughing and sneezing." Me: "Oh, sometimes." Driver: "Well, when ya do, get in bed and cuddle up. Put ya knees under ya chin and ya won't rupture yaself. I had hay fever when I was in the Army and the doc tole me to do that. And he tole me to put my eye over a fountain and it would wash away the germs. There's a fountain in the park and I could bring ya there and ya could try it." I said, "Thanks, but I think I'll wait until I get home, as my husband is waiting for me." A hint I thought I should drop about that time.

Meanwhile he kept taking side streets and eventually reached Fifth Avenue, which runs parallel to the park. Suddenly, he screamed, "Sorry, lady, I brung ya by the park. I just wasn't thinking." I replied, "That's okay, just as long as I don't go *in* the park." A few more blocks and he said, "Did ya ever try penicillin? I call it the wonda drug. Do ya wanna know why I call it the wonda drug?" I, weakly: "Why?" He: "Well, they give it to me in the Army and it cured me. And my pop, he's an ole man, from the ole country, and he never washes his teeth. So he gets this terrible toothache and his face is all swoll. So he comes to me and he says, 'Son, I'm in awful pain and I don't know what to do.' So, I tell him, 'Go to the doc and tell him to give ya some penicillin.' So he goes to the doc and the doc gives him a shot in the ass and it's his tooth that's hurting. But the next day he comes to me and he says, 'Son, you're right. It's a wonda drug. I ain't got no pain and I'm peeing purple.'" Me: "Wonderful." After a few more exchanges we reached the Osborne and I handed him the fare. And he said, "Naw, lady, keep the money and buy yaself some penicillin."

In 1949 I was on the first weekly half-hour live dramatic network TV show on the air. It was called "Man Against Crime," a private eye series originating from New York on CBS. I played Mike Barnett, and whenever I introduced myself to other characters during a performance I always added, "With two *t*'s."

Incidentally, I had worked in the same studio some years earlier on a visit to New York. In the mid-thirties Worthington Miner, director of many Broadway plays and one of the first national TV programs—"Medic," with Richard Boone—did an experimental two-hour program consisting of amateur groups and a professional or two. It was directed to the two or three hundred sets in New York City on Thanksgiving Day from this same studio in Grand Central Station.

At the same time—1949, that is—I was also starring in *Detective Story*. This meant rehearsing every day for the TV show and doing the stage play at night. "Man Against Crime" went on the air on Friday night from eight-thirty to nine. It was done at the only available broadcast studios, on the third floor of Grand Central Station, because the radio networks hadn't yet installed facilities for TV.

I finished "Man Against Crime" at about two minutes to nine every Friday night and rushed to a waiting elevator that took me down to a waiting squad car. With the siren open we would go up Sixth Avenue on the left-hand side of the street to the stage door of the Hudson Theatre on Forty-fifth Street, where they held the curtain till nine o'clock. The stage manager was waiting in the alley. When he saw me arrive safely (we ran into a fire truck one night) he would signal the curtain to go up. I would run to my dressing room upstairs and quickly change into my wardrobe for Jim McLeod in *Detective Story* and just barely make my first entrance cue.

Things aren't done that way today.

Those were truly the covered wagon days of TV. Everything was experimental: story, acting, camera, scenery and lighting. And it is lighting—especially lighting at CBS—that lingers in my memory.

Today we have wonderfully creative and expert lighting men who can make anyone look better than he really does. But in those days the lights were controlled and placed solely by the electrical department. They consisted of large inverted pans, about four feet by two feet, containing four or five long incandescent lamps hung directly over each set. They threw a glaring bluish-white light onto the poor actors, magnifying every line or blemish or imperfection in their faces and giving them hollow eyes.

Those were also the days of kinescope, a film-tape impression taken at the broadcast mechanical source and mailed in reels to all the local stations. The network cable hadn't yet been built. When those ghoulish figures were transposed to kinescope the actors looked like invaders from another planet and one's closest friend couldn't recognize him on TV outside of New York City. And even in New York City he might think rigor mortis was setting in.

After the dress rehearsal of "Man Against Crime" one Friday evening we had a half hour before going on the air and I was talking to one of the electricians. I asked him if they didn't have some kind of hooded lamps that could be clamped onto the sides of sets about head-high. Something that would compensate for that overhead X ray. Something that would let the viewer see the actors' faces. He said he thought they had a lot of them but that it would take a requisition from Mr. Paley to get them. They'd never before been used for TV.

I worked on this friendly electrician for a couple of weeks and eventually persuaded him to sneak in some clamp lights after the dress rehearsal when the stage was quiet and fairly deserted. I walked into the playing area of each set and he surreptitiously clamped a lamp on each side, aimed in toward that area. We managed to get them onto all the sets.

When we went on the air a little while later there was a noticeable mild confusion from the cameramen during the performance. Afterward they all said, "What was on the sides of the sets? Every time we went into a set we had to duck something sticking out from the sides that wasn't there before." The technical crew and the director came running out from the control room and said, "What happened? Everyone looked wonderful."

The confession had to be made, and from that time on there was light on the actors' faces at CBS. And who knows? Maybe this was the beginning of modern TV studio lighting.

In those pioneer days, something vital was expected to go wrong at each performance—something like the sound going out, a camera breakdown or an overloaded circuit blowing out. One typically uncomfortable moment comes to mind, though the problem was not a mechanical one.

A rather elaborate pawnshop interior had been constructed for a scene of about twenty seconds, during which Mike Barnett accosted the pawnbroker back of his counter, asking if he had any guns. The pawnbroker was to say he had some and then take Mike to a bin from which he produced several guns, naming them, "a Beretta, a Lüger, a Smith and Wesson," etc. Mike had no intention of buying a gun. The scene was simply to draw the name of a wanted criminal from the pawnbroker—just a few seconds of questions and answers mingled with the discussion of guns.

On the air, when I entered and asked the pawnbroker—a nice little gray-haired, frightened actor—if he had any guns, there was no response. I could see he was "frozen," a term for complete panic. Seconds are important on the air. When your time is up, something else comes on the tube. I thought if I said something close to his lines it might help to relax him and restore his memory.

"It looks like you have a bin full of guns over there," I said. I walked to the bin and picked them up one at a time. "A Beretta," I said, hoping the words would restore him, "and a Lüger and a Smith and Wesson."

He hadn't moved from back of his counter, nor had he spoken. The seconds were going fast and we had to get on with the show. But I had to have that name. That was the only reason for the scene.

So, going back to him at his counter, I said, "By the way, did you ever hear of a guy by the name of Nick Riley?"

He finally spoke. "No," he said. It was the only word he'd spoken in the whole scene. If he'd said "Yes" we could have got somewhere.

"Well," I said, "it's just come to me. I think that's the name of a fellow I've been looking for."

Not very brilliant or inventive dialogue to ad-lib, I'll admit, but I was almost in panic myself. I left the pawnshop without even a "thanks" or "goodbye." And eventually I got Nick Riley, I should add.

Horace MacMahon appeared with me on "Man Against Crime" one time. He was playing the police lieutenant in this episode and we had a scene together in his office. We were on the air. He was sitting at his roll-top desk and I was on a chair behind him, leaning toward him, over his shoulder. The camera was shooting through a trap door in the wall just over his desk, so that our two heads and shoulders were included in the shot. Suddenly Horace "went up" in his lines.

I knew what he was supposed to say and tried several times to help him, mainly because time is so important on the air. But, like Brownie in *Dancing Mothers* in Des Moines, Horace resisted all my efforts to rescue him. Finally, after much pointless ad-libbing, he turned and faced me, his back to the camera, and spat: "I know guys like you! You come a dime a dozen!"

To keep from laughing at the meaningless non sequitur, I too ad-libbed for a minute, my face to the camera, and then we got back on the track.

We also had our difficulties when we went to film. TV was still new and budgets didn't allow for anything but essentials. We made each film in three days and one of those days was always outdoors, no matter what the weather, to lend realism. Any scene away from the studio is known as "location." We had no allowance for locations, so we stole them, or slipped a little something to guards or security people or whoever might be involved. In this way we managed to shoot inside the Statue of Liberty, even up into the torch; in and around Grant's Tomb; inside Palisades

Amusement Park on the New Jersey cliffs one windy, icy winter day; outside on construction-work scaffolding on the fortieth floor of an office building in the heart of New York City; etc.

One snowy, windy day we were stealing a location at what was then the world's largest outdoor picture theatre, at Bruckner Boulevard and the Hutchinson River Parkway in the Bronx. It was a quick scene, with the camera pointed toward the screen. I was in the foreground about thirty feet in front of the screen. The camera was to pick up a car about a thousand feet away to the left. It was to come down the outside aisle from the camera's left, as the camera panned it to the front of the arena, level with my position, and followed it as it rushed up to me and screeched to a stop. Then an actor would jump out and run to me, and we'd have a few words, then two "over shoulder" shots. And that was to be that.

The wind was blowing. It was snowing. It was cold. We were all set up. Our director, Ed Montagne, signaled to the assistant who was standing beside the car in the distance, and the assistant waved the actor-driver on and ducked out of sight. Nothing happened. Montagne cupped his hands and shouted to the car, "Come on!" Again, nothing happened.

The assistant, dimly seen through the wind and snow, rose from his concealed position and seemed to be talking to the actor-driver.

Eddie again cupped his hands and yelled, "Send him in!"

The assistant shouted something indistinguishable.

"Can't hear you!" shouted Eddie.

The actor stepped out of the car, cupped his hands and in a stentorian voice shouted, "I don't know how to drive!"

The assistant drove the car, with the camera going, while the actor ducked on the floor of the back seat. The car stopped at its designated place and the camera cut to another angle. The actor, who had now changed places with the assistant in the parked car, jumped out and ran up to me. We played the scene in the wind and snow and went our way.

Our society underwent a noticeable change of attitude right after World War II. I think it came about because of improved affluence that accompanied increased employment in all fields—

thanks to FDR—and the sense of security that went with it. One small manifestation was that before the war when you went into a shop or store, you were given service fit for royalty. After the war when you undertook the same venture (a tough one), the clerk—if you could find one at all—would wait on you as if he were doing you a favor.

Pride in workmanship and service was becoming negligible. Machinery was doing a lot of what had been done by hand, and demand for services exceeded skilled workers, so that personal contribution was diminished. A job was a job. With coffee breaks and holidays.

Far be it from me to begrudge workers the benefits they've achieved. I hope they get more in the future. I headed a union for twelve years and helped improve conditions and wages for actors. My point is that a bureaucratic, protected, impersonal attitude toward all work, from top to bottom, has resulted, and I think it's bad when this attitude is compared to older philosophies that called for hard work, sacrifice, hardship and a sense of obligation and responsibility, along with the other cliché success formulas. I think we've lost something, personally and collectively.

All this first impressed me one day on location when we were filming "Man Against Crime."

Because we "stole" our locations, we had to get in and out quickly to avoid arguments or possible pay-offs or security infringements or trespassing charges. And the cast rarely knew where we were going till we got there.

On this day we found ourselves in the 238th Street repair yards of the Interborough Rapid Transit New York subway, deep in the Bronx.

The scene was part of a chase. The camera was set up and I was told to leap over live rails (I didn't realize they were live until I'd leaped over a dozen of them) for about a hundred yards to a lone subway car, climb aboard and enter at one end of it.

As I completed this death-defying feat, a workman in overalls who had been sitting at the other end of the car watching all this strange behavior, said, "Actors really work, don't they?"

"Sometimes," I replied facetiously. "Don't you?"

"I haven't done a day's work in the fourteen years I've been here," he said. "I found out the first day I came here that if you walk around as if you're going somewhere, with a tool in each hand, no one questions you. I spend every day wandering around the plant with a couple of tools, visiting my friends."

Maybe the IRT man was ahead of his time when he began this procedure. But many others, in all pursuits and all ranks from top to bottom, have caught on to his disregard for his job and himself and they're emulating him. It's too bad.

We've been disillusioned by men in power—Hitler, Mussolini, Stalin, Farouk, Jimmy Walker, Lester Maddox, Harding, William Hale Thompson, Mayor Hague, Agnew, Nixon and others to whom we've given public trust. If we don't look out, we'll become accustomed to saying, "It's always gone on."

The United Nations had better do something other than debate. We must have world government, one language, one currency, one set of standards.

Groups and individuals have always opposed each other. Good opposition based on ideas and ideals is healthy and necessary, but too much of it is based on self-aggrandizement and greed. We're all seeking some kind of immortality. This is a valid urge. It implies a justification for having been given life. But the effort has to be honest and compassionate.

There used to be a code, right or wrong, which tried to embrace all of this. Now we seem to have an indefinite code, based on the old one and revolting against it. It threatens all concepts, including its own. There has to be a system, an establishment. Certainly it should be constantly challenged and altered. But without an establishment there would be no society. We're close . . .

End of sermon.

Barney Brady was properly named. He's about five foot eight, stocky, black-haired, with glistening blue eyes that light up a face which looks as if it just reached port on a freight ship from Ireland, on which there were many laughs, drinks and serious physical disagreements during the long slow voyage. Barney has a gravel-throated voice. He's from the Bronx and gallantly carries the accent. He's a delight.

Barney was the assistant property man for the filming of "Man

Against Crime." The head property man, because I liked him, shall be anonymous for the following reasons: He had been head property man for years on the road and in New York with one of our most famous actresses. In his declining years he'd found a willing and conscientious assistant in Barney, and he was tired. Each morning he'd arrive at the studio just before shooting with a brown paper bag, held perpendicularly under his arm, and proceed to a dark corner of the prop room and during the day slowly drink the contents of the brown paper bag, knowing that Barney had accumulated the necessary props and had everything under control.

One day I was strolling through the old Edison Studio, at Webster and Decatur avenues in the Bronx, where we shot "Man Against Crime." I saw Barney in an abandoned upstairs office. He was leaning back in an old-fashioned swivel chair with his feet up on a table-desk. He held a telephone receiver between his ear and shoulder and was reading aloud from a prop list, to a property rental company, necessary items for the forthcoming show. This is his description of one of the items: "Two eye-den-tick-al wall brackets. Dey gotta match, pal. An' dey gotta be te-riffic. Dey're goin' in a ten-million-dollar shit house."

The stagehands had been together for several years and they liked each other without exception, which is rare. There's frequently at least one misfit.

Barney needed a patio at his house in the Bronx, so the entire crew volunteered to go there one Sunday and lay the concrete. They would bring their wives, with potato salad, cold cuts and cake, and make a day of it.

Barney ordered ready-mixed cement to be dumped on the front lawn before the gang arrived. When they did, the girls went to the kitchen with their contributions, while the ten or so men were left standing in the living room, each with a brown paper bag under his arm. Though it was only about 9 A.M., it was suggested that they have a sip before construction began.

Somehow the jolly stagehands never got round to the business of the patio, and eventually the cement had to be removed with a jackhammer.

That's how TV films were made in those days.

Melville Burke directed "Man Against Crime" for two years

while we were "live." Edward Montagne became producer after a year and a half or so. Mel had a distinguished background, having directed numerous Broadway plays, stock companies in Denver, Skowhegan, Maine, Newport, Rhode Island, Minneapolis, Cincinnati, Louisville, and acting as managing director of the Municipal Theatre in Northampton, Massachusetts, as well as having directed pictures, radio and TV. He was a delight to work with and we played many practical jokes on each other.

Eddie Montagne both produced and directed after we went to film. He was born into the picture business and had experience in all areas of it except acting. He was, and is, a jolly fellow with a quick laugh.

We were two years "live" and three years on film. I asked Eddie if he'd be so kind as to jot down a few memories of our enterprise. His amusing account recognizes Mel as well:

"A few happy memories of 'Man Against Crime':

"Sid Lumet [Sidney Lumet, the highly successful feature picture director today], then our A.D., crooning into the phone to the cameraman (from the control room to the cameraman on the floor over walkie-talkie, short-wave mouthpiece and earphone hookups). He always crooned, encouraged and complimented as he cued the crew.

"Mel Burke, the director, flower in his buttonhole, cigar in his mouth, always the perfect gentleman. That is, until the night he received a memo from Al Foster (the advertising account executive) requesting him to cease smoking cigars while directing a show sponsored by Camel cigarettes. I've always suspected that you wrote that memo to get a rise out of Mel. If so, you succeeded because his language was livid—elegant but livid. Then, if I'm not mistaken, you nailed his cigar to a table one night.

"Remember the night the corpse walked? If you recall, Dennis Patrick was playing the murdered man. You, as Mike Barnett, were supposed to prop the corpse in a chair and pretend to talk to it so that the killer would disclose himself. The only trouble was, Dennis had forgotten and had gone to take off his make-up —result, no corpse. So you had to do a monologue. My great fear was that Dennis might walk in in the middle of the scene. Fortunately, he didn't.

"Breakdowns were common on live TV. Remember the night the microphone went dead right in the middle of the plot scene? The second mike was unlimbered and rushed across the stage. You could hear the actors' voices getting louder as the mike approached. Then a stagehand's voice yelling, 'For Christ's sake, get out of the way!'

"We were on the air fifty-two weeks a year and I remember how we would struggle to give you some time off. Even bringing Bob Preston in for five weeks as your brother Pat. Another time we created a new show called 'The Hunter,' with Barry Nelson, so you could get some rest.

"I remember one time we had a show with three girls. One, named Anne Italiano, was particularly bad and poor Mel had a terrible time with her. Anne Italiano turned out to be Anne Bancroft.

"We also gave breaks to Jack Warden, Eva Marie Saint, Nita Talbot, Jack Lemmon, Jack Albertson, just to name a few. That's when New York was full of good actors who wanted to work. If you remember, we could get people starring on Broadway for minimum.

"Remember when we started integrating film into live shows? As I recall, Mike Barnett was touring Europe, so we wanted to get some European flavor. I found stock (from film libraries of travelogues and old pictures) on different cities for which I paid fifty cents a foot because it was a scratch print, which meant there was a wide scratch down the middle. We couldn't afford any more, so we used it on the air. Things were so crude in those days, nobody noticed. Probably thought it was their set.

"When we went to film, the adventures began all over. If you recall, we shot at the old Edison Studios, built in 1904, the oldest in the United States. On that one stage, Ralph, we did one hundred and eight half-hour shows in two years!

"How can you forget Barney Brady and his adventure with the animals? If you recall, we wanted to do a picture in the Bronx Zoo. After giving us an okay, the curator changed his mind the day before we were to shoot. In desperation we called a company that imported animals for zoos and circuses. They had a couple of chimps, a tiger and a baby elephant the size of a great Dane. We built a few cages and started shooting. Barney went downtown in a truck for the animals. He knew every minute was important because we only had a little to do without the animals. The truck broke down on the Grand Concourse. Barney was stuck. But not for long. With typical Barney Brady audacity he stepped out onto the Concourse and hailed a cab! Before the driver knew what was happening, Barney had the two chimps, the tiger and the baby elephant in the cab. 'Bedford Park Studios!' he ordered, and ten minutes later we had the animals. You know, Ralph, I've told that story dozens of times and no one believes me. But you, Barney and I know it's true.

"Remember how we used to use the Botanical Garden as our back lot? What with the Bronx River and its rapids and falls and exotic foliage, we could be anyplace. I do remember, however, we were doing a picture supposedly in the Canadian wilds, but had to wait occasionally because the elevated train could be heard.

"Remember the day a Western Union messenger came to deliver a telegram and we discovered he'd been a director for Thomas Edison at this studio?

"The way we used the city was something I recall proudly. Remember we'd throw the equipment in a station wagon which the assistant cameraman would drive, the crew would get in one car driven by Frankie Mayer (unit manager), the cast in another, driven by me or you, and we'd be off. Whether it was the Battery, the Statue of Liberty, Palisades Park—anyplace—we traveled light. I look at some of the convoys they use today and I marvel at how well we operated with so little.

"Another time, we were turned down when the N. Y. Yankees decided they didn't want a murder at the stadium. You called Ed Feeley of the Giants and we arrived at the Polo Grounds to find Chesterfield ads all over the place. We managed to keep them out of the picture, but Winchell ran a story saying we had Chesterfield ads on the Camel show.

"Weather meant nothing to us. We shot in rain, snow, hail, hundred-degree weather because we couldn't afford to stop. The Palisades Park show comes to mind. It was in midwinter and I don't think the temperature ever went over fifteen degrees. You and the other actors had to rub your faces as the camera was coming up to speed so you'd be able to talk. That's when you and the stunt man were staging a fight in the roller coaster and he froze. I remember the two of you in the icy structure seventy-five feet high, trying to hang on for dear life.

"Remember the female impersonator we used on one show that we shot on location and the great debate in the restaurant at lunch time, which toilet he should use, and the panic that ensued when he went into the men's room in full make-up?"

Incidentally, when we started the show live it cost $3,800 a show. On film it eventually went up to the staggering cost of $37,000. Today a half-hour show costs from a couple of hundred to three hundred thousand a show.

On one of the vacations Eddie mentions, my wife, Alice, and I and a couple of friends, Mildred and Ed Cantelmo, booked a freight ship for Europe. Our ship, the *Ida Baake*, burned at the Brooklyn docks. We were able to book a Spanish freighter and eventually arrived in Rome with documents for an almost-private audience with Pope Pius XII, acquired by Ed Cantelmo from Cardinal Spellman.

Ed and I went to Vatican City to present our credentials. I was in awe of the centuries-old architecture and the splendor and reverence as we sat waiting in the reception hall to be interviewed. Suddenly in the still silence, from across the hall, in a deep voice, I heard, "Mike Barnett with two *t*'s."

Back of a desk sat a huge priest with a face that had roots in County Cork or Tipperary.

He was grinning widely as Ed and I approached him. "I'm from Brooklyn," he said. "I've followed you through your dangerous escapades against crime for years." He was a jolly fellow and our business was done in no time.

It was summer and the Pope was at Castel Gandolfo. We passed the Swiss guards and were ushered into a waiting room with ten other people, where we stood, facing a wall decorated in Italian motif.

I don't know about the others, but presently I felt a presence from behind us without a sound. Then he appeared. Pope Pius XII greeted each of us by name, prompted by an assistant. He chatted with the Cantelmos and us in English. He knew our interests and occupations.

Then he moved on down the line, chatting in German, Chinese and Italian.

Finally he stood in front of the whole assemblage, raised his arms and called for a blessing on all of us.

I had, and still have, the feeling that that's probably as close as I'll ever come.

And I'm not a Catholic.

At the conclusion of the five-year stint on "Man Against Crime" I went on the road with *Oh, Men! Oh, Women!*, which ended in Chicago. *Fearful Decision,* a TV production on the "United States Steel Hour" the previous season, had been so successful that Armina Marshall of the Theatre Guild, who produced the show, telephoned me there to ask about repeating it. We did and the reception was as enthusiastic as for the original.

Then I came to Hollywood to do a TV show. When it finished another followed immediately. I was about to return to New York after that when a call came to meet some agents and Abe Lastfogel (head of the office) at the William Morris Agency. There was another TV offer, to be done a few days later.

I said it was fine with me if the schedule was such that I could be back in New York by December 5 to emcee the "Shannooka Festival" at Madison Square Garden, to which I was committed.

There was a pause as the four or five of us stood in the Morris office hallway.

Then Abe Lastfogel said, "*What* are you going to emcee?"

"The 'Shannooka Festival,'" I replied.

After everyone, except me, recovered from overwhelming laughter, Abe said, "You'd better learn how to say it if you're going to emcee it."

Emceeing the Chanukah Festival at Madison Square Garden for four consecutive years was one of the most moving of all my experiences. Admission was by the purchase of Bonds for Israel, and Madison Square Garden was sold out and people were banging at the doors each year. Over the four years I introduced Golda Meir, Abba Eban, "the General" and many others. And always present and participating were Isaac Stern, Richard Tucker, Robert Merrill and other greats. It was always a long evening that went too quickly, with ethnic dances, spectacular panoramic pantomimes, orchestral music with what seemed like hundreds of instruments, virtuoso solos and, of course, stirring and emotional addresses by the guest speakers. I'm sure everyone left Madison Square Garden, as I did, with a large lump in the throat.

Through this period I appeared on both sides of "What's My Line?" at various times with Arlene Francis, Dorothy Kilgallen, Bennett Cerf and John Daly. And I was on the panel of "To Tell The Truth" for a year with Kitty Carlisle, Polly Bergen, Bud Collyer and various guests.

I did four other TV series—"The Eleventh Hour" in the 1963–64 season, "The Survivors" in 1969, "The Most Deadly Game" in 1970 and "Hunter" in 1976.

A series is great if it goes. But it's hard work. It requires all the discipline one has acquired, and all the knowledge. The procedure is quite different from making a feature picture. There is so much money and so many days to make a TV episode. The same might be said of a feature, but the money and the number of days are quite different. The average half-hour TV film is made in three days, the average hour TV film is made in seven or eight days (sometimes less) and the average two-hour film for TV, three five-day weeks. A feature picture can have from six or eight weeks to six or eight months, with a correspondingly adequate budget.

The luxury of many "takes" in TV is not allowed, so one learns to "spoil" a take so it can't be used if it isn't going right. The actor is always aware that he's the one on the box. The viewer doesn't know, or care, about difficulties on the set. The actor must always be at his best on the first take because in many cases—if someone doesn't fall down in the scene—the first take will be printed and "coverage" (close-ups, two-shots, over-shoulder shots) will be relied upon. But no one knows what the cutter will select.

So the challenge is always there. The actor must come to the studio completely prepared for the day's work, with everything thoroughly thought out and letter-perfect. Of course accidents happen—unfamiliar technical terms in the dialogue, a last-minute dialogue change, a complicated "piece of business." These and other distractions can "throw" an actor. In *Flight 402* I had a line about some kind of "infarction" that became a stumbling block. It took about eight takes to get it, much to the amusement of all the "passengers" on the plane each time I "blew." But I must say I don't blow often.

While we were making an episode of "The Eleventh Hour," President Kennedy was killed and we got the news on the set. We were all shocked, as everyone else was. After a while the producer asked me what I thought we should do—go on or go home. I said something about the old cliché "the show must go on" and I spoke with Ann Harding, our guest star that week, and Jack Ging, my co-star, and they agreed. We tried, but we couldn't get through a scene. Everyone was in a daze. So we went home.

One morning when I came on the set of "The Survivors," there was a group of front-office and company officials in a glum-faced huddle. I asked what the problem was and they said that at about our halfway mark in the thirteen-week round of the series the entire budget for Lana Turner's wardrobe had been used up. They were trying to determine who should go to Lana's dressing room and tell her. My stated reaction to them was that they had nothing to fear from Lana—she'd just say, "That's all right. I'll just go home and when you get some more money, let me know." And that's almost word for word what did happen. By the way, they got some more money. But I guess that was one of the most expensive and unfortunate series in so many ways, including too much story and continual rewrites.

The less said about "The Most Deadly Game" the better. Its concept was unusual and well written by Mort Fine and David Friedkin, who did "I Spy" so successfully. We sold it to the network with a twenty-minute "presentation" rather than the usual pilot. We had excellent talent in every department. Aaron Spelling was the executive producer and Joan Harrison, who produced the Alfred Hitchcock show, alternated with David and Mort as producers, and David and Mort wrote most of the shows and acted as story editors.

The regular cast was Inger Stevens, George Maharis and me (you'll notice I include myself as "excellent talent"). But before we started shooting, Inger's tragic death cast a pall over the whole undertaking from which we never recovered. Yvette Mi-

mieux replaced Inger and did an excellent job, but we just never got over the spell cast by the circumstances of Inger's death (suicide). It's hard to understand with all that talent, but that's my estimate of what happened. We were just jinxed into a state of shock from which we never recovered.

"Hunter" was at best a familiar pattern which had a good look at "I Spy." It went wrong, I'm told, by network insistence that the audience be let in on the identification of the antagonist and his maneuvers before the members of the cast. The idea and the scripts on which the series was sold were just the opposite, containing an element of surprise to the audience. This meant rewriting scripts, which became emasculated and rather confused. Of course it's always easy to make excuses for failure. On the other hand, some shows with less than mediocre appeal have stayed on the air for years. Anyone who can predict or create with a sense of absolute certainty of acceptance in any of the media has yet to be born.

Two of the most active and gifted directors of live television in TV's heyday were George Schaefer (remembered mostly for "Hallmark Hall of Fame") and Sidney Lumet, now a highly successful picture director. Here is George Schaefer's assessment of that heyday:

"There were about ten golden years between the time television had developed a large enough audience to afford expensive, original productions and the time tape and film became the order of the day, when live, dramatic programming was in its prime.

"To me, this form was most exciting and creative and unique. Programs would run ninety minutes or, very rarely, two hours. They would be cast and rehearsed just like a Broadway stage production. At the end of an intensive rehearsal period, which usually was two to three weeks, the company would move into a studio and spend from three to five days in sets and costumes rehearsing with multiple cameras, usually four or five. This would lead up to the single broadcast performance, in which all the elements of performance and technical expertise would blend.

"There are many stories of disasters and mistakes along the way, but when it all came together properly the electric excitement of that opening night performance taking place on your home screen at the very second it was being given in a studio created the majority of television's early great memories. I should add that from the viewpoint of the director and producer one great advantage of the live days was that with the pressure of getting the show together against incredible odds, there was neither time nor necessity for the 'helpful' participation of the sponsor or the network or the agency. The program was in the hands of the actors, the technicians and the director, and it went out just that way to the audience."

And here are the observations of Sidney Lumet, who left a brilliant mark on that era:

"To me, the most moving and memorable thing about the live TV days was the amount of talent it provided: writers, directors, actors, technicians. And the thought that keeps persisting most for me was not that we were a particularly talented group, but that this amount of talent and creativity obviously exists all the time and only needs an opportunity to emerge. I've never felt more fortunate, even at the most despairing moments in work, that I was at the right age at the right time, which is sheer historic luck. I know that if a new technical development opened up today, an equal amount of creative American energy would emerge as it did in our day. What came out of New York in those days is still coming out in painting and ballet. We have more than six full-time companies dancing right now on Broadway. Certainly the fantastic technical advances in tape recording, the total simplification that it now means, have created a continual outlet for young people. So when people talk about the Golden Age of live television in New York, it seems to me they should be talking about the Golden Age of opportunity."

Actors have always sought the company of actors. There were three actors' clubs in New York—the Lambs, the Players, and the Friars. I belonged to and served a term each on the board of directors of the Lambs and Players.

The days are gone now when New York was the national center of theatre activity and actors needed and enjoyed each other's companionship between engagements.

The Lambs no longer exists.

The Friars' members are mostly variety actors, who are active and affluent today with Las Vegas, TV and nightclubs, and they are still thriving.

There used to be a saying that the Lambs are actors trying to be gentlemen, the Players are gentlemen trying to be actors and the Friars are trying to be either or both.

Understandably, the Friars don't especially like this saying, but they've remained the healthiest.

I still belong to the Players and I'm a member of the Dutch Treat Club, which is composed of writers, editors, publishers and professional people.

It's been the custom of the Players Club to do all-star revivals for one performance now and then.

I had been chosen to play the Porter in a TV production of a Players all-star revival of *Macbeth* on NBC.

You will recall that the Porter is awakened from a drunken slumber in the middle of the night to admit Macduff through the gate.

Walter Abel played Macduff.

I came mumbling and grumbling to the gate with a lighted torch held head-high. The torch was a small length of broomstick, on the upper end of which was a wide-mouthed coffee can painted black and containing gauze saturated with flammable fluid that had been ignited.

During my ramblings about the aftermath of drink, I unbolted the gate and Walter passed me as he and his entourage entered. I closed the gate and turned to him. He was beating the sides of his head as our dialogue continued, which he'd never done at rehearsals.

Afterward I said to him, "Walter, what the hell were you doing, beating your head after I let you through the gate?"

"You set my wig on fire with your torch as I passed you," he said. "I was beating out the fire."

While we're on the subject of all-star revivals, when Howard Lindsay was president of the Players he once told me the following story about a revival of an Oscar Wilde play:

At the opening of one of the acts the curtain went up on a stage without actors. There was an entry from a hallway upstage left (right to the audience). Two curtained floor-to-ceiling windows comprised the back wall and a fireplace at a raked angle occupied most of the upstage right wall (left to the audience) with one "flat" below it. There was a large chair left center, a straight chair against the back wall between the windows and another straight chair against the wall downstage right.

As the curtain rose, the stage cat (there's one in residence in almost all backstages) walked across the warm footlight trough on this rather chilly night (most backstages aren't warm on chilly nights until the warmth from the audience wafts toward the stage and combines with the heat from the footlights). The cat, oblivious of the audience, was looking for a warm place to stretch out. And it found one. The fire in a "practical" fireplace on the stage consists of chunks of translucent glass the size of pieces of coal, covered with crinkled, crumpled or torn magenta "mediums" from the border or footlights, with flickering clear bulbs buried at the bottom of the coal basket and a small fan out of sight to give the whole thing life.

The cat found the warm bed created by the heat from the light bulbs and reclined on its stomach facing the audience.

Naturally the audience laughed. But the laugh came just as Dennis King entered in full Edwardian attire: tight trousers with straps under his insteps, coat with tails, double-breasted waistcoat, ruffled shirt cuffs, stock tie, curled hair, holding his top hat upside down just to the right of his stomach.

There was no one else onstage as he took his bewildered position, stage right near the fireplace, facing the audience—and unaware of the cat. The confusion on his face caused the audience to laugh louder. Dennis began to examine his attire, particularly the area between his crotch and his waist.

The audience laughed louder as Howard made his entrance in the same Edwardian garb, and the cat was now asleep. Howard was thrown off balance by the laughter as he took his position alongside Dennis, both of them facing the audience without a word and both clutching their upside-down top hats.

Howard glanced at the area just described on Dennis and Dennis simultaneously inspected the same area on Howard as the audience laughed louder. Then the two Edwardians bent slightly forward and thoroughly inspected themselves as the audience went into convulsions while the very portly and impeccable Francis L. Sullivan entered in the same wardrobe and a chest-high cane.

The audience was now in an uproar. The cat was still asleep and not a word had been spoken. But none of this fazed Sullivan, who confidently proceeded to the large chair downstage left and sat, scanning his two friends, still without a word. The audience was now hysterical.

As Sullivan sat, his legs spread a bit and his trousers were open from the seat upon which he sat, halfway up his considerable stomach to his considerable waist.

They had to pull down the curtain and start over again, without the cat.

It's difficult to explain, or even articulate, the attraction the theatre has for actors. They've been called "exhibitionists," "children," "eccentrics," "drunks," "psychopaths" and many other labels. There's evidence, too, that many such characteristics were validly applicable to quite a few actors before, and for some years after, the beginning of this century. Now, however, the actor is generally accepted as a respectable member of society, but this is a fairly recent status. It has been only within the last twenty to thirty years that actors have abandoned the notion that because they appear before a public of all political persuasions, they should not make public their own personal political preferences and philosophies for fear of alienating themselves from theatre-goers of opposing concepts. And they're no longer social outcasts. Perhaps some may warrant one or more of the earlier descriptions, but to no greater extent than followers of other pursuits, even including the clergy, for that matter.

I can only say from my own observation and experience that wherever the personal professional attraction to the theatre comes from, there is none deeper or more dedicated. The disappointments and sacrifices are beyond those of making the effort to climb to a satisfactory career in any other field. And I have to interpolate here that no reputable actor, at any point in his career, will claim satisfaction. The striving for more knowledge and experience and variety and perfection persists. In the meantime, that rapport with the audience, even on film—when one learns it's there and how to exercise it—is like food and drink and a breath of fresh air in the command it gives the actor over the control of the author's emotional and intellectual communication with the audience.

The phrase "the show must go on" has been ridiculed and denigrated, but the fact that it's still used at all in any connotation is proof of its validity. The actor has an obligation to the public, the rest of the cast, the author and the producer not only to be there, and on time, but to do his best at all times. Particularly if his name draws a following, but also at any professional level. Most of the time whatever physical or emotional discord that exists before a performance or rehearsal, or day's work in a studio, will have disappeared when the work is done. I'm not a woman, so I can't make a flat statement on this. But any actor will agree with me.

There is a growing tendency that I deplore in the theatre for actors to telephone the stage manager and say, "I have a headache (or whatever). Please put my understudy on tonight." And this is not only from women, who, in the chorus, have a day a month at their disposal anyway. Some people are so temperamentally constituted that the discipline of repeated performances in a long-run stage play becomes irksome. Discipline, I believe, is one of the cardinal demands of the profession of acting. Absolute discipline, with particular reference to the aforementioned obligations as well as a special obligation to oneself. It's well to believe that the audience is there to see *you*. *At your best*.

Actors are generally thought to be languishing in cars, boats, farms, money, servants and luxury. Some are, but comparatively few. And most actors don't work steadily. A recent study showed the mean number of weeks worked in the theatre to be eight. There are about eighteen thousand members of Actors Equity Association and over twenty thousand members of the Screen Actors Guild. In the late twenties and early thirties there were about three hundred theatre productions a year, and most failures went on the road for a number of weeks. Now there are about forty productions a year and virtually no road. In the early thirties there were about six hundred Hollywood pictures a year. Now there are about two hundred.

Competition is unequaled in any other endeavor. Many people cling to a hopeless acting career. Luck plays a big part. But so do ability, experience, discipline, obligation, personality and the capacity and aggressiveness to stick it out till luck comes along.

No other pursuit I know has the hazards, the hardships and the heartaches of the acting profession. But at the same time, no other pursuit contains the same sense of achievement and gratification with respect to personal contact with people: the audience.

And you always hope and try to improve.

Many actors, I'm positive, pursue their careers at least partially as a means of defying the traditional patterns of conformity. Acting allows the actor to communicate with the masses and to influence or at least provoke them. True, actors only speak the author's words, but it is they who stand and articulate them. And, more often than not, the actor is remembered more vividly than the author.

It would be impossible to communicate the depth of devotion that most actors give to their profession. Of course there are some who work at it for money; some who fall into it by the accident of a good voice or photogenic features, or both; and some who cling to it into unemployable circumstances. And some who never should have pursued it but won't recognize their lack of qualification.

But those who elected to become actors and had the stamina and good fortune to start building a background leading to versatility, style and technique during the halcyon days of the theatre, before radio and talking pictures and TV, those who would do any odd jobs that would enable them to keep contact with theatrical agencies and producers, and who suffered long periods of unemployment, frayed clothes and meager or missed meals but who were always optimistic in their self-assurance and ready when opportunity arose, and who climbed from insignificance to recognition through dedication, hard work and heartache—those are the actors whose careers produce a kind of satisfaction that is nearly complete.

Many actors can't stand to look at themselves on the screen

because they see what they should or shouldn't have done. And most would like another chance at the same performance. Those actors are a breed apart, always restless, because of the goal of perfection they've set for themselves, and often feeling they've been discarded during long periods of unemployment.

Acting, it seems to me, is an urge for justification, a fulfillment of ego by communication. Its greatest achievement is its perpetuation in the memories of the audience, and its finest postmortem is something like "Kilroy was here!"

Every actor craves recognition, and most would like immortality.

Unfortunately, the immortals are becoming fewer, largely because of a lack of facilities for training—the repertoire companies, the stock companies, the tab shows, the tent shows, the road companies, vaudeville, burlesque.

Dramatic schools don't supply adequate training. No one can be taught to act. An aspiring actor with talent can be guided and developed within his own capacities but he can't be taught to act. Acting is a very personalized effort. If it weren't, one actor would be like another and all actors would receive the same salary.

Much the same applies to actors' labs and showcases. This is subjective, introspective behavior in most cases, for their benefit rather than the audience's. Incidentally, the first sign of an amateur or neophyte is the folding of arms, more by young women than men, the moment they get a cue to speak. And the second is ending sentences in incomprehensible whispers.

The Actors Studio is often chided for the habit of some of its members of mumbling and disregarding the author's lines and instructions. It's a valid criticism, as I discovered when I worked with one of them in the original "Defenders," on which the series was based.

Herbert Brodkin produced the original "Defenders" live in New York with five cameras. He also produced the series. The cast of the original production included William Shatner, Steve McQueen and Martin Balsam, among others, and it was directed by Robert Mulligan.

At the camera rehearsal, on the day of the live shooting, I had a scene with one of these "method" actors. He was not in any of the positions we had rehearsed for the past ten days or so, and I couldn't hear him. When he'd stop speaking I'd guess that was my cue and speak my lines. There were just the two of us in the scene and we stumbled through.

Afterward, he left for a following scene on another camera in which I was not involved. I was left alone, in limbo for the moment. The cameraman who had just shot the two of us, and who was also "at liberty," beckoned me to join him back of his camera.

"Do you know what an Actors Studio actor reminds me of?" he asked.

"What?" I inquired.

"A man in a dark suit, standing on a busy corner in a pouring rain, peeing in his pants," he said. "It's such a nice warm comfortable feeling, and nobody else knows what's going on."

As a generalization, Actors Studio actors seem to me to have an inarticulate delivery and an introspective, subjective approach to acting.

Naturally there are a few exceptions, but I believe *they* would have been distinguished without or in spite of the Actors Studio.

Herbert Brodkin was a daring innovator. He's still at it, having just produced "Holocaust," and before that "The Missiles of October," and many memorable productions earlier. He is one of the most tasteful producers, demanding and giving perfection. Here's his account of early TV days:

"What can I tell you about early live TV that you don't already know?

"It was a great time to be involved in TV, to learn, to experiment and to once in a while be successful.

"My memories revolve around shows like 'The Defenders,' originally done on 'Studio One' as a two-hour show with you playing the lead and Steve McQueen doing a relatively small part, and later on of course your refusal of the lead in the series of the same name (played by E. G. Marshall). Other dramas such as 'Child of Our Time' and 'Judgment at Nuremberg,' both directed by George Roy Hill, stand out. Live television in the fifties was well on its way to developing into a very special dramatic form combining both film and legitimate stage technique, and adding a few things of its own. It would have been marvelous to watch its unfolding into a brave and exciting new medium. It will never happen now. Murder by film and tape."

On another trip to Hollywood for TV Alice was with me. We stayed at the Beverly Wilshire Hotel, where Alice made a luncheon date with an old friend of ours for one of my working days.

The old friend was Annie Isaacs, one of the two sisters of Broadway producers Edgar and Arch Selwyn.

Annie was in her eighties, short, stout and with the typical Selwyn dancing eyes. Her hair was dyed brown, she was alert, to the point and inquisitive, like all the Selwyns.

Alice met her in front of the hotel. She drove herself, sitting on a cushion so she could see the road, in an ancient, glistening, wire-wheeled sedan.

After luncheon the chatting slowed down and then paused for a moment. From that pause, apropos of nothing that had been under discussion, Annie said, "How's Ralph in bed?"

Alice was stunned into temporary confusion. Then, not wanting to be trapped into replying in any intimate detail to such a brazen question, and being brilliantly noncommittal, she said, "Oh—average, I guess."

"I thought so!" said Annie. "All those actors are lazy."

With Harry S Truman on stage at the Hudson Theatre after a perform-ance of *Sunrise at Campobello* (*Joseph Abeles Studio*)

With Eleanor Roosevelt (*Alfred Eisenstaedt*, Life *magazine*, © *1957 Time Inc.*)

As FDR in *Sunrise at Campobello*, 1958 (*Alfred Eisenstaedt, Life magazine,* © *1957 Time Inc.*)

Also from *Sunrise* with Mary Fickett and James Bonnet, 1958 (*Joseph Abeles Studio*)

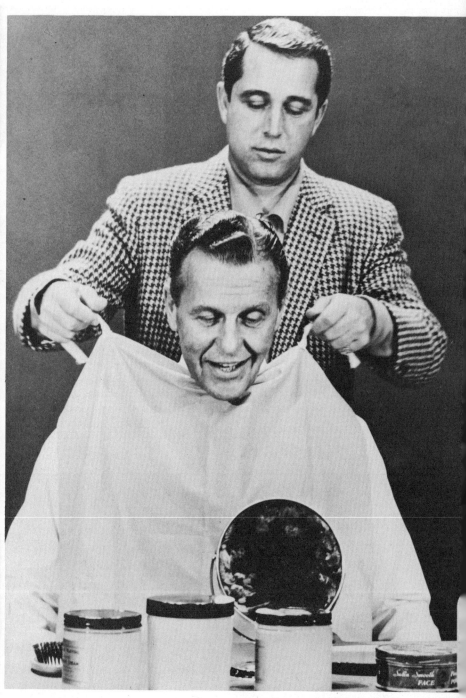

Preparing for a bit of FDR on Perry Como's TV show, 1959

UN radio, 1958 (*Copyright Lawrence Fried*)

With my wife, Alice, in Atlanta during the closing week of *Sunrise* on the road (*Photo by Floyd Jillson*)

With President John F. Kennedy at the White House correspondents and photographers greeting in Washington, D.C. His first public appearance after his election

With Harry Morgan and Jack Webb on the set of "Dragnet" (*Jack Webb Productions*)

From *Rosemary's Baby* (*Copyright © 1968 Paramount Pictures Corporation*)

With James Cagney and the Frank McHughs at the American Film Institute festivities the night Jim was honored

With Rock Hudson in NBC's novel for television, "Wheels," 1978 (© *1978 Universal City Studios, Inc., All rights reserved*)

PART X

In the middle of the run of *Detective Story*, I was nominated for the presidency of Actors Equity Association on an independent ticket and won the election without a campaign. It was the first of four three-year terms, from 1952 to 1964. I had been vice-president for two years before that.

These were troublesome times for the theatre, as they were for so many segments of our society.

Crime was rampant (more than usual).

The Kefauver Senate hearings had their sensational day and accomplished little.

McCarthy went on a rampage and accomplished nothing, except to ruin careers, individuals and himself.

Communist baiting became an epidemic, and Senator McClellan took up where Kefauver left off with more crime investigations, which actually did slap a curb on and/or put away some offenders—among them, construction and truck-operating groups and some just plain gangsters.

Much of this had an effect on the theatre. In some cases it was impossible to curtail some unscrupulous and/or nearsighted and/or politically ambitious union leaders who inflicted unreasonable conditions on various areas of the theatre which created exploding economics. This unquestionably reduced the number of plays produced, which resulted in high unemployment, among other injuries.

The performer unions were wracked by the Communist issue, spurred by McCarthy and two ex-FBI men who published a periodical called *Red Channels* that named and accused suspected

Commmunists. They set themselves up for clearance for those who felt inclined to appeal to them. Advertising agencies, sponsors and radio and TV networks had clearance apparatuses in their casting procedures. Actors turned against actors. It was a vicious time.

All the performer unions drew up anti-Communist resolutions. Several set themselves up as judge and jury in consideration of association with groups, or "suspect" individuals (victims of hearsay, gossip and name-calling). Some put themselves in a position to suspend or expel under hysterical action, threatening livelihood.

I was determined that Equity would produce a resolution tempered with intelligence, rationale and calm. We formed a five-man committee to produce such a resolution. And we did. The gist of it was that only an admitted or proven Communist member (proven by legal procedure apart from Equity) could be examined.

No one was ever invited to appear.

I sent copies of the resolution for comment to Attorney General Brownell, Cardinal Spellman and Bernard Baruch. I did not hear from the attorney general. Cardinal Spellman sent a letter of approval and Mr. Baruch invited me to meet him at 7 A.M. at his home overlooking Long Island Sound in Oyster Bay.

I had to get myself together at 5 A.M., which didn't bother me, in anticipation of meeting Baruch, the appointee of several Presidents, as well as one of the most respected men in the country, a man whose father performed the first appendectomy in the United States, in 1888.

I was really set up as I drove through Queens County to Northern Boulevard and out to Oyster Bay.

At 7 A.M. I was met by the butler at the entrance to the sprawling, spacious old house and led into the generous living room, where the familiar gentleman sat reading the morning paper.

He saw me and rose to his six feet four or five, saying, "Hello, Bellamy. Sit down." He motioned to a large overstuffed chair and then sat himself.

I started some pleasantry as he fidgeted with something in his upper vest pocket. He looked at me and said, "Wait a minute, till I get on the air," and he adjusted his hearing aid.

He was charming and hospitable and we discussed the ugly times. Finally he said that communism was a definite threat to us and since no one else seemed to be doing much about it, he had to go along with McCarthy. His words were, as nearly as I can recall, "McCarthy's doing the job for me."

I must say I was shocked.

He had no comment on our resolution. But in the light of his sentiments, his estimate was implicit.

I have to add that I still respect and admire "Barney" Baruch for his service to the country and his "park bench" philosophies and his non-partisan advice to several Presidents. He was a grand and wise old man who, I would say, made one mistake.

Live TV was distinguishing itself during the fifties and I was lucky enough to become a part of one of its best scripts, the aforementioned *Fearful Decision*. It was the story of a boy kidnapped for ransom, whose father goes on the air with a huge pile of money on the table before him and says to the kidnapper, on camera, out over the air, "This is everything I own in the world, all the cash from my bank, the cash from my investments, the money from the mortages on my house and everything in it, and my car. But you're not going to get one cent of it. I'm going to spend it to find you. And I will."

And the boy is returned. It was a powerful script, produced by the Theatre Guild for United States Steel. I got an Emmy award nomination.

About the same time, I did a guest spot with Sid Caesar and Imogene Coca and Carl Reiner, who was acting in the show as well as writing for it. It was about the talkative milkman who delivers the milk early in the morning, waking everybody up, and they come to the kitchen door rubbing their sleepy eyes. He comes into the kitchen and talks—and talks—and won't go. It was a funny sketch.

Pay TV was in the experimental stages, and I got interested because of the alarming unemployment in Equity. I took up the cudgel. I've been in the battle since its inception, not only because I felt it would help relieve Equity's unemployment problem but also because of my firm belief that it is a coming adjunct to the theatre and commercial TV. And I still have that firm belief.

Agents had become more prevalent with radio and TV. Most of that activity was in New York (later moving to Hollywood). There were not only new agencies but Hollywood agents had branch offices in New York to accommodate their picture clients who were now invading both radio and TV in droves.

My agents in Hollywood were Berg and Allenberg, who later merged with William Morris, but at that time they had no New York office. So for New York work I became a client of William McCaffrey, the old-timer who, you'll remember, began as a vaudeville booker for the B. F. Keith circuit—which he related in his letter—but who was then, and still is, one of the most distinguished and exclusive agents. Among his present clients is Art Carney.

Bill's general factotum, office manager, bookkeeper and excitingly attractive executive vice-president in charge of everything was Alice Murphy, whom I married thirty years ago. We've had nothing but fun and a good life together, and each year is better than the last. She's intelligent, understanding, has a good sense of humor and she's my best friend and companion. And still as exciting as ever. We both like the same things. We've traveled a lot around the world on freight ships and ocean liners and planes. And she's the best of all cooks. What a lucky man am I!

Alice lived at the Osborne Apartments at Seventh Avenue and Fifty-seventh Street when we were married. It was the second-oldest luxury apartment building in the city, built in 1885. The Dakota at Seventy-second Street and Central Park West was older, built in 1881.

We took a larger apartment and lived there for several years.

Two of our closest friends still live there, Martha and Wladimir Selinsky. He's a composer and conductor. He was a child prodigy, conducting symphony orchestras in Europe at age seven. He's now active in TV and picture work.

One Halloween I prepared for visits from trick-or-treaters with various bits of candy, apples, gum, etc. I really get a kick out of kids at Halloween. Their behavior is so mild and amusing compared to my earlier Halloweens, which called for removing people's gates and hanging them on lampposts, smearing windows with soap and throwing pebbles at windows.

We were apparently on a blacklist this Halloween. No one showed up.

Alice called Martha and Vladi to tell them the joke was on me. We'd been boycotted.

Then, a half hour or so later, about eleven o'clock, the doorbell rang and Alice ran up the marble stairway that led to the entrance to our sunken apartment.

She opened the door and there stood two frightening apparitions that could have walked right out of Charles Dickens' slums. They were demanding trick-or-treat.

After the shock we beheld Vladi in a coat and dress of Martha's—lipstick, hat, shoes, *et al.*—and Martha in Vladi's suit, shirt, hat, shoes, *et al.*, with a moustache.

They did the trick and we all had a treat.

The pursuit and machinery and personalities of politics are at once awesome, confusing and irritating, and sometimes inspiring, humorous and mysterious—and, with the late Watergate revelations, contemptuous.

When I was president of Actors Equity Association I had some contact with the system in Washington in pursuit of an arrangement for a more equitable interchange of alien (principally British) actors, the result of a long-standing but unacknowledged feud between British and American Equity associations. It was caused by an unequal number of British actors invading our Broadway theatre and in many cases undercutting American Equity's minimum salaries. To some degree this condition still persists.

Granted, each country's best actors, musicians, singers and artists in all fields should have the freedom to go to all countries and be encouraged to make themselves available to the greatest exposure. But all performing unions have difficulty with medium- or lower-income foreigners who will work for less and thus deprive their members of work and income.

There is not, and probably will not be, any kind of quota arrangement. Each case will probably continue to be determined on its merit, under certain specifics—such as the professional standing of stars or featured players, locale of the play, type of company with respect to how long it's been together (such as the "Old Vic"), content of the play or plays. These specifics are a part of the rules resulting from experience on both sides of the Atlantic.

After years of mild friction and lack of any kind of formula for reciprocity, I think that's the way it should stand, with due consideration and respect on both sides of the Atlantic.

British Equity has an agreement with its Immigration Department to present it with recommendations in each instance, and the recommendations become the department's findings. We had that arrangement for a while, but it became too bureaucratic and now American Equity makes its own decisions. Incidentally, at one of the meetings with the director of our Immigration Department, I was told that actors were not the only complainants. He said wrestlers were even more vociferous in their protests, demanding that the department keep aliens out entirely.

In the early sixties the theatre was in particular distress and Equity's unemployment situation was desperate.

Two things happened.

Equity had a request for concessions for the operation of an experimental theatre in downtown New York City. Its aim would be to encourage new playwrights, actors and directors.

Equity granted salary minimum concessions on a conditional basis, principally that an actor could leave, without notice, if he were offered a job on the standard contract.

A couple of weeks later we heard from another prospective "Off-Broadway" producer, and we granted him similar concessions.

Others appeared before the Equity Council and they hired a lawyer. Some were now doing classics and revivals. As their number grew we were forced to negotiate with them. And we now have a well-entrenched Off-Broadway theatre.

Actually, Off-Broadway now adheres more to its original purpose than it did shortly after its innovation. Many well-known actors, directors and playwrights, who were unknown previously, have come from Off-Broadway. In some respects, it serves as the old tent and rep and stock companies did.

Another innovation was Equity Library Theatre, which was the inspiration of Broadway producer John Golden, who proposed it and financed the first effort when employment was at an all-time low. It had acting companies appearing at public libraries, at minimum salaries, with the subsequent financing to be underwritten by a loan from Equity, which has finally become an annual grant. It has been a boon to older actors and a showcase for young actors, many of whom have been discovered and are now familiar names. Equity still grants an annual "loan."

Also, while president of Equity I had contact with the House Ways and Means Committee and Chairman Wilbur Mills in an effort to gain the right for actors to spread their taxable income over a period of years, averaging good years with bad. This effort was finally brought to fruition after eleven years and now includes everyone, not just actors. It's the tax-averaging device which allows for a five-year spread.

The day in February 1963 after I made my last appearance before the committee, I bought the evening papers and boarded the plane at Dulles International Airport en route to California. When I opened the paper my picture was on the front page accompanying the story of the adoption of the tax-averaging plan. It was a feature story in every paper in the country and on TV. It was a nice warm feeling after eleven years. That and pensions were the two issues that gave me the most satisfaction in my four-term twelve years as president of Equity.

During one of my Equity missions to Washington I visited a Senate session. As I was seated in the front row of the gallery, big, imposing Senator Alben Barkley—not yet the "Veep"—was standing on the Democratic side of the aisle, gold-rimmed glasses halfway down his nose, reading a prepared speech. After a couple of minutes he was interrupted by Senator Robert Taft on the Republican side of the aisle.

Senator Taft rose, standing on one foot, the knee of his other leg bent and resting on the bench at his desk, and said, "Will the senator yield for a question?"

Barkley looked over his glasses across the aisle, right into Taft's eye, and said, "I would if I thought the senator would understand the answer!" And he continued with his speech, all to the amusement of the entire Senate, including Taft.

At another visit to the Senate, during another one of my Washington missions, they were in a wrangle of some kind and Senator Lyndon Johnson, then the majority leader, looked across the aisle to Senator Everett Dirksen, the minority leader, and signaled with a nod of his head to meet him at the rear of the Senate floor. There Johnson put his arm around Dirksen's shoulder, as they stood with their backs to the chamber, whispering. In a minute they returned to their seats. Senator Dirksen asked for the floor and offered a proposal that was a compromise on the problem before them, and it was resolved.

Probably the most forceful President the country has seen was FDR. He appeared at a time of social and economic chaos and he made daring moves to recover. The crises he inherited and the public attitudes toward him and his decisions were reminiscent of those of the presidencies of Washington and Lincoln, each of whom faced the same personal and philosophic division of acceptance.

FDR had the advantage, though, because of four terms and the microphone, which certainly had an interconnection. The fireside talks were reassuring and informative to the majority of us, in the midst of confusion. He was an inspiration to that majority, and ahead of his time philosophically. Of course, I'm prejudiced.

President Eisenhower was an engaging man personally. He was completely honest, had a good sense of humor, and he fairly exuded the discipline of his military background. I met him three times. First at the Lambs Club, at a dinner in his honor when he resigned his membership in the club because of his election to the presidency. In his opening remarks he said, "I hope you'll always call me Ike."

He was charming and entertaining. He liked people and he was a good listener. He had the gift of making you feel what you had to say was the most important subject of the moment.

The second time I met him was at a Gridiron dinner that I attended with Ed Murrow the night after my wife and I appeared on "Person to Person" with Ed in New York.

Before that broadcast, Ed and I were chatting while testing

the voice and picture levels between our apartment, where my wife and I were being interviewed by "remote," and the studio, where Ed was broadcasting. He said his wife had forgotten to pack a white tie for his trip to the Gridiron dinner the following night and he wasn't going home to his farm in Dutchess County after the broadcast. He asked me if I'd bring along a tie for him. I did, and we were a couple of Beau Brummells at the dinner.

Ike was both amused and amusing at the dinner and had time to chat personally with many of us, with friendly and interested ease, before it. He may not go down as one of the greatest Presidents, but I believe he was characteristically American in that he had all the traditional American virtues. He was Midwestern, self-disciplined, forthright and humble.

The third time I met him was at one of his stag dinners at the White House. There were eleven of us, including the President, as I remember. I'm sure, though she denies it, that that invitation, as well as the one to the Gridiron show, came about through Ann Whitman, Eisenhower's secretary and an old friend of my wife's and mine.

I attended this one with Ed Murrow, too. But this time he brought his own tie. The ten guests represented varied pursuits and the conversation could have been covered by a newspaper index.

There was a pocketknife at each place. The President explained that he wanted a little memento for each of us and that he liked knives. He'd made the selection himself. I still have my knife and my place card and a commemorative coin that was struck later, all preserved in an envelope. Corny, perhaps, but a tangible reminder of a pleasant evening.

Winging back to New York in the small morning hours, I told Ed Murrow that I thought the evening was a memorable one and that Ike was concerned and dedicated and doing his best.

"And the most naïve man who ever sat in the White House," Ed added.

PART XI

In the early 1930s it was considered wise publicity for Hollywood people to make "personal appearances" in vaudeville theatres. There was a whole new roster of actors for the screen, recruited from the stage—actors who could speak lines and create and sustain performances without a director dictating every move, mood and reaction through a megaphone. It seemed necessary to acquaint the public, personally, with this new invasion of actors.

My agent, Sam Jaffe (not the actor, but of the same name), advised me to go on such a tour. I told him there was nothing I could do in such an appearance. I couldn't sing or dance, and my one experience in vaudeville with a sketch had been disastrous. Jaffe said not to worry, he had a writer friend, Herman Mankiewicz, whom he'd ask to produce some suitable material.

I never had the honor of meeting Mr. Mankiewicz, whom I knew by reputation to be an astute, erudite, brilliant man. In fact, so much so that he turned the vaudeville assignment over to a young writer friend who was just getting started in pictures, under contract to Columbia at fifty dollars a week. Dore Schary. Dore wrote a talk act that called for me to be on microphone talking about Hollywood, interrupted from time to time by a stooge sitting alone in a box who appeared to be part of the audience. It was a pretty bad act.

I didn't meet Mr. Schary before presenting myself and my stooge to the public, but about a year and a half after the short tour from Chicago to the East, I was having lunch at the Hollywood Brown Derby and the waitress brought me a note that read something like, "Hope you knocked 'em dead on the Big Time." I looked across the restaurant to see a fellow peering at me through his glasses and grinning.

Of course I knew at once it was Mr. Schary. His partner was with him, who'd collaborated on my touring vehicle. I had written them to thank them for their effort and I had given each of them one of those watches worn in the breast pocket of the jacket at the end of a strap secured by a button at the other end slipped through the lapel buttonhole. And I think I had some appropriate inscription engraved on the backs of the watches. Dore says he still has his.

Our paths didn't cross again for twenty years. One night after dinner in New York, I was checking my lines for the part I was rehearsing for a TV show when the phone rang. It was Dore Schary, who said he had a play he'd like me to read. It developed that we were living across the avenue from each other, he at the Alwyn Court Apartments at Fifty-eighth Street and Seventh Avenue and I at the Osborne Apartments at Fifty-seventh and Seventh.

He sent me the play.

Alice read it while I finished studying my TV part. She'd finished about the same time I'd finished and she said, "I think this is it."

I read it and called Dore about midnight, after I'd recovered my emotions, and I said, "If you're serious, I'll meet you in the morning and sign a contract."

That's how I became identified with *Sunrise at Campobello*, which was to be the highlight of my professional career.

A peculiar thing about *Sunrise* is that everyone knew the story before they came to the theatre, but in spite of that there was a suspense.

I think the appeal was the indomitability of the human spirit— the courage and will to live.

And the response from international figures who came backstage, people I didn't know personally, was remarkable. They were there in recognition of FDR and his battle, not to congratulate me. And I don't think they were completely aware of it.

At the time it never occurred to me to ask how I came to be

considered for the role. I guess that's a sign of a pretty good ego. And I never heard the story until I received this letter from Dore Schary:

"Well, it happened this way: When I had finished the script of *Sunrise at Campobello* the Theatre Guild and I began casting around for the acting company. (For the sake of all concerned I shall not mention the names of those who turned down the part of FDR.) We had discarded the names of other possibles and had also rejected a few lesser-known actors as candidates.

"By now things were moving along rapidly; we had selected most everyone else—but we had no FDR. It was early October—rehearsals were to begin in late November and the wasps of panic were beginning to buzz. Lawrence Langner had been at me to sign Anthony Quayle but I had resisted the suggestion on the basis that to use an Englishman to play FDR would not be satisfactory. I told Lawrence, 'Granted Mr. Quayle is an extremely good actor—but let's use him, if we come up with a hit, in London.'

"The pressure mounted day by day—and our engagement of the Cort Theatre was in jeopardy—actors we had selected were getting 'antsy.' We had signed contracts for scenery, costumes and lighting and the Guild, with some justice, was laying heavy weights on me to accept Quayle.

"On that particular Friday night in October, Miriam (my dear, darling Miriam) and my associate Walter Reilly had an early dinner at our apartment in the Alwyn Court Apartments on Seventh Avenue after which I said, 'We have to find an actor for FDR . . . now—tonight.'

"Walter and I got at our lists and went over each name. We added, then crossed out other names. Miriam kept saying, 'There's one name you're forgetting.'

"After a while I asked, 'Who?'

"She said, 'You know.'

"I said, 'Know who?'

"She said, 'Him.'

"I said, 'Who is—*him?*'

"She said, 'For years you've known him. He plays tennis.'

"I said, 'Don Budge? Please, Miriam—give me a name.'

"She said, 'I'm thinking.'

"I said, 'What was he in?'

"She said, 'Lots of pictures.' (Miriam, you understand, is not very good at names, except those of people she knew up to the time she was eighteen.)

"I said, 'What pictures? Name one.'

"She said, 'Westerns, costumes, kings—like that.'

"I said, 'What the hell is—"like that"?'

"She said, 'Beards and history parts. He's tall.'

"I said, 'Miriam, let us alone.'

"She said, 'You had him in pictures at M-G-M.'

"I said, 'Miriam, lots of actors were in pictures at M-G-M— when I was there we made almost three hundred.'

"She said, 'He was a President.'

"Reilly said, 'Let's see, a President—eh? Washington, Jackson— Lincoln? Maybe?'

"Miriam said, 'Yes.'

"I said, 'Fonda?'

"Miriam said, 'No.'

"I said, 'Oh, Massey—Raymond Massey.'

"Miriam said, 'Yes—that's who.'

"I said, 'He can't play FDR.'

"Miriam said, 'You're right, he'd be awful.'

"I said, 'Miriam, shut up.'

"Walter and I returned to our lists. About twenty minutes later, when we were at the edge of desperation, I was about to call Langner and tell him to call Quayle. Miriam, who hadn't said a word for those twenty minutes, now cut in.

"MIRIAM: I've got the man.

"DORE: Oh no. Not again. Who this time? Wallace Beery? He's dead.

"MIRIAM: No, really—I know this one is right—and you know him very well.

"REILLY: Miriam, for Chrissakes!

"MIRIAM: Listen, the two of you. He's perfect—he's got light eyes—tall—good-looking—light hair—

"DORE: Miriam, what the *hell* is his *name?*

"MIRIAM: I don't know.

~ 243 ~

"DORE: Damn, damn—you're driving me crazy.

"MIRIAM: You had him in a picture—

"DORE: What picture?

"REILLY: Don't be silly—Miriam doesn't remember.

"MIRIAM: That's right.

"DORE: What was it about? Can you remember what it was about?

"MIRIAM: A kidnapping.

"DORE: A kidnapping?

"REILLY: A *kidnapping*?

"DORE: What picture did we make about a kidnapping?

"REILLY: The only one I can think of is *Ransom*.

"DORE: Miriam, that one was with Glenn Ford.

"MIRIAM: No, it wasn't.

"DORE: Wasn't what?

"MIRIAM: That was the picture. But not the actor.

"DORE: Please, Miriam, don't argue with me. Glenn Ford was in the picture. We bought it from a television show, *Fearful Decision*—in the TV version it was played by—

"REILLY: Ralph Bellamy!

"MIRIAM: I told you!

"DORE: Ralph Bellamy! Ralph! Miriam, you're a doll! A genius! Of course, where the hell have we been! Why didn't we think of him? Why didn't Lawrence? Or Armina? Or you, Walter? Why—he'd be perfect!

"I reached for the phone and called Lawrence [Langner], who must have kept a phone book the size of a standard one issued by Bell Telephone. When I told Lawrence we had the man —Bellamy—he agreed—gave me your number and I called, kicking myself again and again for not having remembered *State of the Union* or *Detective Story*, and wondering if your damned phone was out of order—or whether you were out—or in Europe —or—or—then you answered.

"Well, the rest you know. You loved the script and so did Alice and you and I shared a success that meant something precious and unforgettable.

"The remainder of this story is yours to tell."

During the rehearsal period all kinds of assistance was afforded us. Ed Murrow made FDR speech recordings available to me; the Institute for the Crippled and Disabled, where FDR learned to use his braces and crutches, allowed me to work out with paraplegics, one of them with an affliction similiar to FDR's; and the Roosevelt family was most generous and helpful —especially Mrs. Roosevelt, who opened Hyde Park to us and produced much memorabilia and family background and characteristics.

Life magazine did an extensive cover story on *Sunrise at Campobello*, with photographs by Eisenstaedt. Dore, Vincent Donehue, the director, and all the cast—including Mary Fickett, who was so good as Eleanor; Henry Jones, who played the role of Louis Howe so brilliantly; Alan Bunce, who turned in a striking performance as Al Smith, and Anne Seymour, who played Mama —spent the morning at Hyde Park, guided by Mrs. Roosevelt, for Eisenstaedt's pictures.

Luncheon was prepared for us across the road and up the hill at the smaller house where Mrs. Roosevelt was living.

We congregated in the living room before luncheon and Mrs. Roosevelt said to her secretary, "See what everyone will have for a cocktail. I'm going upstairs to write my column. I'll be down soon."

It developed that everyone would like sherry. The secretary disappeared for ten minutes or so and returned very embarrassed, to reveal that the liquor cabinet was locked and that Buzzy Dahl had gone to New York City with the keys in his pocket.

Presently Mrs. Roosevelt reappeared and asked the secretary why there were no cocktails. The secretary repeated the unfortunate circumstance and Mrs. Roosevelt left the room. In about a minute and a half she was back with a bottle of sherry.

"How'd you get the door open?" asked the secretary.

"I took the spikes out of the hinges," replied Mrs. R. A knowledge gained from the furniture manufacturing business she and a friend operated, no doubt. Or maybe she knew Alma and George Morgan.

Dore and I became fast friends, which we remain today, and as the opening came nearer our anxieties and hopes magnified, until Christmas night 1957 in New Haven, our first public performance.

We were well received, but we had work to do. We eliminated a prologue which, incidentally, Dore's friend Moss Hart said didn't belong when he saw the play. He further speculated that Dore wrote it after he'd written the play, which was true. Pretty astute.

From New Haven we went to Boston, a town of critics, both press and lay, and we fared well there, too.

When one thinks of Boston in terms of politics, it's usually "Democratic," but there's also Beacon Hill and the Brahmins. One night Dore was sitting in the audience with his wife, Miriam. At the end of the first act he heard a man's voice from the seat behind him say, "If I'd known it was about this fellow, I don't think I'd have come! I had enough of that son of a bitch when he was alive."

That was a jolt for Dore, but he'd had jolts before and he could handle it.

When the house lights came up at the end of the second act, the gentleman's voice was heard to say, "He really had a tough time, didn't he!"

That was some relief for Dore. At least the substance of the play was coming across.

When the play was over and the audience was preparing to leave, Miriam started to rise. Dore took her wrist to hold her back, hoping for a parting shot from behind.

It came. The Beacon Hill Brahmin gentleman was now obviously standing and tugging, as if helping someone with a wrap. In the midst of this act of gallantry he said, "You know, dear, if I'd known all this a few years ago, I might have voted for him."

Then, after a final affectionate tug, he added, "Once."

Then on to Philadelphia, where we felt we'd added the finishing touches. Jimmy Roosevelt joined Dore and me after the play one night. He was the only one of the family to have seen it up to that time. He seemed pleased with the way things were developing but he said, "I must warn you of something. Mother's going to see this soon and she'll be very moved. She's reluctant to expose her emotions and there's no knowing what she might say. It could be brusque or unpleasant or at least misunderstood."

Dore and I made a mental note of this.

The cold opening night of January 30, 1958, in New York was unique in the theatre. Ambassadors and diplomats from all over the world, Cabinet members, Supreme Court justices, lawmakers and political figures of all descriptions were there. So was the entire Roosevelt family, with the exception of the man the play depicted.

Mrs. Roosevelt, with an escort, sat in the last row at her own request.

The entire press corps was there, of course, and they hovered behind her, hoping to catch any quotable remark.

Finally, after the play was over and the lights had come up, it came. Her escort asked, "What did you think?"

"A good play," she replied, "but about as much like the Roosevelt family as some people from Mars."

It should be noted here that the manuscript had been approved by each of the family and much of the dialogue was verbatim.

Well, word of this quote of Mrs. Roosevelt's passed through the theatre to backstage and to the world, I guess, like a hurricane.

Those of us connected with the play had been invited to the apartment of Secretary of the Interior Oscar Chapman for supper afterward. My wife and I had just got there and left our wraps when Mrs. Roosevelt arrived, alone. Jimmy rushed up to her and said, "Mother! What's this I hear you said about the play?"

And she said, "What?"

"That it's 'about as much like the Roosevelt family as some people from Mars.' You didn't say that, did you?"

"Yes, I did," she replied.

"You didn't really mean it, did you?"

She was visibly moved, and with quivering lips and downcast eyes she said, "No, I didn't." Then she wrapped herself up again for the cold January night and left.

The run of the play in New York was sensational. Standing

room every performance, and it was a delight to do because the audiences loved it.

I was able to leave the theatre soon after the last curtain because I wore no make-up. I only had to change clothes and straighten up a little.

One afternoon after the matinee I was hurrying up the street to get home quickly for a nap and a bite to eat before the evening performance. I was aware of two ladies who had just seen the play and who were walking ahead of me, discussing it. I, understandably, slowed up.

"Wasn't it wonderful?" one of them said.

To an actor this is better than food and drink.

"It was just great!" the other replied. "So moving! So human! So inspiring!"

I could hardly contain myself. This is what every actor tries to achieve with the material given him.

Then, as an afterthought, she continued, "There was just one little thing—I can't stand Ralph Bellamy!"

Fortunately for me, critics were a little more charitable. I include the following excerpt from an article by Walter Kerr in the New York *Herald Tribune* on February 9, 1958, not so much because it praises me but because of its reference to the old stock companies.

"By pure accident, I may be the best-informed man in New York on the acting range of Ralph Bellamy. When I was considerably younger, and when Mr. Bellamy was considerably younger, I spent quite a few Monday nights convincing a lean, wiry, fortunately gullible man named Rexford Bellamy that I deserved free admission to the stock company he operated in my home town. Rexford Bellamy was Ralph Bellamy's father, Ralph Bellamy was the juvenile star of each and every production, and I did wind up on the press list, for reasons which are obscure even to me.

"This meant that I'd no sooner get used to the actor Bellamy as José Vallejo in *Cradle Snatchers* than it was Monday night again and he'd be playing Duke Merrill in *Kempy* or Sheridan Scott in a perfectly dandy mystery thriller called *The Rear Car*. To this day all the theatrical heroes of the late twenties look like Ralph Bellamy to me, and I'm not just thinking of the dismayed lovers and surprised husbands of *Three Live Ghosts, Bringing Up Father,* and *Married—and How!* What I remember is the switch from the Mortimer Snerd gurglings of a subnormal detective in *The Ghost Train* to the passion-wracked eyes of the Reverend Davidson in *Rain.* Never saw a better Reverend Davidson in my life.

"It thus comes as no surprise to me that Mr. Bellamy is perfectly able to play Franklin Delano Roosevelt . . . There never is a false stress in the actor's thoughtful, touching sparring-match with the world around him. The grin is genuine; what goes on beneath it is subtly, honorably implied.

"Rexford Bellamy would be proud."

As I've mentioned before, my father and my brother Dick ran the "front of the house" of my stock company.

We played *Sunrise* a year and a half in New York. And I must say that I couldn't have done the job at all without the understanding and help of my wife, who put up with all the annoyances and inconveniences of my continually playing FDR recordings and practicing the wheelchair and crutches in our rather small New York apartment. To say nothing of my reading the part aloud while learning it.

The stage play of *Sunrise at Campobello* was, as I've said, *the* highlight for me and I received a lot of awards. I mention this so that I can include a quote about awards from two rather well-known actors. It was sent to me by my producer friend A. C. Lyles.

In the April 1978 issue of *Oui,* Richard Burton says to Ivor Davis in an interview: "I remember talking to Olivier about awards. We were both one of five nominees for a 'Tony' award in New York, and we both knew that Ralph Bellamy was going to win for playing Roosevelt—and he did. Afterward, Olivier and I went to the Plaza Hotel. We had a drink and I said, 'Anyway, these bloody awards—it's disgusting to create false rivalry between actors. We shouldn't have such things.' And Olivier said, 'I agree with you—except, of course, when one wins them oneself.'"

After our New York run, we went to the National Theatre in Washington, D.C., for a four-week stay that was extended to six weeks, through the middle of the summer, including the Fourth of July.

There was lots of activity in Washington. The McClellan hearings were in progress, with Bobby Kennedy acting as legal counsel. The whole government hierarchy seemed to be there at a time when vacations were normally in order.

Before we left New York, I'd been invited by phone to address the National Press Club in Washington at luncheon. After accepting the invitation I spent a most uncomfortable few weeks wondering what I could say at my appearance. There was only one area in which I felt qualified and that was FDR, the man I was playing in *Sunrise*. But the men I'd be addressing had known him intimately. How could I dare pose as an authority?

I concluded that my only course should be an account of FDR's battle with polio through his political rise. And I would finish with some familiar gestures—putting on the glasses, clenching a cigarette holder in my teeth and tilting it upward, and raising an arm and hand in a waving salute to the audience with a typical grin.

Then, following custom, I would answer questions submitted from the audience to the Press Club president, who reads them aloud for the guest. The president was Bill Lawrence of the New York *Times*.

I was going along pretty well. The speech was accepted nicely and now the questions were coming forward. One of them read, obviously facetiously, "I'm a Roosevelt hater! Do you think I'd enjoy seeing your play?"

I don't know where it came from, because I'm not usually that quick. But just as facetiously I replied, "I've noticed that most Roosevelt haters have a wide sadistic streak. So I imagine you'd have a great time watching FDR struggle with his infirmities for two and a half hours."

I saw two arms shoot upward in the center of the room and then fall to the table and a head fall on the arms.

I met the man afterward. He was a nice fellow and he came to the play, and he liked it.

After Washington, we had a four-week vacation before starting a nationwide road tour in Columbus, Ohio.

My wife and I set out in our car for the Florida Keys. On the way we stopped for a week at Sea Island, Georgia, a typical southern resort in every respect. There were palms, palmetto, magnolias, dripping Spanish moss, honeysuckle, camellias, a hospitable host (Irving Harned), friendly people and comfortably warm Atlantic Ocean water.

While we were there my New York agent called about an unresolved point in my contract, which had been revised for the road tour. Actually, Dore and I had an agreement on it over the phone but the agent said it should be in writing even though it was a minor point. He asked me to write an informal letter to Dore and mention our telephone agreement, then mail it to him, the agent, who would forward it to Dore for initialing.

I complied, beginning "Dear Dore," after which I told him about our trip to Sea Island and how lovely it was and a few other pleasantries. Then I referred to our telephone agreement and concluded with "Affectionately, Ralph."

I sent the letter to my agent and forgot it. A few days later a fat envelope arrived for me at Sea Island. It contained a letter from my agent saying he'd submitted my letter to the legal department of the agency and that I would find an accompanying revised letter, which the legal department advised me to sign and send to Dore.

It began "Dear Dore" all right, but that was all of my original letter that was left until "Affectionately, Ralph." It read something like "Dear Dore: Pursuant to our telephone conversation and mutual agreement relating to the revisions of my original contract for services rendered in the play *Sunrise at Campobello*, and with special reference to new services, namely a nationwide tour of said play *Sunrise at Campobello*," and on and on in legal gibberish until "it is my understanding that there shall be the following changed conditions, beginning after the second comma in the third sentence of paragraph three on page four of the original contract" and on and on until "If this conforms with your understanding of the above-mentioned telephonic agreement, please initial and forward to my agent at the earliest possible moment. Affectionately, Ralph."

I sent it to Dore with an explanatory letter. For a long time thereafter, we signed our correspondence with each other "Affectionately," with the quotation marks.

After our vacation, we began the nationwide tour in Columbus. We'd broken the house record for attendance in Washington at the National Theatre and did the same at the Blackstone Theatre in Chicago, the Curran Theatre in San Francisco and the Biltmore Theatre in Los Angeles. And we closed in Atlanta on FDR's birthday, January 30, 1960, returning to Los Angeles to make the film of *Sunrise*.

The Warner Brothers' picture was made with some replacements. Greer Garson played Eleanor, Hume Cronyn played Louis Howe and Ann Shoemaker was Mama, among others.

Incidentally, in the stage play a very young boy named Richard Thomas played John Roosevelt and James Earl Jones was Edward, a friend and employee.

I was still president of Actors Equity and chairman of the negotiating committee which was meeting with the producers in New York to draw up a new contract while we were shooting the film. The phone was off the hook on the sound stage at Warner Brothers through a good deal of the shooting. Negotiations had gone on for weeks, but an impasse had now been reached and the meetings were broken off. All the legitimate theatres were closed. Times Square was dark for about a week, long enough for some small businesses to go broke.

In the midst of the Times Square blackout, our company went East to shoot exterior scenes at Hyde Park, New York City and Campobello Island. On the night we arrived in New York Dore and I went to his apartment, where I was to stay for a couple of days. No one but my wife and Dore knew I was there. Or so I thought.

In the middle of the night I was called by John Shubert of the League of New York Theatres. How he knew I was there I'll never know. He said it was essential that we meet and continue the talks. I said we were more than willing. We agreed to select splinter committees from each side, to include Dore for the League and my first appearance for Equity, so that two new faces could be introduced, and Moss Hart agreed to serve as a kind of moderator. There were three on each side, with Moss in limbo.

We met in secret at the One Fifth Avenue Hotel. We had to put the two groups in separate rooms because, together, there was nothing but name-calling. Most of the important negotiating had been completed. This meeting was really a way to find a kind of face-saving device.

Moss and I went back and forth from room to room, but we couldn't penetrate the wall of difference.

Finally, David Merrick, president of the League, Herman Bernstein, Dore, Moss and I were in the producers' room and there was silence.

A crazy idea hit me. I asked if anyone knew how many people on Broadway were working for minimum. No one knew and I called Equity.

There were thirty-seven people working for minimum.

I told David that the actors had made the last concession and if the producers would come up one dollar on the minimum I would try my best to convince the actors, with Moss's help, to accept that and everything else that had been negotiated and call it an agreement.

"Not one cent more!" David said.

I looked at Dore, who was standing behind David. He took David back of a partition and in a minute or two David came back and said, "All right, one dollar more on the minimum. But if it's turned down, everything we've negotiated so far will be withdrawn."

Moss and I went back to the actors, and after some persuasion the dollar increase was accepted.

Of course, each side had to sell the proposal to its members, which they did. The strike was ended, the lights in Times Square came back on again and the theatres reopened—for thirty-seven dollars.

Herman Cooper, Equity's lawyer, was a part of these negotiations, as he had been in most of the negotiations during my tenure. He was one of the most able, practical, forceful and respected lawyers I've ever met (I hasten to say I haven't had to deal with many, professionally). Herman eventually became my personal lawyer and close friend, even though he's on the other side now: management-union.

And while speaking of old friends at Equity, I must certainly mention the executive secretary, Angus Duncan, son of Augustin Duncan and nephew of Isadora Duncan. Angus was a dedicated, honest, warm fellow who loved actors and Equity. He was one of the best things that ever happened to Equity. He's now retired and living in Florida. My good friend.

But the gutsiest member of all the negotiating committees during my negotiating experience was Frank Maxwell, vice-president of Actors Equity Association, and now on the board of the Screen Actors Guild. We and Herman Cooper often ended together in negotiations. Sometimes it seemed as if we'd spent a lifetime together.

After four three-year terms, I was elected President Emeritus of Actors Equity Association.

When I became president of Equity our treasury consisted of $600,000—in checking accounts. When I left, our treasury amounted to over $3,000,000. And it was due, after persuading the Finance Committee that it should be done, to the wise counsel of Lester Degenstein. Lester has been my personal financial adviser for over twenty years, and he and his wife are close friends. "Degie" knows the hazards of, and protections for, this eccentric business.

Every actor is asked by interviewers what his favorite part has been. Naturally I have to say FDR in *Sunrise at Campobello*. And though I got every award there was for the play, the most cherished reward is my friendship with Dore and Miriam.

Another incident that typifies Mrs. Roosevelt's reluctance to expose herself publicly, as well as her well-known compassion for others, is worth mentioning here. She lived in New York for a while at the Park Central Hotel at Seventh Avenue and Fifty-sixth Street. The papers carried a story of her being a hit-and-run victim one cold, slushy, early spring day.

I asked her about it a little while later and she said, "It wasn't hit and run. It was really my fault. I was crossing Seventh Avenue, going west against the traffic light. A taxi hit me and knocked me down. The driver stopped immediately and helped me to the curb, where I sat on the southeast corner. I was a little dazed, but I was soon sure that I was all right. A crowd had started to gather and I realized things could go badly for the cab driver. So I told him to get on his way quickly, that I was not hurt. He did. I sat on the curb for a few minutes, and then some of the people who'd stopped walked me across the street to the hotel. Fortunately no one thought to take the license number of the cab."

When we went to the National Theatre in Washington with

Sunrise, I called my old friend, Ann Whitman, President Eisenhower's secretary, extending an invitation to Eisenhower to see the play. She called back, saying the President thanked me but that he didn't go to the theatre. When he had time to relax he preferred bridge. Alas, poor Ike!

In the summer of 1961 I went to Saigon to do a documentary on the Hope Ship for NBC. Fred Rheinstein was the writer-director and Dexter Alley was the cameraman. We had no script. Fred would write something as we experienced it, I'd learn it while Dexter set up his camera and we'd shoot it.

Dr. William Walsh was the founder and guiding light of Project Hope and he'd flown on from Indonesia, Hope's last six-month stop, and joined the ship downriver from Saigon. The Communists bombed a hole in her hull as she rounded the last curve approaching the Saigon dock.

The Hope Ship with her many missions, on invitation from underdeveloped and needy countries, is one of the greatest people-to-people, humanitarian, diplomatic, good-will, peace projects ever to emanate from this country. The doctors give their time for three months, without remuneration, and they're the best doctors in the country, from almost every state. The nurses are on leave from, and in the uniforms of, their hospitals in the States, and they receive only expenses. The ship is on lease from the Navy for a dollar a year. Every new medicinal and surgical discovery, from pills to operating room radio equipment, is given to her by the manufacturers. It's a thrilling institution floating around the world. She goes to a country by that country's invitation, not only treating people but teaching doctors new techniques by remote TV aboard the ship.

At her departure, she leaves an American staff behind for a time, to see that the local unit of native doctors and nurses that she has set up runs smoothly.

Now Hope staffs operate in the United States as well as abroad.

The Vietnam war hadn't got to its worst in 1961, but one never knew who was who politically. Even among individual families.

Fred and Dexter and I met, aboard ship, a nine-year-old with exotropia, meaning that he had no depth perception and his eyes focused together only briefly. He was Ta Van Tu, and he also had a second thumb on his right hand. We took to him immediately and used him as the protagonist in our little film. The operations on his eyes and thumb were successful and he became, as it were, the commanding officer of the ship. When President Ngo Dinh Diem came aboard, we persuaded him to visit and chat with Tu as he lay in bed after his operations. Tu was overwhelmed. Our last shot was of me walking away from the ship and waving to Tu, who was still recuperating aboard.

We went on a junket by plane into the interior. After we landed, we went by jeep with armed guards to the village of Phung Hiep, where they'd never heard of a doctor. On our trip there we were preceded by tanks and trucks full of armed men, passing lookout towers with armed men at every crossroad and armed soldiers with their trousers rolled up to their knees in rice paddies with farmers and water buffalo. We set up a screened hut in Phung Hiep, opposite a spot where the heads of two DDT exterminator officers had been found nailed to a post that morning.

Many incidents, almost like miracles, occurred there. A sick, withered baby was relieved of its pain and sent with its mother back into the country with a packet of medicine that said on the face of the envelope, in the native language, "The people of the United States wish you well." Everyone got an envelope, even if it was only a couple of aspirins.

A man came forward, supported by a friend at each arm. Dr. Walsh tried to get information through the interpreter but had no luck. He had the man stripped to the waist and examined him. There were crude crisscrossed tapes over his nipples, which Dr. Walsh removed, to reveal two ugly gashes forming crosses. Through the interpreter it was learned that the night before, sitting on a box in the open mud street, their equivalent of a witch doctor had performed the operation and inserted human placenta. Presently the man collapsed. They administered paramedic treatment and medicine and sent him to the ship, via our jeep and plane. When I left the ship about two weeks later, the man was up and about and exercising daily.

The "Hopies" as they called themselves, worked with the Vietnamese hospitals, such as they were—no windowpanes, crowded, the dead on stretchers in the hallways to make room for new patients and the smell of sweat and medicines. But that's all changing, thanks to Hope.

While I was there I became acquainted with a local barber whose badly wall-eyed son was cured with acupuncture.

Our little unit visited and photographed an acupuncture practitioner at work in his three-sided house in a compound on the outskirts of Saigon. His patients, about twelve or fifteen of them, sat next to each other in a rectangular U-shaped formation. He squatted on his heels in oriental fashion as he questioned a patient about symptoms. Then he would refer to a book of plates (red and blue and sinewy), to find a figure that fit the patient's symptoms.

In the margins surrounding the plate were arrows going to the pertinent points, and he would place needles (gold to instill heat, silver to extract heat) following an indicated course (the needles stuck through the clothes) from feet to eyelids to fingernails. In half an hour he'd remove the needles. He said he could cure anything that didn't require an operation in three treatments. Through an interpreter I asked how old the practice was. The interpreter replied, "He says forever."

There was an old lady in black lying on a couch in a corner when we arrived. She had the pins stuck in her. I asked about her through an interpreter. The doctor replied, through the interpreter, that she'd been carried in with a stroke a couple of days before. She was paralyzed. This was her second treatment. Before we left, the pins were removed and she walked out as if she'd never had a bad day.

The Hope Ship is one of the most charitable and humane projects extant.

My visit to the Hope Ship was one of the most moving experiences of my life.

On the subject of treatments and healings, I was butchered a few years ago by a surgeon who performed a double hernia operation.

I subsequently had the job redone by another surgeon, one hernia at a time.

During the first of the two later operations I came to on the operating table in the midst of the proceedings.

"You're not supposed to be with us," said the surgeon.

"But I am, and I don't feel a thing, and I'd like to watch the performance," I said.

After some discussion, an automobile rear-view mirror was procured and clamped to a portable standing metal post, facing down so that I could see my innards as I lay on the table. There was no feeling. It was as if I were watching an operation on someone else.

Later, while on the TV mini-series "Wheels," I had a severe intestinal attack and returned to my surgeon "just in time" he said.

With the same assistant and anesthesiologist in attendance, I asked for the mirror arrangement again.

Seeing my abdomen wide open, and feeling nothing at all from the knife, I said, "I don't see how anyone, observing the intertwining and intricate formation of the human organs, can deny a God or a Supreme Being or Whatever. All that couldn't be an accident."

There was a quite audible, affirmative, simultaneous response from the two surgeons, the anesthetist and a nurse.

It's customary for the White House correspondents and photographers each to give an evening for the incoming President. At John F. Kennedy's request the two were combined, and the event marked his first public appearance after his inauguration.

Merriman Smith, as the senior and dean of White House correspondents (the one who says, "Thank you, Mr. President," at the conclusion of press conferences), was in charge of programing. Smitty was an old friend and he telephoned me in New York asking me to open the program as FDR with specially written material that would relate not only to the President but also to members of the press and others in the audience.

I quickly said, "No, thank you." Having played FDR on the stage in New York and on the road for two years, and then having made the picture, I had determined not to appear again as FDR. I was afraid of becoming so typed that it would interfere with other roles, both on the stage and in pictures. But Smitty was persuasive. It meant I had to ask Dore Schary to get the wheelchair out of dead storage and brush up on FDR.

The occasion took place at the Shoreham Hotel, which has an enormous auditorium and stage. The President and his Cabinet, the Vice-President and the justices of the Supreme Court sat on a raised dais against the wall to the left of, and at a right angle to, the stage as one faced the packed audience. Included in the crowd were most of the Congress and ambassadors and diplomats from all over the world, as well as all the national and international correspondents and photographers.

I opened the program in the wheelchair without introduction. The material was personal, pertinent, conversational, somewhat abrasive, but humorous and curt. It took about six or seven minutes and it went well. Then Joey Bishop came on as emcee, with a list of brilliant entertainers. Meanwhile, backstage, Smitty asked me to get straightened up and come back for what I thought would be a company bow after the program.

I did as requested and I was standing casually offstage with a drink in my hand when I heard Joey say, onstage and at the microphone, "And now, Mr. President, the man who impersonated FDR at the beginning of the show would like to say a few words as himself." And he introduced me. There I stood, offstage, with a drink in my hand, having had no foreknowledge of this "honor." There was nothing to do but to put down my drink and walk out onto the stage. Joey passed me, backing off and applauding me.

Well, it's one thing to address the President of the United States, the Cabinet, the Supreme Court, Congress and the press and diplomats of the entire world if you know in advance that you're going to do it. And that's a fairly ego-cracking prospect in itself. But to have it come at you unexpectedly, with a drink in your hand, is mind-blowing. Unless you're Winston Churchill.

I have no idea what I said. If my life depended on it I couldn't say. I only recall that during my unconscious suffering I suddenly heard hearty laughter and instinct made me come to the end of a sentence after which I said, "Thank you," I think, and walked off to applause, as Joey passed me, now backing onstage and joining the applause. As he reached the microphone he said, "Ralph, you'll be invited to the White House to play touch football tomorrow."

Afterward those of us who had appeared on the program retired to a side room where the President greeted us. He stopped and chatted with each of us as we stood in line. I had headed a theatre committee for him during the campaign. Though we had never met, he knew about it and thanked me and then passed down the line.

Then he hesitated and backed up and, recalling the campaign incident in Texas in which I had been instrumental in blocking the formation of what could have been devastating pressure against him, he said, "And thank you for what you did for me in Texas." A photographer snapped us as we were both laughing.

The Texas pressure was to have come from a chain of newspapers. At a social gathering down there I sat between the owner of the chain and an oil operator friend. They were declaring their dissatisfaction with some aspects and personalities of the campaign and proposed to get the governor to exert state-wide political pressure and to place a front-page box in the papers quoting the governor and stating the editorial position of the chain, in opposition to the Kennedy-Johnson ticket.

I said some naïve thing like "This is the President of the United States you're talking about. I don't know anything about Texas politics and it's probably none of my business, but corny as it sounds, why don't you let Kennedy state his position and face you on it before you take such drastic action?"

They looked at me strangely and said, "Can you get him down here?"

"I don't know," I said, "but I can try."

I went directly to a telephone and called my columnist friend Jack O'Brian in New York, who I knew had connections with the Kennedys. The result was that Kennedy went to Texas, the opposition was removed and he carried the state. By not too big a margin, as I remember.

The photographer who snapped me with the President in Washington sent me a copy. Sometime later I emceed a dinner for the President at the Palladium in Hollywood. Before leaving for the gathering I told my wife, "I'm going to take the picture with me and hope he'll autograph it. What have I got to lose? He'll either do it or he won't."

As luck would have it, I sat a tier above him and directly

behind him on the stage next to the podium. When he had a quiet moment I said, "Mr. President—?"

He turned, smiled and said hello. I exposed a part of the face-down picture and said, "Would you?"

Still smiling, he looked around the auditorium, produced a pen from his pocket, turned back to me and said, "Slip it to me!"

I did and he did. And it's one of few personal autographs, under a warm and flattering inscription. A treasured possession from a unique and inspired man.

Out of the blue one day came an offer to replace Hugh Downs on "The Today Show" for two weeks while he was on vacation.

This was a new experience and I hied to New York with much trepidation. Having watched the show for years (and been interviewed on it the morning after the opening of *Sunrise at Campobello*) I was, and still am, impressed with the organization and ease with which it's presented, almost as if it's been rehearsed.

I was picked up at 4 A.M. each morning from the Tuscany Hotel by limousine and taken to what looked like a storefront on Forty-ninth Street between Fifth and Sixth. Large windows opened to the street, so that passers-by could look in and watch proceedings, which were set up back in the "store." A long desk accommodating three or four was backed by a plain wall and there was an area with a couple of chairs for guest interviews, and of course, the control room to one side. Three cameras and TelePrompTers moved about as needed, and the participants could see the whole show on small TV sets built horizontally into the desk at each place.

There were people who appeared on Forty-ninth Street every morning with folding camp chairs and sat peering into the windows.

Everything was plotted masterfully from the control room and there was a floor manager with earphones on the set.

They were ready for any emergency. And one arose one day. Something had gone wrong and the floor manager said to Barbara Walters and me, "When the weather's through, be out on the sidewalk and interview the passers-by."

This was another "first" for me. But after the initial encounters all went well and it seemed as if we talked to everyone in New York.

The whole experience was fun and everyone on the show was helpful and kind. I enjoyed it.

I've sometimes told actor friends who've been depressed about their careers: if you ever feel discouraged, which all actors do at times, stand across the street from a big office building, preferably in New York City, at five o'clock in the afternoon and watch the people disgorge themselves.

They hate what they do, they hate each other and they're rude as they push and elbow their way to a cab, a train, a bus, a subway or whatever, to get home to have dinner and go to bed to get up the next day and do it all over again. Then think of how lucky you are.

Actors are among the few people who are doing what they want to do and liking it and, hopefully, making a living of it.

Michael Crichton says he's a newcomer. And he is.

So I thought it might be interesting to know his reaction to what he's doing so successfully now, in connection with the evolution of his medium. And his thoughts on what's gone before. Here's his reply:

"I have a paradoxical thought, very often. I wish it were back in the days of Zanuck and Cohn and the real dictators. For a couple of reasons. One is that this is inherently an insecure business, and it helps (actors especially) to be told what you are going to do next, and that's that. Now that everyone is obliged to make a choice on every project, you often find people tying themselves into neurotic knots instead of just seeing it as a job and doing it and having some fun and working hard. It's also true that as production had dwindled, nearly everyone works too infrequently. (Paying enormous fees to movie people is also a bad idea for that reason. A while back someone observed that Paul Newman had just made about ten million dollars on his last few movies, and he really didn't feel the need to work right away soon. That's understandable and nobody would begrudge him his bucks, but I think that writers and directors and actors and everybody work better when they work steadily. You take time off, you get out of shape, you lose your sharp edge.) The final thing is that although everybody has horror stories about the days of the magnates, I nevertheless hear overtones of respect in the stories. Today it seems as though there are fewer, and milder, horror stories—but no respect at all. Agents run the business now, deal-makers who haven't got any taste or knowledge or even, in the final analysis, any particular affection for movies. They could just as well be selling salami or rugs or vaginal deodorant. I think that's too bad.

"I guess the overriding feeling that I have is that at one time, movies were a business. Today they aren't a business—TV is the business, and it seems to work pretty much the way movies did. Movies are some kind of weird megabucks art form and enormous crapshoot in which the costs are astronomical and so are the potential returns. I think without question movies are dying as a form. Eventually they will be just too expensive to make and distribute, unless something can be done to alter the basic way they are conceived and put together and gotten out to the public.

"Myself, I'd rather be back in the days when movies were a business. It must have been more sane.

"I notice, for example, that performers who go back to earlier periods are much less crazy and much more professional in their attitudes. I just finished a picture with Dick Widmark, a wonderful man, but a professional in the sense that has almost vanished from pictures today. And I think in other areas, including writing and directing, there has been a pronounced increase in self-indulgence by the people making movies.

"It's a mixed bag, now. Some of the best movies ever made have been made in the last ten years, I think, as well as some of the most lucrative. So it can't be all harmful. But at the same time I have the sense that the average movie today is less well conceived and less skillfully executed than the average movie twenty years ago.

"On the other hand, making movies is really fun. I think it's a privilege to be able to do it at all, and whenever it gets irritating, and whenever the executives in their English suits and their suede loafers with brass buckles start driving me crazy, I remind myself that it's a privilege. I mean, where else are you going to get millions of dollars, literally, to spend on your private fantasies? To make them real?

"I often think that if someone were to come in and listen to me talking, while I work, that I would be bundled off to the nearest nuthouse. I mean, it's true. On the set, there's all that talk: 'Kill the baby and lose the gobo . . .' And right down to the final mix, where you sit around trying to decide if the door slam has enough low end and if the level is right. Change the music: 'Let's tacit the strings.' It really is a lunatic world, with these intense preoccupations about fine points that no one in the audience will probably ever be aware of, but still . . . somehow you believe it's important."

Before signing off I have to record an unforgettable moment. My mother lived to be eighty-eight. My father lived to be ninety-three. They had a small house in Hollywood and many friends whose company they enjoyed. My mother failed rapidly toward the end, more in the area of senility than physical disability.

I visited them frequently, and one early evening when I arrived, my mother was in bed. I went into her room to say hello and chat. I said, "Hi there! How're you making out?"

She looked up, smiling, and searched my face. Then she said, "Your face is familiar, but I don't seem to be able to place your name."

It's a long way from "All that you do, do with your might; things done by halves are never done right."

The intervening years in Chautauqua, resident stock, traveling rep shows, Broadway, radio, TV and ninety-seven feature pictures have been colorful, cultivating, confidence-producing and crammed abundantly with friends.

One hears so much of growing old, of declining years. They decline only if you let them.

One can't live on memories. One becomes bored and dies with only memories.

Most memories have to do with challenges and accomplishments. So it seems the thing to do is to store up the fun, the sorrow, the experience, the fulfillment of each day and look forward to tomorrow.

Sentimental?

Sure, but it's true. If you've read this far, I hope I've made the point.

AFTERPIECE

This is a time not only for looking back at the disappointments and pleasures but also for new beginnings.

Everything ends.

But there are always new beginnings.

My friend of nearly fifty years, Jim Cagney, and I pack our painting kits and quite frequently attend classes with his old teacher, and now mine, Sergei Bongart, a native Russian and one of the most sought-after painters of this, his adopted country.

That's a hobby Jim and I share. Another of mine was collecting pre-Columbian and African sculpture. I've given 169 pieces to the L.A. County Museum. Jim has quit acting, after a brilliant career. But he still has interests in conservation issues and some of our sadly decaying concepts, many of which interests I share.

I can't quit acting after some two or three hundred plays in stock and rep; a couple of Broadway flops and several Broadway hits; my own stock company; ninety-eight feature pictures, four TV series and what seems like a thousand TV shows.

I like to think there's still a lot to do. And it's fun to talk about it, especially with young people who seem to want to know what it was like back there.

But there's a danger too. One has to watch out for living in the past. I hope that never happens to me. The future is really the thing.

Once having become an actor one realizes that acting is one of the most precarious pursuits. Unlike many other professions and trades, there's a lot of unemployment, discouragement and very possible, or even certain, economic difficulty. And of course, competition with already established actors. And unless you're born into the profession ("in a trunk" as they say), I think there's usually opposition to a sibling or friend choosing to be an actor. Not so much now perhaps, as, say, the middle teens.

In China, where the theatre probably began, prostitutes, barbers and actors were once social outcasts.

Today, I like to think, certainly actors, and most barbers (including mine—Jimmy), and probably prostitutes, have overcome.

Often, even experienced actors in plays have been known to allow themselves to be lifted into the euphoria of a successful opening night and overextend their individualities, forgetting there's an author, a director and the rest of the cast.

As a case in point of this mishap, there's an anecdote about George M. Cohan that's applicable here: After the opening night of a highly successful play which received glowing reviews, including references to the performances of the actors, and after the second performance, the cast arrived to give the third performance the next night to find a notice on the call board which read "Rehearsal at 10 A.M. tomorrow!—To take out the improvements." (Signed) George M. Cohan.

In case I haven't made myself clear, let me quote David Garrick, who was one of the first "natural" actors. He said, in a piece written in 1776 called "A Short Treatise upon Acting. By Which the Players May be Instructed and the Town Undeceived": "Acting is an entertainment of the stage, which by calling in the aid and assistance of articulation, corporeal motion and ocular expression, imitates, assumes or puts on the various mental and bodily emotions arising from the various humors, virtues and vices incident to human nature."

Certainly an academic statement if there ever was one. But it's valid, I believe, because it admonishes the actor to exercise reserve and taste and simplicity and sincerity.

Audiences, and a lot of actors, don't recognize the difference in acting technique between the stage and the silver screen. On the stage one plays for the last row in the gallery. In pictures the most fleeting facial movement can express an emotion or reaction that would require a broad gesture and emphatic facial expression to convey the same action or reaction on the stage.

Paul Muni wrote, "To act in motion pictures is to act in a

world in which mechanical problems beset the actor on all sides
—his steps are caged by chalk marks and focal distances, his
voice is directed by microphone, controlled by dials. Finally it is
unrolled, projected, seen through a lens and heard through a
horn before an audience hundreds of miles away from him."

Leslie Howard said, "The modern talking picture sets itself up
as a vehicle for the spoken drama, and as the logical successor to
the flesh-and-blood theatre—a fact which can be borne out by
comparing the behavior of an audience at a successful play with
that of a similar audience at a successful picture."

And, if all that's valid, it applies to television too.

You might guess from all this that I love the theatre. I do. I
also have a deep respect for moving pictures. They reach thousands of times the audience, and as they gain in theatrical and
dramatic importance they become more socially influential, more
enhancing of an actor's recognition. And, more and more, television is embracing the same advantages. Many of our TV programs go round the world. But I still have the deepest affection
for the theatre. There is no question that any actor who has had
experience in all the media, when asked which he prefers, will
unhesitatingly say "the stage." And the reason is the audience.
Each audience has a collective personality. It's like meeting a
new person each performance.

The profession of acting has always been surrounded by an
aura of glamour. It has a hypnotizing, magnetic attraction causing many of us to make great personal sacrifices in order to
hopefully bathe in its flattering light and to bow to its thrilling
applause.

I remember my beginnings very well. I also remember each
heartache and obstacle.

But today I can say it's been worth it.

And I look to the future eagerly.

FINIS

INDEX

~ 271 ~